TEMPERANCE SERMONS

DELIVERED

IN RESPONSE TO AN INVITATION

OF

THE NATIONAL TEMPERANCE SOCIETY

AND

PUBLICATION HOUSE.

NEW YORK:
The National Temperance Society and Publication House,
NO. 58 READE STREET.

1873.

JOHN ROSS & CO., PRINTERS, 27 ROSE STREET, NEW YORK.

CONTENTS.

Contents.

Common Sense for Young Men

ON THE

SUBJECT OF TEMPERANCE.

"There is a way which seemeth right unto a man; but the ends thereof are the ways of death."—Prov. xiv. 12.

THIS is peculiarly applicable to those who are young, who are going, as it were, along unknown paths, and who see, branching out to the right or to the left, roads planted with flowers, overhung with vines, and full of tempting sights and beckoning pleasures, all of which look to them secure and most joyful. But these roads, once entered upon, are difficult to leave; and the sights that tempted them, and the pleasures that beckoned them, are gradually exchanged for harder and harder fates. The smooth road soon becomes precipitous, the easy and apparently safe course soon becomes full of peril, and at last they are plunged into remediless destruction.

This is the career of thousands. They enter upon ways which are enticing, which are covered with beauty, which promise great remuneration.

which fulfil only in part the things promised, and which, having deluded them, at last destroy them.

There are a great many such ways, but there is only one of them which I propose to speak upon, to-night, and that is the way of the drinker.

It is a part of every Christian minister's duty to keep his congregation instructed on the subject of temperance from the Christian point of view. It is especially my duty, because this church has, from its very foundation, reckoned the cause of temperance as a part of the great Christian movement of the world. It is my duty, because in many ways a generation has come up in our midst without that special and sedulous training which we had in our youth. Those who are at about my time of life remember the beginning of this education, and how strong and various were the influences and impulses and instruments by which the attention of the community was aroused. There was, first, novelty; and then, at last, fashion and public sentiment concurred. This movement has run through one generation, and also has run through a kind of moral period, and a reaction has come on, and a generation of young persons have arisen who are less informed, perhaps, on this subject, than those who immediately preceded them. It becomes important, therefore, that churches and ministers should renew the instruction of the young on the dangers of drinking.

I do not propose to go into a denunciatory tirade against liquor dealers, or against dram-shops, or against the drinking usages of society. I propose, to-night, to speak to the young men of my charge, and to the community, in so far as my words may be borne out to them; and I propose to speak as an elder brother, and to address this subject, with all moderation, and yet with all earnestness, to their best judgment. I do not propose to carry you away by exciting your feelings; but I propose, if possible, to convince you through your reasoning faculties. And I ask you to consider the subject of entire abstinence from all that intoxicates, from motives which bear upon your personal welfare, from motives which bear upon the welfare of the society in which you live, and from motives which spring from religion itself. And I remark,

1. A healthy nature never craves intoxicating drinks. Men are not drawn to the use of intoxicating drinks as they are drawn to the use of food, or ordinary drinks. I suppose that ninety-nine in a hundred of the men that drink, learned, and had to learn, to love intoxicating beverages; and I suppose that those who indulge in them most, and most ruinously, have to do it with a testimony that they are not palatable. You are not, therefore, called to follow any great instinct in drinking. The sin of indulging in intoxicating drinks is not like a passional sin; it is not like obedience to some master-passion that lies within demanding gratification. There is no such excuse for men who drink as that of natural hunger or thirst. Men may be naturally hungry or thirsty, but men are not by nature thirsty for wine, nor for whiskey, nor for brandy, nor for any

other compound; so that in drinking there is no obedience on the part of men to any radical instinct or radical impulse.

Hence, the use of intoxicating drinks is not necessary. It is not prompted by anything that is natural in yourself. If you say: "Yes, I have a natural craving for it," then to you I say: That is the very reason why you should not take it. If you have no craving for it, why should you cumber yourself with it? And if you have such a craving, surely, if you are wise, you will not put yourself in peril by indulging it. If you have the appetite in you, then by all means, unless you are utterly reckless in regard to your own welfare, you will take warning, and shun the danger which threatens you.

2. Alcoholic stimulants are not needful. Not only does a desire for them not spring from any constitutional impulse or necessity, but experience has shown that they are not needful as elements of diet. I do not undertake to say that they have no place medicinally. I express a well-matured judgment when I say that I think they have been employed medicinally in a manner that is very rash, and that is not scientific; but I do not propose to interfere with the doctors' sphere, except to express the wish that they might study the moral interests of their patients as much as they do their physical well-being, and as little as possible put men under temptation by prescriptions which require the continuous use of alcoholic stimulants. That they are to be excluded wholly

from the range of medicine, I do not undertake to say; that I would not employ them under medical prescription, I do not undertake to say; but I do undertake to say that, except as medicine, they are not necessary. They are not needful for health, and they are not needful for strength. They are not a part of a man's normal diet. You are not, therefore, required to indulge in them for the same reason that you are required to indulge in meat, or in bread, or in milk, or in water.

3. Alcoholic stimulants are not usually palatable. Young men who drink seldom love at first what they drink. They serve an apprenticeship to a bad habit. I have alluded to this already; but there is in it a still further point to be developed. There are many things that men do which they do not like to do, and for which they have no natural appetite; but then, they gain something by doing them that is worth the toil required to overcome the barriers that surround them. Very few there are who like the methodical industry which is required to master a trade. So young men are obliged to do what they do not want to do, and are kept from doing what they want to do. The result is that, at the end of five or seven years of apprenticeship, they have learned what is equivalent to the labor which they have performed during those years.

The young man who studies a profession, studies against his will a great deal of the time; or rather, he obliges himself by his will to study for the sake of that which he will gain by study.

And so we are continually, in one sense, going against nature; that is, we are continually going against the lower nature for the sake of the higher. There is an upper or spirit nature, and there is a lower or flesh nature; and the upper demands the denial of the lower. When, therefore, men study long for a professional life, or practise long with the hand for an artist or artisan life, they go against their natural tendency. And they gain something that is worth all the self-denial and all the painstaking to which they subject themselves. But when men learn to love drink, for which they have no natural appetite, what do they get in return, but habits that are fraught with danger? They gain no equivalent for what they give. They force nature, and force nature for the purpose of bringing themselves into a condition in which their whole life will be full of peril.

4. Drinking habits are not economical. And economy, though it is a very homely virtue, and is not reckoned among moral virtues, and is spoken of as a commercial virtue, has a most important relation to a young man's prosperity, regarded not only commercially, but morally. I need not speak of it as a matter of commerce. Great moderation in the expenditure of money—great frugality in the early part of a man's life—is a part of that education which every man is expected to gain who means to acquire a fortune, and become a responsible and influential man in the community.

Now, the administration of one's wealth, or of

one's affairs, in a close, careful, and successful way, is morally beneficial, inasmuch as it means self-denial, forethought, arrangement, with a purpose, followed by a definite action of the will. All these things are self-governing elements. Self-government may begin with pecuniary matters, as well as with other affairs. And thousands of men take their first step in moral life through the drill which economy requires. And no young man, whatever his situation in life may be, has a right to despise economy, or has a right to be careless or profuse in the expenditure of his means. No matter if a man's hands are in mines of wealth, he has no right to make a wasteful use of that wealth. No man has a right to go from youth to manhood without having formed rigid habits of economy. If you are poor, then the way out of poverty into wealth is through economy; if you are rich, then you should administer your riches so that your example shall be a blessing and not a curse to the community. You are God's steward, and you have no right to recklessly spend money that you did not earn—though young men seem mostly to think that they have a right to scatter all the money that they can lay their hands on!

The majority of young men, when they enter upon life, have but little at the beginning. More than half—yes, more than two-thirds, probably—of the young men who come to New York to seek their fortune, come with a very slender pittance. They are obliged to live upon a very small income. And it ought to be a matter of pride with every young man to be able to live on his income, however small it may be, and inside of it. It is not necessary that you should live here as you lived at home. It might be more agreeable, but it is not necessary. There is something higher than living at a first-class boarding-house, or at a hotel. There is something better than having a luxurious table. It is not necessary that a young man should go to a boarding-house at all. If your means will not allow it, it is not necessary that you should go any higher than to buy your loaf and eat it in your own room.

"But," you will reply, "what sort of a life is that, where a young man works all day, and then goes like a dog to his kennel at night, and gnaws his loaf, and drinks his cold water, and creeps under his straw, and gets up in the morning, and gnaws his loaf again, and then drags himself out to work once more?" I think there should be provision made for a more respectable method of cheap living; and yet, until that provision is made, even such a life, voluntarily assumed, is nobler than for a young man to live at a higher rate, and steal the difference between his salary and his expenses, as you are not ashamed to do, often! It is better for a young man to feel so proud that he will not go one penny beyond what he lawfully owns. And even if a young man is wealthy, it is noble for him to live on a moderate allowance. But when young men come to the city, and have but a small pittance of salary to live on, how often do they split up and divide that pittance, and waste a large portion of it on tobacco and drink!

I shall not now enter upon a crusade against the use of tobacco, though I think it is entirely needless. The most self-indulgent and the most selfish of luxuries is that of tobacco. I never knew a dozen men that used tobacco that cared anything about whether they smelled agreeable to other people, or whether they carried themselves so that other people were happy, or not. They will foul the house, they will foul the boat, they will foul the car, if they are not arbitrarily restrained. They forget father and mother, and wife and children, and all others, and go through life smoking, stenchful and disagreeable; and when they are expostulated with, they laugh! The use of tobacco does not make a man a monster: it only makes him selfish in respect to the comfort of people round about him. Though I consider this to be a most disagreeable and selfish habit, I do not look upon it as being at all equal to drinking in its evil effects; but it is a very wasteful habit. There are few young men that are beginning life who can afford to smoke.

And, much more, there are few young men that can afford to drink when they are beginning life, for, if you drink cheaply, you drink meanly. If you drink wholesomely, you drink dearly. Drinking involves an expense that very few at the beginning of life can afford to incur.

Drinking habits take hold indirectly upon the whole framework of a man's prosperity They lead to very many expenses besides the daily expense of the cup. They bring one into society, and introduce him to customs which are constantly a levy and a tax upon him. They place him in a position where he is subjected to a great many expenditures which, under other circumstances, he might avoid. For they who come together for drinking purposes are seldom persons who are careful to engineer their way, little by little, and step by step, up to a strong and safe manhood. Out of the circle where drinking is carried on for purposes of pleasure there open, day by day, hundreds of doors that never open without a fee; and a young man who forms the habit of drinking takes on an expense that wastes his patrimony, and will continually keep him down.

This may not be the case with all, and it will be the case with some more than with others; but I think that, with the majority, reasons of economy should be sufficient to dissuade them from forming drinking habits.

5. Drinking habits open the door to many temptations which no man has a right to encounter. Vices come with drinking habits. Young men who are susceptible, wide-awake, and unformed in their habits, are inclined to smoke a little, and drink a little, and gamble a little, and "see life" a little; and this group of little vices are very apt to invite the company of larger vices. Drinking habits throw young men into associations, and under cricumstances, where it is far more likely

that their lower nature will be solicited than that their higher moral nature will be solicited.

We see in the poets much about the cup—much about its generosity. Many glorious things are said and sung about "the wine in the cup;" and yet, after all, it is the *beast* that drinks the cup. In nine hundred and ninety-nine cases in a thousand, it feeds the lower nature wholly, and not the higher nature at all.

Now, there are many that are frail in the hour of temptation, and that must needs utter that petition of the Lord's Prayer, "Lead us not into temptation"—as if we should go down if we came into its presence, as we should, many of us. The majority of us are so weak that we have no right to bring ourselves into temptation by forming habits of drinking.

6. There cannot be a doubt as to the fact that habits of drinking withdraw from a young man the confidence of those who watch and gauge young men. Young men who are preparing themselves for life, by drinking lose the confidence of those who desire to employ respectable and trustworthy men. The knowledge that a young man drinks, destroys his reputation for trustworthiness.

I do not say that that is the case in every country. If a man is born under a vine in Italy, and is accustomed, from his youth up, to participation in the wine-cup, I do not say that he will not be considered trustworthy. We are very much creatures of the institutions and habits of the country where we are; but in this country, where you are, and where I am speaking to you, it is not the habit of the population to indulge in the use of wine or strong drink, and it is so far opposed to an intelligent, correct public sentiment among us, that it unquestionably leaves a mark upon a young man who indulges in it.

If you were looking out for a confidential clerk, and two young men presented themselves, in all respects equal, except that one of them was accustomed to indulge gently in drinking, and the other was not at all accustomed to it, you would not hesitate in your choice. Even if you did not scruple at putting wine on your own table, you would take the young man that was temperate. Many a man who is vicious, wants his wife to be pure; and many a man who drinks, will not allow his clerks to drink. And if young men are addicted to even a mild indulgence in drinking habits, it is prejudicial to their good name and to their chances of success.

This is a habit which is not required by any natural impulse, which is not necessary to your health, which is full of perils, which exposes you to various temptations, and which throws a shadow over the threshold of your business life. And why should you voluntarily form such a habit, or place yourself in such a position that you will almost inevitably fall into it? What reason is there for your entering upon such a course?

7. Drinking may either develop a tendency which lies dormant in you, or it may create a

tendency which does not already exist in your system. As a matter of fact, it is certain that there are many persons who inherit such an abnormal condition of the nervous system that, on suitable provocation, there spring up in them paroxysms which are almost as ungovernable as are convulsions or the paroxysms of neuralgia. There is such a thing as a latent tendency of the constitution that will slumber all one's life, if it be let alone, if those things which excite it be rigidly withheld, but that, if it be once roused up, will assert itself with a force that is well-nigh omnipotent. And there is many a man who, by taking alcoholic stimulants early in life, arouses that hereditary tendency in himself; and, once being aroused, tiger-like, it destroys its victim. And thus thousands are destroyed irremedilessly.

But if there is no such tendency in you; if your father, and his father, and his father, or if your ancestors on both sides, have sent down to you a constitution unimpaired, it may nevertheless be the fact that, from other causes, there is a condition of your system which predisposes you to that tendency which, if created in you, you will transmit to your posterity. And I cannot think of a cruelty greater than that which shall lead a parent, from reasons of mere self-indulgence, to roll down on his posterity, to many generations, a tendency which shall be one long and terrible curse to them. And yet there are multitudes that are doing it.

Whoever consumes his own nervous system by excessive indulgence in any manner, prepares the way for those who come after him to be blighted in their whole nervous constitution. And if, in the use of intoxicating drinks, you drive up your jaded faculties; if you, for the sake of fulfilling tasks that are beyond your power, resort to unnatural stimulation, you prepare yourself to hand down to your posterity the blight of intemperance, if ever they shall touch the intoxicating bowl.

8. No man has a right, under all the conditions that I have mentioned, to put himself in peril by either or all of these mischiefs. No man has a right to buy a ticket in this lottery of death. If a lottery should be started, if the wheel should be opened, and if you knew that there was one in each hundred of the tickets that would bring death and destruction to the person who should draw it, you would not have anything to do with that lottery. You never would run the risk of losing your life, where the chances of death were one to a hundred, even if one of the tickets was marked ten thousand dollars, another two thousand, and another one thousand. Who would patronize such a lottery? Who would not say that a man who did it courted death? But here is a lottery in which the death-bearing tickets are more than one in every hundred. And what earthly reason is there that should induce a man to put in a venture where the risk is so great? What great good is there that he can hope to gain? There is none. What great happiness is there that he can reasonably expect to obtain? There is none.

What customs impose on him the necessity of thus placing himself in jeopardy? None that are not better broken than observed. What inward need impels him to it? None.

Thus far, I have argued this question on the lower grounds of expediency. I present, now, higher motives for the young to live a temperate life.

1. Every man is bound to present himself to his age and country as noble a specimen of manhood as is possible to him. Every man is bound so to develop every part of his nature—his physical vigor, his intellectual strength, his moral powers—that when he presents himself to his country he shall be worth that country's accepting.

It was the custom among the Greeks, when a man had done well, when he had made great achievements, to have a statue of him in some temple of the gods; and their temples became museums, filled with statues of those benefactors of the state, who were able to buy statues of themselves, which had been voted a place there. These statues were ranged in long successions about the temples. And every man is bound to case himself, not in marble, but in flesh and blood, in mental powers, and in the higher attributes of the soul, and present himself, a living man, to the state, that he may be, not a mere lifeless *simulacrum*, but a man of life and vigor, and an instrument of good, in the age to which he belongs.

I love to see young men with a noble carriage, and with blooming health. I cannot bear to see young men, that have every reason for building up a noble manhood, walking with a discolored face and an unwholesome skin, which are signs of intemperance. Perhaps there is nothing more disreputable than for a young man to present himself a miserable wreck of what he might have been, and a burden, to the state and to the age in which he lives; and perhaps there is nothing more creditable to a young man than to present himself to the state and to the age in which he lives a monument of health and vigor and true manliness. Temperance brings you to this higher and nobler condition of manhood, and intemperance takes you from it.

2. No man has a right to sport with all the interests that are centred in a moral being, and to put himself in peril for such reasons as mostly induce young men to drink. As I have said, there is no natural appetite in you for intoxicating beverages. There is nothing in your normal condition which leads you to want them. There is a curiosity that many young persons feel in regard to them. I remember that, from what I had read in the Bible and other books about wine, I had the impression that if I tasted it I should be lifted up to the seventh heaven, and I had a great curiosity to know how wine tasted. And finally I *did* taste it. But I was not lifted up by it as I expected I should be. And since this curiosity exists, I cannot say that if my child had heard of champagne, and wanted to taste it, I never would let him taste it. I think it very likely that if I did not he would

gratify that curiosity, that abnormal desire, by stealth; and it seems to me that if he is going to know what it is, the knowledge had better be conveyed to him by parental revelation and teaching, mostly. And a child that has had one taste of it, usually wants no more. And when young men have once tasted wine, and satisfied their curiosity about it, why should they continue taking it? Though they do not like it, they are ashamed among their companions not to hold up their heads, and toss off a drink, just like any other man. They are ashamed to be deficient in so manly an accomplishment! They are ashamed to stand up and say, "I do not relish it; I do not need it, and I will not have it." They cannot bear the ridicule which such a declaration would subject them to. They are ashamed to have it thought that they cannot afford to have what rich and fashionable people have; and yet they cannot, and it is a lie for them to pretend that they can. You drink because great men around you drink. The head of that firm up there drinks, and so you poverty-stricken clerk down there drink. And you are going to drink what fashionable people do—you, that have not a rag of fashion, and will not have for years to come. And you will do it knowing that it is beyond your means, that it is contrary to good health, and inconsistent with manliness. For miserable, unmanly reasons of pride and vanity, you drink. You do not dare, going out at one o'clock at night, with half a dozen young fellows that have "the flush of health" on their faces, when they ask you to step in and take some "bitters" with them, to refuse. You do not dare to meet their taunts and gibes. You do not dare, when you hesitate and draw back, and they say, "What! afraid? You are probably one of the virtuous young men that came from the country," to say, "Yes, I am; and I intend to remain so a good while." How many men are there that, in a matter vital to their virtue, vital to their good habits, and vital to their manliness, flinch, and go down before their companions, and drink what they do not like, and what they know is damaging to them, putting everything in peril, because they have not the manliness to say "No"!

You go to a wedding, and the fair hands of the entertaining company present the cup to you; and you say, "Of course, I must drink here." Oh! that it were only just here; but there are so many *just heres!* Soon after comes the convivial entertainment; and the same hands again present you with the cup; and you drink again. Temptations follow at frequent intervals, and on each succeeding occasion you yield more easily than at the previous one. It does not make you a drunkard, but it weakens your power of standing on your conscience and manly independence, and saying, "Such things I disallow, and will not do." It is the beginning of that inclined plane down which you are preparing to slide. It is one of those ways which are pleasant, and which seem to be safe, but the ends of which are death. To stand in the blooming presence of beauty, and to be smiled upon, especially if the persons that smile upon you are a little higher in society than you are, they standing on five thousand, while you stand on five hundred, is very flattering to your vanity. And if, having invited you, they offer you wine, and say, "You certainly will take it from me," you cannot refuse. You think, "If I am admitted into that family, my prospects will be bright; my fortune will be made."

What a casuist the devil is when he wants to get people in his power! How delicate he is! How he makes the road to sin smooth and delightful!

So, under such beguiling influences, young men take the cup, and drink, and drink again, and drink many times. And many, under such circumstances, are ashamed of themselves; they rebuke themselves; they go home with an unquiet conscience; they feel humbled; and yet, they repeat the same round of dissipation again and again. And I put it to any man who has any self-respect, whether he ought to be cajoled or dragooned into using what he does not like, what does not like him, what exposes him to all possible perils, what is unfitted to his circumstances, and what is subversive of all his thoughts of manhood?

I am ashamed of a young man who cannot resist the temptation to drink; or, rather, I am sorry for him. I think very likely that I should feel embarrassed, and blush, and submit, as you do. But it is no less a peril; and I warn every young man not to allow the customs of society to seduce him from a sober and matured purpose, to stand utterly clean and clear of this mischief.

3. This is the great social battle of the age which we are fighting between the flesh and the spirit—between the animal and the man. We are living in a time when nothing can save us but moral principle in the individual. Our government is an equal government, as such. We have cast in our destiny on this great principle of popular government, and we must go up with it, or go down with it. It is for us to maintain our institutions, if they are maintained at all; and unless we can teach individuals and the masses self-respect and self-control, we are utterly ruined. It is a mere matter of time. There is no salvation for institutions like ours except in the principle of self-control. And there is no single evil, social or political, that strikes more at the foundation of such institutions than the drinking habits of society. If you corrupt the working-class by drink; if you corrupt the great middle-class by drink; if you corrupt the literary and wealthy classes by drink, you have destroyed the commonwealth beyond your power to save it. And we are making battle for the preservation of this moral principle. It is the great patriotic movement of the day. Therefore, we must have clear heads; we must have right consciences; we must have all the manhood that is in men, or that can educate them to it. The good that is in society will not be a match for the evil that is continually pulling it down.

Now, young men, which side are you to take in

this great struggle? Will you go for license? Will you go for passion? Will you go for corruption? Or will you range yourselves on the side of those who are attempting to lift men up toward spirituality; toward true reason; toward noble self-control? You can afford to go but one way. Every young man who has one impulse of heroism, one generous tendency in him, ought in the beginning to take his ground beyond all controversy, and say, "I work for those who work for the good and beautiful and true."

4. You have no right to allow your example to seduce the weak. I have spoken of the effects of drinking habits on yourselves. Now comes an auxiliary consideration. Even if you are not yourselves personally injured by drinking, your example injures others.

I am aware that men oftentimes revolt from the application of this thought in regard to example, saying, "Man is independent. I am not bound to conform to the vulgar opinions of ignorant men. I am not bound to take the pattern of my development from the undeveloped and uneducated below me. They must come to me. I shall not go to them."

A man has a right to shock public opinion whenever he is endeavoring to bring in a higher morality; whenever there is a greater degree of refinement after which he is seeking; whenever custom is to be set aside, and a new and better state of things instituted. He is a moral coward who fears to do it under such circumstances. But you have no right to be content with simple conformity to custom, and to be indifferent to the effect of your example on those beneath you. There are many persons who are apt to consider themselves exempt from this duty of taking care that their example shall not be a stumbling-block, but a safe guide, to others. Those who are influential by reason of wealth, or position, or culture, are wont to throw off the responsibility of their example; but none more than they should watch their example with a conscientious regard for any who may be affected by it. In proportion as God has made you strong, either in your mental attainments or in your outward circumstances, he lays on you the responsibility of the example which you set for those who are not so fortunate as you are.

A man cannot help being influenced by the example of those who occupy elevated positions in society. A man will inevitably be affected by the example of those who are high in station. If a man is rich, and lives in splendor, his example will surely influence those by whom he is surrounded. And it is the duty of all that are endowed with the power of benefiting or injuring others by their example, to see that that example is beneficial, and not injurious. Those who are at the top of society are largely responsible for the ideas of those who are at the bottom. And if God has advanced you among men, it is not to give you more license, but to make you more careful of your example before others. No man has a right to let his example work mischief upon those in the midst of whom he moves. And the unfeeling indifference of men (and more, perhaps, in this matter of drinking than in any other) as to the welfare of their neighbors, shows that their hearts have become seared by prosperity, and degraded by the things which should, in the providence of God, have made them more tender and considerate.

5. No man has a right to be neutral in the great work of temperance, in this age, and in this country. Every man, from considerations of personal safety, from moral considerations, from considerations of his relations to his fellow-men in social life, and from considerations of patriotism or of state, ought to take sides in this matter, and let his position be known of all men. It is too notorious to require any proof, that, to a very great extent, especially in the cities, our legislation begins in the grog-shop. The seed of judges is planted there. Our administrations spring out of the ooze and mud of drinking holes. Our national councils are begun there. The machinery of government is arranged there. There is no part of the community so active as that which lives in the indulgence of the animal appetites; and there is no part of the community which should be watched over with such sleepless vigilance by those who, by sound morality and superior judgment, are fitted to wisely administer the affairs of the nation. And the time has come when all good men, who have so long staid at

home, and left the management of political affairs in the hands of dissipated and unscrupulous men, should come together, and take the side of purity and temperance. We must produce a radical change in the public sentiment of the country on this vital question, or we shall be destroyed by the overwhelming deluge of the drinking habits of society.

Now, I have purposely avoided exaggerations in the discussion of this subject to-night. I have avoided the presentation of extravagant views. I have attempted to address myself to your reason. And, in closing, I desire to ask you two questions:

First: Have I not presented considerations sufficient to make it every man's duty to think about this subject? If you have indulged yourself hitherto thoughtlessly and carelessly in drinking habits, is it not your duty to consider seriously whether it is not best for you to become a total abstainer from everything that is intoxicating? If your example in this matter has been such as to lead others into temptation, ought you not to consider the propriety of reviewing your course, and so rectifying it that it shall be a blessing, and not a curse, to your fellow-men?

The second question which I desire to ask, is, whether it is not your duty to decide this question on strictly moral grounds? I do not say to men, "You shall never drink wine or ardent spirits." I say to them, "Ought you not to make a decision on this subject? And ought you not to make that decision on moral grounds? Is not this a matter that you ought to consider, not only in the light of your own personal welfare, but also in the light of your relations to individuals with whom you come in contact, to the community in which you live, and to the nation to which you belong?"

I can well understand how a man may, on his death-bed, look back upon his career in life, and say, "I am sorry that I ever touched the cup;" but I cannot understand how any man can, on his death-bed, look back and say, "I am sorry that I have always been abstemious of the cup." There is one way that you know is safe, and honorable, and proper as regards others; but the other way, even if it is possible for it to be safe, is one in which there are a hundred chances to one that, directly or indirectly, it will be mischievous—if not to you, to others.

Can you form a decision on such a subject as this, and not take into consideration these great verities? And are you that are safe justified in taking the first steps in a course which is so full of peril? How much wiser and better it will be for you, whose lips are still clean, to go through life with them undefiled! Do this, and you will have reason all through your life to thank God that in your early days you were induced to take a stand of strict, invariable temperance. Temperance will do you no harm. In a thousand ways, it will do you good. Even occasional drinking will do you no good; and entire abstinence from drinking will do you no harm.

Take the right side; the manly side; the patriotic side. God help you and keep you. And by-and-by, may there come from the lips of many a man who hears me to-night this testimony: "I thank God that I heard that sermon by Mr. Beecher on that Sunday night. It saved me. It made me live a better life all the way through."

THE MORAL DUTY

OF

TOTAL ABSTINENCE.

"Wine is a mocker, strong drink is raging: and whosoever is deceived thereby is not wise."—PROVERBS XX. 1.

I PROPOSE to discuss the very important question, What is the duty of every Christian in reference to the use of intoxicating drinks? No question is, at the present moment, agitating more minds than this one. None has a better right to enter the pulpit on the Sabbath; to no other moral question can a minister of Jesus Christ be more imperatively required to return a candid, careful, and most unmistakable answer. In every domain of practical Christian morals, the pulpit ought to make the path of duty so clear that "the wayfaring men, though fools, shall not err therein." A minister should carry no dark-lanterns.

During the past week, I have found my mind disturbed afresh, and deeply, too, by the state of things around us. To the outward eye, the business and the social life of this city have gone on as aforetimes. But the eye of God, looking into the interior moral life of this community, has seen strange and sorrowful things. He has seen struggles with terrible temptation that you have little dreamed of. He has seen several thousands of people strongly tempted to do that which inclination or custom prompted them to do, and yet the very doing of it might be fatal to the body and damning to the soul. He has seen some young man stretching forth his hand, with anxious misgiving, for his first glass of strong drink; and some aged hands reached out to clutch the glass, which should be almost their last. He has beheld thousands of our neighbors entering the door of the drinking-saloon without even heeding that awful inscription written over that door by the hand of Truth—"Whosoever is deceived here, is not wise. Here rich men are made poor; thrifty men are made idle; healthy men are poisoned with deadly disease; parents are made childless; wives are made widows; and immortal *souls*, for whom Jesus bled, are dooming themselves to the outer darkness of eternal despair!" The Omniscient eye has seen some parents setting the sparkling cup (which "biteth like a serpent") right before their own children; and even church-members have offered that ensnaring cup at their hospitable boards to guests, who have been confirmed in dangerous habits by the example of professed Christians! The eye of God has seen the woes, and the ear of God has heard the wails, of the drunkard's home. Beneath all this smooth surface of society, God has witnessed the most terrible passions of lust, sensuality, anger, cruelty, and often of red-handed murder—all fomented and kept in hot fury by the monster curse of the intoxicating bowl. And now, up from this seething caldron of misery and sin, marches the question to-day to every Christian conscience, "What is my *duty* in regard to using or offering these deceitful and destructive drinks?" Surely our All-wise and Heavenly Father has not left us in the dark on so momentous a question of Christian duty. If our Father has made known to us his will in regard to alcoholic intoxicants, where shall we discover it?

I reply that we shall discover it in two clearly legible laws: the one is the law written on our *bodily constitutions;* the other is the law written in this blessed book, the *Bible.* God is the author of both the body and the book. What he has written on the one never contradicts what he has written in the other. Truths never conflict. An established truth of science never contradicts an established truth of revelation. And when any man or any minister attempts to prove that the Word of God justifies and encourages the use of intoxicating beverages, he puts a fatal weapon into the hands of the infidel. For the shrewd sceptic quickly retorts, "I know that alcoholic stimulants are deadly poisons to the human body and mind; if, therefore, your Bible justifies and encourages their habitual use, then your Bible must be false. I prefer to stick to what I know, rather than believe what you make your Bible to say." So reasons the cunning sceptic. But you may be sure, good friends! that I am not going to put such a logical bludgeon into the hands of the infidel; neither shall I put into the mouth of the Christian any excuse for violating God's law, whether written on the human body or in the heaven-sent book. Our bodies, so "wonderfully made," were created to be temples of the Holy Spirit, and not to be dens of debauchery. We are commanded to "glorify God in the body," and every Christian is bound to pray that his "spirit and soul and body be preserved blameless unto the coming of our Lord Jesus Christ."

I. Now let us enquire what law in regard to the use of alcoholic intoxicants, God has written on our bodies?

To this question, both science and universal human experience give answer in a voice as distinct as the thunder of Niagara. Science has made long and patient investigation of the statutes which the Creator has written on the human organism, and has established the fact that alcoholic intoxicants are a poison. Science holds her inquest over the bloated, disfigured body of the man who is drunk, and brings in her verdict, "This man is poisoned!" Alcohol poisons the blood in every vein. It assaults the very throne of our manhood and poisons the brain. It produces such a subtle derangement of the very texture of the brain, that the drinker is tormented by recurrences of thirst for strong drink long after he has broken off the indulgence. There is not a reformed inebriate who does not carry in his brain a powder-magazine ready to ignite at the touch of one drop of strong drink. Alcohol is one of the most malignant of all poisons, for by its horrid sorcery it strikes through, and poisons the immortal soul! Yet, like other narcotic poisons, alcohol has the magical power to deceive its victim by making him absolutely believe that it is doing him no harm! The "father of lies" never made such a liar as alcohol. Even if we never had any Bible, science would inscribe on the forehead of every habitual drinker of intoxicants, "Wine is a mocker, strong drink is raging: whosoever is deceived thereby is not wise."

2. Science has a second testimony to furnish. She declares incontestably that alcohol is not a "good creature" of the God of love; for it is nowhere to be found in the whole domain of nature. While the Almighty has created innumerable fountains of sparkling water, he never created one gill of alcohol! It is the simple product of the fermenting vat and the distillery. It is born of vegetable decay. God made the golden corn to nourish and sustain his mighty family; but distillation throws the golden grain into a vat of rottenness, and presses out of the rotting mass the fiery juice of alcohol. God hung the purple clusters on the vine to gladden the human eye and the palate; but fermentation turns the pure blood of the grape into a maddening intoxicant. Even if we never had an inspired Bible, yet science would have written on the rosy-hued decanter, "Look not on the wine when it is beautifully

red, when it sparkleth in the cup, when it goeth down smoothly; for at the last it will bite like the serpent, and sting like the adder."

3. But science and human experience have a third testimony to offer, and it is the most convincing of all. They reveal to us that God has written on every human body a law of abstinence from intoxicating beverages, by decreeing that alcohol shall lessen the muscular power, and diminish the animal heat, and derange the digestive organs of the human body. All these laws are as immovably true as the law of gravitation. Alcohol is not food. It positively interferes with alimentation. Alcohol, instead of helping digestion, tends to destroy the digestive organs. Yet thousands of deluded people are swallowing doses of gin and whiskey and wines every day, under the ignorant infatuation that these draughts will aid them to digest their dinners. Men will even cling to this delusive lie long after their stomachs have been burnt out by their fiery potations.

If alcoholic drinks do not feed or warm or aid the digestive functions of our bodies, then "surely," says the drinker, "they will strengthen me." No, sir! your "mocker" is lying to you again. Intoxicating drinks actually lessen your muscular power. They waste your vital forces. And they waste them to such a damaging extent, that no sane life insurance company will take a risk on your lives if you are habitually addicted to the use of alcoholic drinks. When the most famous of modern pugilists was asked if he did not use plenty of ale and porter while in training for his brutal prize-fights, he replied, "When I have business on hand, there is nothing like cold water and the dumb-bells." The shameless bully cared nothing for God's law written in the Bible; but he knew too much about God's law written on his body to weaken his giant strength by using alcoholic poisons. I was once told by the most famous American pedestrian, that nothing was so fatal to his success when engaged in a great feat of walking, as even the moderate use of wine or of whiskey.

Science and human experience do not halt at these two individual examples. They point us to the whole mighty and innumerable array of noble feats of the hand, and feats of the muscle, and feats of the brain, and feats of the giant intellect, which have been wrought by men who were clean from the taint or touch of alcohol, and they defy you to match those feats by any performances of bodies or of brains which were poisoned by strong drink. Science and experience point to the fact that every healthy human frame instinctively recognizes alcohol as its enemy, and tries to expel it. Science and experience testify that alcohol does not feed a human body, but impoverishes it; instead of warming the body, it first scorches, and then leaves it to freeze; instead of building it up, it tears it down; instead of prolonging life, it breeds a legion of diseases; and, with the smile of pleasure on its face, it wields the red dagger of the assassin! Science and experience invoke before us to-day the millions of human forms that are scarred, and defaced, and disfigured, and diseased by strong drink; and summoning from their putrid graves the myriads upon myriads who for forty centuries have been murdered by strong drink, they propose to them the question, "What is God's law written upon your bodies?" And from the whole mighty multitude of living bodies and of the dead, comes back a voice loud as the seven thunders of the Apocalypse—TOTAL ABSTINENCE! TOTAL ABSTINENCE!!

II. We have been reading the law of the Creator written on the human body; now let us read and interpret the law written in this inspired *book*. What saith the Lord? In approaching the Word of God to receive its testimony, we must come to it in the spirit of devout candor, and with no disposition to seize upon certain isolated texts, and twist them into hooks to hang our pet theories on. We must study each passage in the light of the whole book. We must look fairly at the general aim and scope and spirit of the entire volume. What is the general aim and spirit of God's glorious Word? No one will dare to deny that the aim of this book is to elevate man, and not to degrade him; to purify him, and not to poison him; to keep his soul and body undefiled, and not to make either body or soul a den of uncleanness. The whole trend of the Bible is towards sobriety and self-control. It enjoins watchfulness and "keeping the body under," and crucifixion of all sensual lusts. It commands us to be holy even as God himself is holy. No virtue was more persis tently preached by our Divine Redeemer and his apostles, than the beautiful virtue of self-denial. No sin is more condemned than the sin of self-indulgence. Our Father sent this blessed book to lead his frail, sinful children up toward heaven, and not to mislead them towards drunkenness and damnation. I therefore assert, without fear of successful contradiction, that from the first syllable in Genesis to the last love-note of Revelation, the whole *spirit* of God's Word is in favor of entire abstinence from every practice which tends to degrade and destroy the human body or soul! The divine law in the book confirms the divine law on the body. All attempts to dragoon the Scriptures into a support of the modern drinking customs—like all similar attempts to dragoon them into a support of modern slavery—only end in making scoffers and sceptics.

Our opponents will say that this is dealing too much in generalities. They demand an examination of particular texts. Their demand shall be gratified. We have no fear of the result. "Let truth and error grapple; who ever knew truth to be worsted in a fair encounter?"

We affirm that the holy Word of God enjoins the duty of abstinence from alcoholic intoxicants. Before this assembly, as before a court, we shall summon witnesses from the inspired record to prove this declaration. First of all, we summon the ancient patriarch Noah, who "planted a vineyard, and drank of the wine, and was drunken!" As we gaze upon the poor old man lying in his debauch, we discover plainly that the grace of God never will protect even a good man from the consequences of sin, while he is breaking God's law written on the body. Had Noah been a "tee-totaler," he never would have been drunk. The very "preacher of righteousness" who could withstand a world of scoffing idolaters could not withstand the wine-cup. What member of Christ's church will dare to tamper with a tempter which laid even Noah on his back?

I next summon Moses, the man of God, who has recorded Jehovah's solemn prohibition of the priesthood from touching wine when engaged in their sacred duties: "Do not drink wine nor strong drink, thou nor thy sons with thee, when ye go into the tabernacle of the congregation, lest ye die." Even that one passage, in the fourteenth chapter of Deuteronomy, which is often claimed as a warrant for tippling, I am not willing to surrender. In that passage, Moses records this permission of God to his people on festal occasions, "Thou shalt bestow that money for oxen, for sheep, for wine or strong drink, or for whatsoever thy soul desireth, and thou shalt eat there before the Lord thy God." This word "strong drink" has a very ominous sound; but it is the incorrect translation of the Hebrew word *shakar*, which signifies a sweet drink expressed from fruits, and often drank in an unfermented state. It is the root of our English word *sugar*. This passage gives no warrant for the use of alcoholic poisons, even on the most innocent occasions of festivity.

Here let me remind you, once for all, that the Word of God speaks sometimes of certain drinks as a "blessing," as innocent in themselves, and as a symbol of spiritual blessings. In other passages, God's book condemns certain drinks as dangerous and deadly. Most unfortunately and ignorantly, our English translators of the Bible often translated both the innocent and the hurtful beverages under the common name of "wine" and of "strong drink." That acute and profound scholar, Professor Moses Stuart, of Andover, has wisely said, "My final conclusion is, that wherever the Scriptures speak of wine as a comfort, a blessing, or a libation to God, they can mean only such drinks as contained no alcohol; but in those passages in which they denounce wine and prohibit it and connect it with drunkenness, they can mean only the alcoholic intoxicant." Facts show that the ancients not only preserved wine unfermented, but regarded it as of a higher flavor than the fermented wine. This unfermented wine, or blood of the grape, could be used without any inebriation whatever. Why, then, shall we not take the sound and safe position that only the harmless and innocent beverages are commended in the Bible, and that it is the alcoholic intoxicant which is there denounced and prohibited?

My next witness is Samson, the stalwart deliverer of Israel; the "muscular Christian," for whom, when he was "sore athirst," God wrought a miracle to give him drink. And that drink was not wine or whiskey, but pure cold water. As this man of giant strength comes on the witness-stand before us, he testifies that he never touched wine or strong drink, nor even ate of anything that cometh of the vine! Nor did his mother do so before him. He thus escaped the danger of an hereditary appetite for strong drink, which is the fatal secret of the drunkenness of thousands. Fathers! mothers! if you would have sober and healthful children, keep the virus of this accursed appetite out of your blood!

Now, what saith the wise man? Let us call up Solomon, to whom God gave an understanding heart, so that there was none like unto him. I will read for you his testimony in close and literal translation from the original Hebrew. Hear his inspired words! "Who hath woe? Who hath sorrow? Who hath strifes? Who hath wounds without cause? Who hath blurred eyes? Those who tarry long over the wine; those who enter in to try mixed drinks. Look not on the wine when it shows itself ruddy, when it sparkleth in the cup, when it goeth down smoothly. For at the last it will bite like a serpent, and sting like a viper." Is there any one in this house who can possibly twist this passage into an apology for "moderate drinking"? Then you might as well say that Solomon believed in a moderate playing with snakes, or in being moderately stung by a nest of adders.

I might summon before you the prophet Hosea, with his solemn declaration, "Whoredom and wine and new wine, take away the heart." And sublime

Habakkuk, too, with that terrific word of warning to every one of us, "Woe unto him that giveth his neighbor drink, that puttest thy bottle to him!" I wish that this thrilling passage of God's Word could be posted, not only over every dramshop door, but also over every table on which false hospitality ever places a decanter.

Many other Bible witnesses, too, I might summon. But let us make room for Paul, the heroic, self-denying apostle, who strove to "keep his body under," and who exhorts us all to present to God even our bodies as a "living offering." He it is who was inspired to utter that fearful announcement, "Nor drunkards shall inherit the kingdom of God." We may reasonably expect, therefore, that he will give his fellow-men no excuse for tampering with that which leads to drunkenness. We are not disappointed. Paul is most emphatic in his counsels to entire abstinence. In his first letter to the Thessalonians, he says: "Let us watch and *drink not*." This is the honest reading of the Greek word, which our translators have rendered "sober." In describing the qualifications for a Christian minister, Paul says: "A bishop [*i. e.*, an overseer of souls] must be abstemious, sober-minded, *not sitting by the wine!*" I translate this vitally important verse thus by the authority of the late Dr. Edward Robinson and other profound scholars. I could not ask for a stronger command to total abstinence on the part of every Christian minister.

So rigid was Paul in his total abstinence principles that, when he writes to his abstaining brother Timothy, he does not recommend him to use wine as a beverage. He carefully says, "Do not drink any longer water only, but use a little wine for thy stomach's sake." He prescribes "wine" only as a medicine, and but "little" at that. (Will some one here please to prove to me that even that little wine was an intoxicating drink?) But lest Paul's position could be possibly misunderstood, he has left to us that memorable utterance so redolent of Gospel philanthropy: "It is good not to eat flesh [*i. e.*, meat offered to idols], nor drink wine, nor anything whereby thy brother stumbleth." It is claimed that this passage enjoins total abstinence on the ground of "expediency." Well, you may use this word if you choose, but I maintain that it is an expediency that has the tremendous *grip* of a moral duty. For if my obligation to do anything which is required to save a fellow-creature from ruin be not a duty, I should like to know where, under the broad heavens, there is a duty? My Bible teaches me that a pernicious example is a sin against the law of love for my neighbor.

We have now briefly examined the testimonies of the chief Bible witnesses on the great question before us. Are there any witnesses to be summoned on the other side? We wait for any to appear. But stop! Here comes an expounder of God's Word who brings forward the example of his ineffable Lord and Saviour, and asserts that Jesus Christ actually manufactured, by miracle, a large quantity of alcoholic intoxicants to be drunk at a wedding-feast!

If we had not heard this portentous assertion made ten thousand times already, we should be horrified. But let us look it squarely in the face. Our opponents will admit that our divine Lord "knew what was in man." He certainly knew also the nature of an alcoholic drink, its temptations, its woes, and its viper-sting. He certainly *could* have created a perfectly innocent unintoxicating wine, similar to the pure blood of the grape. In view of this perfect knowledge and sovereign power of our loving Lord, we defy any man to prove that he actually created and gave to his own children a draught of alcoholic poison. If the Son of God then and there created alcohol, then was it the first time and the only time in human history when divine power ever made what nowhere else exists in nature!

"Thou hast kept the good wine until now," said the governor of the feast, when he tasted of the beverage which Jesus had made. Was that wine "good" which ministered to drunkenness? Was that wine "good" which contained beneath its ruby sparkle the fang of the viper and the sting of the adder? What were considered the best wines in Palestine?

A pertinent answer to this last question is given by the late Moderator of our Presbyterian General Assembly, who declares, in his learned comment on this passage, "All who know of the wines then used well understand the unfermented juice of the grape. The present wines of Jerusalem and Lebanon, as we tasted them, were without intoxicating qualities such as we get here in liquors called wines. Those were esteemed the *best* which were least strong." He is firm in his judgment that the wine at Cana was not alcoholic.

This satisfactory opinion of the learned Professor Jacobus is also maintained by such eminent scholars as Professor Moses Stuart, the lamented Albert Barnes, Professor Owen, President Nott, Dr. Lees, and scores of careful students of the inspired Word. Our divine Lord never made an alcoholic intoxicant! To this firm conviction I have always stood, and shall stand until I meet him on his throne in the day of his glorious appearing. It is even a profanation to couple his holy name with the fiery potations of our times.

I trust you have not been wearied by this brief review of the teachings of God's inspired book. Those teachings may be summed up in four distinct affirmations. Observe each one of them carefully:

1. The Bible, in various passages, points out the evils and the perils of intoxicating drinks. It never pronounces a blessing on an intoxicant, and often warns men against its use. Several passages forbid such use.

2. The Bible, in several passages, approves and commends abstinence from intoxicating beverages. There is not a single verse in this book which condemns total abstinence.

3. The whole spirit of the Word of God teaches

self-control and self-denial, both for our own sakes and for the good of our fellow-men. The only passage in which the word "moderation" occurs has no reference whatever to "moderate drinking."

4. Lastly and chiefly, I find that God's LAW against intoxicants written on the human BODY is not contradicted by his LAW written in this blessed BOOK. Each one sustains and confirms the other.

Here I might rest this argument. I trust that it has been made clear to you that total abstinence from these deceptive and deadly intoxicants is *safe* and *sound* and *Scriptural.* But, before closing, let me speak frankly, though briefly, in protest against certain views advocated by beloved brethren from whom it pains me to differ.

It has been asserted that the use of intoxicating beverages is in itself neither morally wrong nor morally right, but is a "matter of indifference." A man may drink alcoholic liquors without doing any wrong, or he may let them alone without any virtue in the act of refraining. The question of drinking or not drinking, often involves no more guilt or goodness than the question of getting up before sunrise or after sunrise in the morning!

Brethren, I solemnly protest that a question which practically involves the salvation or the damnation of millions is not to be "whistled down the wind" in this summary fashion. I ask you, is it an indifferent matter whether you violate God's law against intoxicants written on your bodily constitutions? Is it a matter of indifference to go against the whole tenor of God's Word? Is it a matter of indifference to partake of that which doth bite like a serpent and sting like an adder? Is it a matter of indifference for you, fellow-Christians, to give your sanction and *example* in favor of those drinking-customs which are cursing society and crowding hell with their victims? The proposition that the drinking of a glass of alcoholic intoxicant involves no moral right or moral wrong, strikes directly at God's law written on our bodies, and the law of self-denial written in his book. There is not a grog-seller in Brooklyn who would ask to have his dramshop-door set open wider than that proposition!

Again, it is often said that as the use of alcoholic beverages is intrinsically a matter of "indifference," it may be left to every man's conscience to decide. Individual conscience then becomes the arbiter. In reply to this postulate, I affirm that it is as much the duty of every man to regulate his conscience by the teachings of God on our bodies and in his book, as it is to regulate his watch by the movements of the sun. But suppose that a man's conscience allows him to use habitually the deceitful glass, will a conviction of conscience save him from the *consequences* of his acts?

Sixty years ago, there was an eminent clergyman in New Jersey who used wine in order to arouse his nervous sensibilities while in the pulpit He conscientiously believed that he could preach more eloquently and impressively while under the influence of alcoholic stimulant. But he soon found that he must increase the amount of his dram in order to quicken his jaded powers, and, before he was aware, he had fallen into drunkenness and public disgrace! He afterwards repented in dust and ashes, and was restored to his ministerial office as a total abstainer. Now, this Christian minister followed the guidance of his deluded conscience until it threw him squarely against a divine law as immutable as the law of gravitation. And this may be the wretched fate of any man who does not enlighten his moral sense by the clear teachings of God and of human experience. Woe unto them that call evil good, and good evil; that put darkness for light, and light for darkness! "There is a way that seemeth right unto a man, but the end thereof are the ways of death."

A third proposition is laid down by those who hold to the "liberty" of using intoxicating beverages, which reads thus: "I may use wine in moderate measure, but if I should at length find the appetite for it uncontrollable, I would never touch it again." We would smile at the verdant simplicity of this idea if it were not too sadly serious for laughter. Millions of drunkards now in perdition have lulled themselves at first with this delusion until they found it as deceptive as the liquors which they drank. When the appetite becomes "uncontrollable," it is too late. With millions of inebriates, the awful appetite becomes their master before they suspect it. For "wine is a mocker." Whoso tampers with it must and will be "deceived thereby." This seductive and blinding quality inheres in the very nature of alcoholic stimulants. And upon this *serpent-quality* of strong drink we base a moral duty to let the adders' nest alone. No man has a moral right to thrust his finger into the cockatrice's den.

Finally, it has been affirmed that this beneficent total abstinence reform—which has been so nobly defended by the Lyman Beechers and the Albert Barneses among the dead, and by the John Halls and the Newman Halls among the living—has no other basis to rest on than the principle of "expediency." Let me here say that I rejoice to welcome to our ranks all good men and women who forswear the intoxicating cup because they believe it expedient to do so. But for one, I practise total abstinence not only because it is expedient, but because it is *right.* The longer I live, the more suspicious I grow as to the use of that word "expediency." It is rather too elastic. It often lacks "bottom" and backbone. As a principle of moral obligation, it will not always "hold water." Nay; I have even known it to be made to hold several gallons of exceedingly bad liquor. I have caught it tippling slyly behind the door. I have seen it tripping up even some good men's heels, when a strong conviction of moral right would have held them as firm as the everlasting hills.

To-day I advocate a total abstinence from alcoholic poisons as a *duty* towards our God, a *duty* to ourselves, and a *duty* to our tempted and suffering fellow-creatures. If the use of intoxicating beverages is forbidden by the law of God written on our bodies, and also by several direct prohibitions in God's Word; if such use is opposed to the well-being of man and to the glory of Jehovah, then is it our duty to let them alone.

I therefore set before you the clear, straight path of total abstinence from all intoxicants. It is the safe path. It is the true path. It has led thousands to that cross of Jesus Christ which is the entrance to everlasting life and heaven's unfading glories. It is a path which has no ambushes, or pitfalls for the unwary footstep.

This is the way, walk ye in it! And remember that no man was ever yet lost in a straight road!

THE EVIL BEAST.

"IT is my son's coat; an evil beast hath devoured him."—GEN. xxxvii. 33.

JOSEPH'S brethren dipped their brother's coat in goat's blood, and then brought the dabbled garment to their father, cheating him with the idea that a ferocious animal had slain him, and thus hiding their infamous behavior.

But there is no deception about that which we hold up to your observation to-night. A monster such as never ranged African thicket or Hindostan jungle hath tracked this land, and with bloody maw hath strewn the continent with the mangled carcasses of whole generations; and thereare tens of thousands of fathers and mothers who could hold up the garment of their slain boy, truthfully exclaiming, "It is my son's coat; an evil beast hath devoured him."

There has, in all ages and climes, been a tendency to the improper use of stimulants. Noah, as if disgusted with the prevalence of water in his time, took to strong drink. By this vice, Alexander the Conqueror was conquered. The Romans at their feasts fell off their seats with intoxication. Four hundred millions of our race are opium-eaters. India, Turkey, and China have groaned with the desolation; and by it have been quenched such lights as Halley and De Quincey. One hundred millions are the victims of the betel-nut, which has specially blasted the East Indies. Three hundred millions chew hashish, and Persia, Brazil, and Africa suffer the delirium. The Tartars employ murowa; the Mexicans, the agave; the people at Guarapo, an intoxicating quality taken from sugar-cane; while a great multitude, that no man can number, are the disciples of alcohol. To it they bow. Under it they are trampled. In its trenches they fall. On its ghastly holocaust they burn.

Could the muster roll of this great army be called, and they could come up from the dead, what eye could endure the reeking, festering putrefaction and beastliness? What heart could endure the groan of agony?

Drunkenness: Does it not jingle the burglar's key? Does it not whet the assassin's knife? Does it not cock the highwayman's pistol? Does it not wave the incendiary's torch? Has it not sent the physician reeling into the sick-room; and the minister with his tongue thick into the pulpit? Did not an exquisite poet, from the very top of his fame, fall a gibbering sot, into the gutter, on his way to be married to one of the fairest daughters of New England, and at the very honr the bride was decking herself for the altar; and did he not die of delirium tremens, almost unattended, in a hospital?

Tamerlane asked for one hundred and sixty thousand skulls with which to build a pyramid to his own honor. He got the skulls, and built the pyramid. But if the bones of all those who have fallen as a prey to dissipation could be piled up, it would make a vaster pyramid.

Who will gird himself for the journey, and try with me to scale this mountain of the dead—going up miles high on human carcasses to find still other peaks far above, mountain above mountain, white with the bleached bones of drunkards?

I will begin at our National and State capitals. Like government, like people. Henry VIII. blasted all England with his example of uncleanness. Catharine of Russia drags down a whole empire with her nefarious behavior. No Christian man can be indifferent to what, every hour of every day, goes on at Washington. While the Presidential Impeachment Trial advanced, some of the men who were to render their solemn verdict on the subject were reeling in and out of the Senate Chamber—the intoxicated representatives of a free Christian people. It was a great question whether several members of that high court could be got sober in time to vote.

Only recently, a senator from New England rises up with tongue so thick, and with utterance so nonsensical, that he is led into the ante-room. He was a good Republican.

One of the Middle States has a representative who very rarely appears in his seat, for the reason that he is so great an inebriate that he can neither walk nor ride. He is a good Democrat.

As God looks down on our State and National Legislatures, he holds us responsible. We cast the votes. We lift up the legislators.

Will the time never come when this nation shall rise up higher than partisanship, and cast its suffrage for sober men?

The fact is, that the two millions of dollars which the liquor dealers raised for the purpose of swaying State and National legislation has done its work, and the nation is debauched. Higher than legislatures or the Congress of the United States is the Whiskey Ring!

The Sabbath has been sacrificed to the rum traffic. To many of our people, the best day of the week is the worst. Bakers must keep their shops closed on the Sabbath. It is dangerous to have loaves of bread going out on Sunday. The shoe store is closed: severe penalty will attack the man who sells boots on the Sabbath. But down with the window-shutters of the grogshops! Our laws shall confer particular honor upon the rum traffickers. All other trades must stand aside for these. Let our citizens who have disgraced themselves by trading in clothing, and hosiery, and hardware, and lumber, and coal take off their hats to the rum-seller, elected to particular honor. It is unsafe for any other class of men to be allowed license for Sunday work. But swing out your signs, O ye traffickers in the peace of families, and in the souls of immortal men! Let the corks fly, and the beer foam, and the rum go tearing down the half-consumed throat of the inebriate. God does not see! Does he? Judgment will never come! Will it?

People say, "Let us have more law to correct this evil." We have more law now than we execute. In what city is there a mayoralty that dare do it? The fact is, that there is no advantage in having the law higher than public opinion. What would be the use of the Maine Law in New York? Neal Dow, the Mayor of Portland, came out with a posse, and threw the rum of the city into the street. But I do not believe there are three mayors in the United States with his courage or nobility of spirit.

I do not know but that God is determined to let drunkenness triumph, and the husbands and sons of thousands of our best families be destroyed by this vice, in order that our people, amazed and indignant, may rise up and demand the extermination of this municipal crime. There is a way of driving down the hoops of a barrel so tight that they break.

We are, in this country, at this time, trying to regulate this evil by a tax on whiskey. You might as well try to regulate the Asiatic cholera or the small-pox by taxation. The men who distil liquors are, for the most part, unscrupulous, and the higher the tax, the more inducement to illicit distillation. New York produces forty thousand gallons of whiskey every twenty-four hours, and the most of it escapes the tax. The most vigilant officials fail to discover the cellars, and vaults, and sheds where this work is done.

Oh! the folly of trying to restrain an evil by government tariff! If every gallon of whiskey made—if every flask of wine produced, should be taxed a thousand dollars, it would not be enough to pay for the tears it has wrung from the eyes of widows and orphans, nor for the blood it has dashed on the Christian church, nor for the catastrophe of the millions it has destroyed for ever.

I sketch two houses in this street. The first is bright as home can be. The father comes at nightfall, and the children run out to meet him. Luxuriant evening meal. Gratulation, and sympathy, and laughter. Music in the parlor. Fine pictures on the wall. Costly books on the stand. Well-clad household. Plenty of everything to make home happy.

House the second: Piano sold yesterday by the sheriff. Wife's furs at pawnbroker's shop. Clock gone. Daughter's jewelry sold to get flour. Carpets gone off the floor. Daughters in faded and patched dresses. Wife sewing for the stores. Little child with an ugly wound on her face, struck in an angry blow. Deep shadow of wretchedness falling in every room. Door-bell rings. Little children hide. Daughters turn pale. Wife holds her breath. Blundering step in the hall. Door opens. Fiend, brandishing his fist, cries, "Out! out! What are you doing here?"

Did I call this house the second? No; it is the same house. Rum transformed it. Rum embruted the man. Rum sold the shawl. Rum tore up the carpets. Rum shook his fist. Rum desolated the hearth. *Rum* changed that paradise into a hell!

I sketch two men that you know very well. The first graduated from one of our literary institutions. His father, mother, brothers, and sisters were present to see him graduate. They heard the applauding thunders that greeted his speech. They saw the bouquets tossed to his feet. They saw the degree conferred and the diploma given. He never looked so well. Everybody said, "What a noble brow! What a fine eye! What graceful manners! What brilliant prospects!" All the world opens before him, and cries, "Hurrah! hurrah!"

Man the second: Lies in the station-house tonight. The doctor has just been sent for to bind up the gashes received in a fight. His hair is matted, and makes him look like a wild beast. His lip is bloody and cut.

Who is this battered and bruised wretch that was picked up by the police, and carried in drunk, and foul, and bleeding?

Did I call him man the second? He is man the *first!* Rum transformed him. Rum destroyed his prospects. Rum disappointed parental expectation. Rum withered those garlands of commencement day. Rum cut his lip. Rum dashed out his manhood. RUM, accursed RUM!

This foul thing gives one swing to its scythe, and our best merchants fall; their stores are sold, and they sink into dishonored graves.

Again it swings its scythe, and some of our best

physicians fall into sufferings that their wisest prescriptions cannot cure.

Again it swings its scythe, and ministers of the Gospel fall from the heights of Zion, with long resounding crash of ruin and shame.

Some of your own households have already been shaken. Perhaps you can hardly admit it; but where was your son last night? Where was he Friday night? Where was he Thursday night? Wednesday night? Tuesday night? Monday night?

Nay, have not some of you in your own bodies felt the power of this habit? You think that you could stop? Are you sure you could? Go on a little further, and I am sure you cannot. I think, if some of you should try to break away, you would find a chain on the right wrist, and one on the left; one on the right foot, and another on the left. This serpent does not begin to hurt until it has wound round and round. Then it begins to tighten, and strangle, and crush, until the bones crack, and the blood trickles, and the eyes start from their sockets, and the mangled wretch cries, "O God! O God! help! help!" But it is too late; and not even the fires of woe can melt the chain when once it is fully fastened.

I have shown you the EVIL BEAST. The question is, Who will hunt him down, and how shall we shoot him? I answer, First, by getting our children right on this subject. Let them grow up with an utter aversion to strong drink. Take care how you administer it even as medicine. If you find that they have a natural love for it, as some have, put in a glass of it some horrid stuff, and make it utterly nauseous. Teach them, as faithfully as you do the catechism, that rum is a fiend. Take them to the almshouse, and show them the wreck and ruin it works. Walk with them into the homes that have been scourged by it. If a drunkard hath fallen into a ditch, take them right up where they can see his face, bruised, savage, and swollen, and say, "Look, my son. Rum did that!" Looking out of your window at some one who, intoxicated to madness, goes through the street, brandishing his fist, blaspheming God, a howling, defying, shouting, reeling, raving, and foaming maniac, say to your son, "Look; that man was once a child like you." As you go by the grogshop, let them know that that is the place where men are slain, and their wives made paupers, and their children slaves. Hold out to your children all warnings, all rewards, all counsels, lest in after-days they break your heart and curse your gray hairs.

A man laughed at my father for his scrupulous temperance principles, and said: "I am more liberal than you. I always give my children the sugar in the glass after we have been taking a drink."

Three of his sons have died drunkards, and the fourth is imbecile through intemperate habits.

Again, we will battle this evil at the ballot-box. How many men are there who can rise above the feelings of partisanship, and demand that our officials shall be sober men?

I maintain that the question of sobriety is higher than the question of availability; and that, however eminent a man's services may be, if he have habits of intoxication, he is unfit for any office in the gift of a Christian people. Our laws will be no better than the men who make them.

Spend a few days at Harrisburg, or Albany, or Washington, and you will find out why, upon these subjects, it is impossible to get righteous enactments.

Again, we will war upon this evil by organized societies. The friends of the rum traffic have banded together; annually issue their circulars; raise fabulous sums of money to advance their interests; and by grips, pass-words, signs, and stratagems set at defiance public morals. Let us confront them with organizations just as secret, and, if need be, with grips, and pass-words, and signs maintain our position. There is no need that our philanthropic societies tell all their plans. I am in favor of all lawful strategy in the carrying on of this conflict. I wish to God we could lay under the wine-casks a train which, once ignited, would shake the earth with the explosion of this monstrous iniquity!

Again, we will try the power of the pledge. There are thousands of men who have been saved by putting their names to such a document. I know it is laughed at; but there are some men who, having once promised a thing, do it. "Some have broken the pledge." Yes; they were liars. But all men are not liars. I do not say that it is the duty of all persons to make such signature; but I do say that it would be the salvation of many of you.

The glorious work of Theobald Mathew can never be estimated. At his hand four millions of people took the pledge, and multitudes in Ireland, England, Scotland, and America have kept it till this day. The pledge signed to thousands has been the proclamation of emancipation.

Again, we expect great things from inebriate asylums. They have already done a glorious work. I think that we are coming at last to treat inebriation as it ought to be treated, namely, as an awful disease, self-inflicted, to be sure, but nevertheless a disease. Once fastened upon a man, sermons won't cure him; temperance lectures will not eradicate it; religious tracts will not remove it; the Gospel of Christ will not arrest it. Once under the power of this awful thirst, the man is bound to go on; and, if the foaming glass were on the other side of perdition, he would wade through the fires of hell to get it. A young man in prison had such a strong thirst for intoxicating liquors that he cut off his hand at the wrist, called for a bowl of brandy in order to stop the bleeding, thrust his wrist into the bowl, and then drank the contents.

Stand not, when the thirst is on him, between a man and his cups. Clear the track for him. Away with the children; he would tread their life out. Away with the wife; he would dash her to death. Away with the cross; he would run it down. Away with the Bible; he would tear it up for the winds. Away with heaven; he considers it worthless as a straw. "Give me the drink! Give it to me! Though hands of blood pass up the bowl, and the soul trembles over the pit—the drink! give it to me! Though it be pale with tears; though the froth of everlasting anguish float on the foam—give it to me! I drink to my wife's woe; to my children's rags; to my eternal banishment from God, and hope, and heaven! Give it to me! the drink!"

Again, we will contend against these evils by trying to persuade the respectable classes of society to the banishment of alcoholic beverages. You who move in elegant and refined associations; you who drink the best liquors; you who never drink until you lose your balance, let us look each other in the face on this subject. You have, under God, in your power the redemption of this land from drunkenness. Empty your cellars and wine-closets of the beverage, and then come out and give us your hand, your vote, your prayers, your sympathies. Do that, and I will promise three things: First, That you will find unspeakable happiness in having done your duty. Secondly, You will probably save somebody—perhaps your own child. Thirdly, you will not, in your last hour, have a regret that you made the sacrifice, if sacrifice it be.

As long as you make drinking respectable, drinking customs will prevail, and the ploughshare of death, drawn by terrible disasters, will go on turning up this whole continent, from end to end, with the long, deep, awful furrow of drunkards' graves.

Oh! how this rum fiend would like to go and hang up a skeleton in your beautiful house, so that, when you opened the front door to go in, you would see it in the hall; and, when you sat at your table, you would see it hanging from the wall; and, when you opened your bedroom, you would find it stretched upon your pillow; and, waking at night, you would feel its cold hand passing over your face and pinching at your heart.

There is no home so beautiful but it may be devastated by the awful curse. It throws its jargon into the sweetest harmony. What was it that silenced Sheridan's voice, and shattered the golden sceptre with which he swayed parliaments and courts? What foul sprite turned the sweet rhythm of Robert Burns into a tuneless babble? What brought down the majestic form of one who awed the American Senate with his eloquence, and after a while carried him home dead-drunk from the office of Secretary of State? What was it that swamped the noble spirit of one of the heroes of the last war, until, the other night, in a drunken fit, he reeled from the deck of a Western steamer, and was drowned? There was one whose voice we all loved to hear. He was one of the most classic orators of the century. People wondered why a man of so pure a heart and so excellent a life should have such a sad countenance always. They knew not that his wife was a sot.

I call upon those who are guilty of these indulgences to quit the path of death. Oh! what a change it would make in your home! Do you see how everything there is being desolated? Would you not like to bring back joy to your wife's heart, and have your children come out to meet you with as much confidence as once they showed? Would you not like to rekindle the home-lights that long ago were extinguished? It is not too late to change. It may not entirely obliterate from your soul the memory of wasted years and a ruined reputation, nor smooth out from your anxious brow the wrinkles which trouble has ploughed. It may not call back unkind words uttered or rough deeds done; for perhaps in those awful moments you struck her! It may not take from your memory the bitter thoughts connected with some little grave. But it is not too late to save yourself, and secure for God and your family the remainder of your fast-going life.

But perhaps you have not utterly gone astray. I may address one who may not have quite made up his mind. Let your better nature speak out. You take one side or the other in the war against drunkenness. Have you the courage to put your foot downright, and say to your companions and friends, "I will never drink intoxicating liquor in all my life; nor will I countenance the habit in others"? Have nothing to do with strong drink. It has turned the earth into a place of skulls, and has stood opening the gate to a lost world to let in its victims, until now the door swings no more upon its hinges, but, day and night, stands wide open to let in the agonized procession of doomed men.

Do I address one whose regular work in life is to administer to this appetite? For God's sake, get out of that business! If a woe be pronounced upon the man who gives his neighbor drink, how many woes must be hanging over the man who does this every day and every hour of the day!

God knows better than you do yourself the number of drinks you have poured out. You keep a list; but a more accurate list has been kept than yours. You may call it Burgundy, Bourbon, Cognac, Heidsieck, Hock: God calls it strong drink. Whether you sell it in low oyster cellar or behind the polished counter of first-class hotel, the divine curse is upon you. I tell you plainly that you will meet your customers one day when there will be no counter between you. When your work is done on earth, and you enter the reward of your business, all the souls of the men whom you have destroyed will crowd around you, and pour their bitterness into your cup. They will show you their wounds, and say, "You made them"; and point to their unquenchable thirst, and say, "You kindled it"; and rattle their chain, and say, "You forged it." Then their united groans will smite your ear; and, with the hands out of which you once picked the sixpences and the dimes, they will push you off the verge of great precipices; while rolling up from beneath, and breaking among the crags of death, will thunder:

"*Woe to him that giveth his neighbor drink!*"

THE GOOD SAMARITAN.

"A certain man went down from Jerusalem to Jericho," etc.—LUKE x. 30.

ALL are familiar with the circumstances which called forth this parable. A certain lawyer, not a lawyer as commonly understood by us, but rather what in our day would be denominated a divine, or expounder of the Scriptures. This man belonged to a class who among the Jews made the Bible their peculiar study, and who were therefore regarded as authorities on all questions connected with the laws of Moses. Having heard of him whose fame filled the land, this lawyer, with a desire perhaps to ascertain whether Jesus was as great a Teacher as reported, put this question to the Saviour, "Master, what shall I do to inherit eternal life?" Knowing who it was that asked the question, and his motive in so doing, Jesus replied by asking a question directly in the line of the interrogator's profession, "What is written in the law? how readest thou?" To this the lawyer replied by reciting the sum of the ten commandments. "This do," said Jesus, "and thou shalt live." Conscious that all this he had not done, yet unwilling to acknowledge it, and thinking he sees a door open through which he can escape from the dilemma into which his own question has brought himself, he asks, "Who is my neighbor?" hoping that if the term neighbor can be kept within narrow limits, he may yet be all right. In reply, our Lord narrates the beautiful and touching story of the Good Samaritan, the parable which we have chosen as the theme of our morning's discourse.

THE SCENE

is laid in a wild and rocky district of country lying between Jerusalem and Jericho, whose mountain caves furnish hiding-places to men as savage as the scenes they infest. The testimony of the Jewish historian, Josephus, as well as that of Jerome and others, confirms the Gospel narrative as to the dangers which beset travellers journeying between these two large cities; yea, so many murders had been committed at one particular part of the road that it was called the Red or Bloody Way; and so unsafe had it become for travellers, that Jerome states the Romans found it necessary to erect a fort there for their protection. It was somewhere among the rocky defiles of this road that the traveller was waylaid by robbers, wounded, stripped, robbed, and left half-dead. Now, if there be a traveller robbed and wounded on the journey of life, it is the drunkard; and, if there be a bloody path in the journey of life, that path is the way which the drunkard pursues; and if there be a class of men to be met with who, answering to the description of those who infested—for the purposes of plunder and murder—the road between Jerusalem and

Jericho, is it not that class who waylay the unwary at every turn, and prey upon the vices, weaknesses, and excesses of the thoughtless drunkard?

THE OBJECT.

(1.) *In the injuries he received.*—This traveller was wounded and left half-dead; loss of blood and exposure would doubtless, if help had not been rendered, have speedily deprived him of life. Does it fare any better with the victim of strong drink?

(a.) There are the *physical* injuries he receives. I need not prove to you that alcohol from its very nature cannot be received into the human system without doing it violence. The drunkard does not need a doctor's certificate with 2,000 names attached to convince him that intoxicating drink is his enemy. What are his feelings subsequent to a debauch? His head aches dreadfully, the skin is dry, the mouth is parched, and thirst excessive. Look at his eyes—where is their wonted fire? Listen to him when he speaks—his very voice is changed. There is not a blood-vessel that does not suffer from the scorching liquid. Every vein in his body is made a highway for torture to travel on. There is not a nerve in the whole animal economy escapes the withering influence. The heart, the lungs, the liver, the stomach, all suffer. Their natural action is destroyed, and the train is laid for a variety of diseases.

(b.) There are *mental* injuries. It is not the body alone which suffers. The wound reaches

back to that mysterious nature which sits modestly concealed behind its veil of clay. Alcohol, though affecting more or less the whole system, is peculiarly a *brain poison.* Now, as the brain is the organ of the mind, you cannot injure, alter, or poison the brain, without equally injuring, altering, and poisoning the mind. A few doses of laudanum will at once convince the greatest sceptic of this fact. But alcohol not only attacks the brain and mind; it affects particular portions of the brain, and hence particular faculties of the mind, in different ways. Thus all observation proves that it weakens and subverts the will, confuses and perverts the intellectual powers, diminishes and lowers the consciousness and other moral sentiments, whilst it, at the same time, intensifies the imagination and other æsthetic faculties, and goads on the mere animal faculties and propensities to mastery and dominion over all. You may tell me that these results only follow excess; if only enough be taken to produce "exhilaration," "pleasurable excitement," no such effects are produced. No doubt this exhilaration, by heightening the æsthetic faculties, produces a greater flow of language, eloquence, and wit. But is it not the fact that, when people are thus exhilarated by drink, they will say and do improper things they would otherwise have left unsaid and undone; they will tell secrets, are more rash and venturesome, and oh! how often is "the wine-strong Hercules struck down by his own club"—his strength gone, he reels, and babbles, and falls, as if affected by the paralysis of the insane; yea, how often does the scene close in insanity.

(c.) There are the *moral* injuries. Who can drink without a deterioration of the moral faculty, a deadening of conscience? What is the meanness and dishonesty to which a drinker will not condescend; and from which he would recoil but for the depraving influence under which he has placed himself? Like a hot-blast furnace, alcohol intensifies a man's natural depravity, and develops principles of evil which might never have reached maturity but for the vigor which it imparts to them.

2. *The Sufferings Endured.*—What must have been the mental anguish of this poor man when left by the robbers? Even at the present day, travellers tell us that of all the roads travelled, this between Jerusalem and Jericho is the most dangerous, and that travellers are rarely allowed by the Governor of Jerusalem to proceed to Jericho and the Dead Sea without an escort, so thickly is it infested with robbers. How did this poor wounded man know but that his assailants might return and complete their work of blood, or that others as merciless might finish what they had begun; or, if let alone by man, there were vultures and wolves who might sweep down upon him at any moment? Oh! the anguish of mind as he there lay to die thus; the thought is agonizing! And it is when we consider the mental anguish of the poor victim of intemperance we realize somewhat of the curse and climax of his sorrows. The mind has capacities of suffering

of which few but drunkards know aught. While the low and ignorant drinkers are not strangers to this mental anguish, how dreadful must the sufferings be in the case of those of superior minds and cultivation. A man may deny the Bible, he may argue himself into the disbelief of eternal realities, and yet, without the ministry of a Nathan, the hour will come when conscience will be more dreadful than the voice of any earthly prophet, as it peoples the scene around him with the remembrance of unforgiven sins and the ghosts of murdered joys. The inebriate awakes from his delirium delight to find himself in a very hell of agony. Others can gather joys from the past, but not he. What memories can he call up that he would not rather have buried for ever? "Oh! the agony! the agony!" said one to me, the other day—a gentleman known throughout the whole land, endowed with as fine a mind as ever God gave to mortal, and whose sympathies and affections are as tender and loving as his intellect is great and noble, but who, yielding to temptation, became a victim to the "cup"—"oh! the agony! the agony of these few days! All the trials and sorrows and griefs of my past life (fifty years), and they have been neither few nor light, are not to be compared to the suffering of these few days. For," he added, "in these I have had consolations and alleviations, but in this none. The essence of my misery is, it is *self-procured.*" No wonder, rather than endure such agonies, many seek refuge in the death of the suicide.

3. *There is the Loss Sustained.*—The thieves stripped the poor traveller of his raiment, robbed him of his money, his time, and his strength. All this and something worse befalls the drunkard: he is robbed of that which is dearer to him than all—character. When character is gone, all that gives to human existence its worth and significance is gone, and man becomes no better than the brute, no better than a graven image; he sinks to a level with the beast he drives, or the acres he ploughs. Now, of all the causes which contribute to ruin character, the most formidable is intoxicating drink.

I have seen, and you have seen, men in every department of human pursuit, of the noblest natures and highest attainments, sacrificed to rum. I have seen, and you, too, perhaps, ladies of high birth, of generous affection, of accomplished manners and cultivated mind, excluded from the very society in which they were made drunkards, pensioned off in some cases, and doomed in the private asylum to a life of ignoble restrictions; and in others, cast out for children to hoot at, and passers-by to sigh over in sentimental pity. Oh! what has not this accursed vice wrought in the way of ruining character? What character so noble and so sacred that it has not blasted? Touched by its hell-fire flames, I have seen, and you have seen, the laurel crown changed into ashes on the head of morning genius, and the wings of the poet scorched by it, and they who once played in the light of sunbeams and soared to Alpine heights of fame basely crawling in the dust—the finest mind paralyzed, and the noblest intellect turned into drivelling idiotcy.

Statesmen of no mean fame nor talents we have helped to lift out of Boston gutters. The ermine of the judge and the sacred robe of the divine we have seen sweeping the polluted floor of the bar-room. In all this, I speak what I know, and testify to what I have seen. Men of God! in whose pulpits we have spoken, and under whose preaching we have sat, and from whose hands we have received the communion elements, we have seen dragged from the altar, deposed from the ministry, and degraded before the world as drunkards, and sent, blasted in character and reputation, with quivering lips, and a hell burning within the breast, to homes where once nestled loved ones, but whom they have beggared and disgraced. And these men—whom once I would have as little expected to fall as some of you—as you believe it possible that this vice shall yet degrade me from the pulpit, and cause my boy to blush at mention of his father's name—some of them lie in dishonored graves, some are teaching school, while others are seeking to eke out a living as pedlars of stationery and canvassers for books, and one, as common hostler in a public livery-stable of Boston, has more than once curried the speaker's horse. Oh! the tales we could narrate. Away down in the lowest stratum of human misery and degradation, how many formerly opulent merchants and prosperous tradesmen have we found in our explorations! But is the drinker the only sufferer? No, no! Who has not heard a thousand times repeated the story of the drunkard's home and the wrongs of wife and children. Oh! the domestic sorrows, the miseries caused by drink! Who shall tell of the tears of deserted, starving, wretched, bruised, bleeding, dying women produced by the drinking habits of husbands who once loved them, but who are now dead to every humane feeling, who have violated every sacred vow, and sundered every holy bond? Who shall tell of children trembling at their own father's footsteps, and hiding from his violence? Who shall tell how scenes of domestic bliss have been embittered and converted into scenes of the blackest, saddest misery and woe? The history of these broken-hearted wives, starved, murdered children, like Ezekiel's roll, is written within "with lamentations and weep ings and woe."

Nor in all this do we refer only to the homes of the poor, though scenes in such homes we have witnessed enough to make a man exclaim with Jeremiah, "O that mine head were waters, and mine eyes a fountain of tears, that I might weep day and night."

One man, a fine mechanic, earning the highest wages, was once the head of a happy family, but drink entered, and happiness fled. His is the old story of descent. One night, I remember it well, this man came to his wretched home, as usual, a reeling drunkard; his wife, who had been sick for some days, was at this time very ill indeed. The sight of her sobered to some extent the husband, and he acceded to her request to go and get some medicine. Taking the prescription in his hand, he went to the druggist, got the medicine, but on his return was met by some of his associates, who urged him to go and take just one drink with them. He yielded, drank, and forgot his errand and his suffering wife, and only left that bar-room when he was driven forth by its landlord. On reaching home he was too stupefied to help either himself or his wife. So he rolled himself over on the bed beside the suffering one. During the night the poor woman died—but terrible was that night. The heavens seemed on fire, the lightnings flashed, and the thunders roared. The terrific storm awoke the sleeper; and on opening his eyes he saw beside him the corpse of her whom, before the speaker, at the altar of God, he had sworn to protect and cherish until death. Talk of the refined cruelty which the savage Indians of this land formerly exercised towards their victims! Oh! what prolonged torture did that unhappy woman undergo, week after week, at the hands of her husband! And drink did all this. A kinder husband, when he let drink alone, never lived.

Done! Oh! what could we not tell? The money we have given to the girl, that the mother might buy a coffin in which to lay the form of her dead child, has been taken from that girl by the father in spite of the entreaties of the suffering mother, and, leaving the naked corpse of his child lying upon the table, where we found it, he has gone and spent the money for drink! But there are homes never visited by the police in search of crime or to stay violence, nor by the missionary to feed the hungry or clothe the naked—homes of the outwardly respectable and even affluent, where there are ruined means, broken hearts, careworn faces, blasted reputations, untold sorrows; and drink has done all! Did time and delicacy permit, I could detail, at length, cases which have come under my own observation, and in which my advice has been sought, during my short residence in Boston, saying nothing of my longer experience in New York, which would call forth your deepest commiseration on behalf of the victims, and rouse your just indignation against that which produces such misery.

But you say we exaggerate. Exaggerate? Impossible! As there are grand, bold, beautiful scenes in the physical world which no flight of fancy, no bold strokes of painting, no graphic powers of language, can accurately describe, so, in the moral world, there are scenes of sorrow, and starvation, and disease, and vice, and cruelty, and death, of which we can give no adequate idea. Let no one fancy we select the worst cases or present the worst side of the picture before them. Believe me, it is impossible to exaggerate; impossible even truthfully to paint the effect of this vice either on those who are addicted to it or those who suffer from it. Are there not many here who can testify to this? Ah! few indeed are the families amongst us so happy as not to have had some one near and dear to them either engulfed in this vice or hanging over the preci pice. I have read of a mother who saw her only son drowned before her eyes. Years came and went ere she could calmly look upon the ocean or hear, without pain, the roar of the billows where her son was lost. How many of you have greater cause for hating the sight of the cup that intoxicates! Take your family record; examine the roll. Is there not one name there that fills your heart with anguish? Oh! what memories are associated with that name! What struggles with temptation it recalls! What mingling of joys and sorrows, of hopes and fears! What solemn vows made and violated! what resolutions formed and broken! and what a sad, sad end! Oh! the beggars, the widows, the orphans, the crimes, the woes caused by these drinks! Truly might they be called the seven vials of his wrath, more destructive in their consequences than war, plague, pestilence, or famine—yea, than all combined; slow, it may be, in their march, but oh! they are sure in their grasp, consigning the body to the tomb and the soul to hell! Yes, the soul; for "no drunkard shall inherit the kingdom of God;" and what standards, scales, or calculations can we command to give us even a faint conception of the worth of *one* soul?

II.—THE INDIFFERENCE AND NEGLECT WITH WHICH THE TRAVELLER WAS TREATED.

While the poor man lay in his wretched condition, a priest and a Levite came that way. So soon as the priest got his eye upon him, he kept as far off as he could; and the Levite did little more, for, although he halted a moment and looked at him, he grudged the aid demanded and hurried away. Here are representative characters of many who treat the drunkard with similar indifference and neglect.

The priest did not so much as stop to look at the victim. It was by chance he came that way. Had he known of this case of bleeding humanity, he would doubtless have gone another way. Also, how many are there who care not to look upon the victims of intemperance—who will not hear of them! They never read a temperance tract, never hear a temperance sermon, nor attend a temperance meeting. They have no sympathy with any of this preaching temperance. Strange that there could be such inhumanity, and that, too, in the church! "Thou shalt love thy neighbor" is a divine command. And "who is my neighbor?" Every man is your neighbor, no matter what his condition, his clime, his nation. If he who could say, "I am a Roman," could rouse in his behalf the sympathies of a whole mighty people, he who can say, "I am a man," should touch the hearts of all mankind. The nature which is endowed with reason and destined for immortality, is not to be passed by as an ordinary thing; and what a picture of a glorious nature in ruins! You may measure the height from which it has fallen by the depth to which it has sunk. The miserable drunkard that reels along your streets carries beneath his tattered rags a soul which kingdoms could not purchase—a wronged, a crushed, a ruined soul, but still a soul; and if God's Son could die for it, who may not care for it? Such, alas! there are. It was a "*priest*" that would not look upon the wounded traveller—a man who, by his profession, was bound to help him; and, O God! tell it not in Gath that professed disciples of *him* who found us in our blood, more than half-dead, robbed by sin, and sinking into death eternal, and died to save us, will pass by the poor victims of intemperance and put not forth a hand to help to save them, but will themselves use the drunkard's drink and thus delude others to drink and become victims!

Not much better are they who are represented by the Levite. The Levite stopped and looked on the spectacle, but offered no relief. So thousands there are who thus treat intemperance and its victims. They may now and again read some temperance periodical, or occasionally listen to a temperance sermon, or give a dime or a dollar to help on the cause of temperance, but beyond that they do nothing. As to putting forth any effective effort to save the drunkard or to prevent others from becoming drunkards, they must not be asked. They would be benevolent, but it costs too much. Neither the priest nor the Levite would have passed by the wounded man if they could have helped him at no expense of trouble or sacrifice. And so many would have no objection to help save the drunkard and stay the ravages of intemperance, were it not for the sacrifices they would be called to make. They would have to give up their own favorite beverage, would be laughed at by some of their associates and ostracised by others.

Yet why should Christians hesitate? In every enterprise undertaken for the benefit of mankind, the Christian public have a part to perform; but more especially when that enterprise aims at the moral improvement of the world. In questions of government, or matters of mere temporal concern, perhaps the Christian may find an apology for his neutrality, as being engaged in objects of a higher and more sublime benevolence. But when vice is to be put down and virtue promoted, he is called upon by a voice which he cannot disregard —by the voice of religion and the voice of God— to take an active and a zealous part. There is no neutrality in this war. When vice prevails, he is an enlisted soldier, and should ever be found in armor. His sword should be always drawn and ready for the conflict. To do good is, and should be, his employment—the business of his life.

That intemperance is a vice we have already seen. Can Christians be indifferent spectators of the desolations of this fell destroyer? Can they view with apathy its ravages, and be guiltless?

III.—THE HELP RENDERED.

After the priest and Levite had passed on and left the unfortunate traveller to die of his wounds, one of a more generous nature drew near. He looked upon the sight; it touched his compassionate nature. And what though the wounded man may be a Jewish merchant and he a Samaritan with whom the Jews have no dealings, but towards whom they cherish a bitter hatred?—he was a needy, suffering man, and he has the means of helping him. So, instantly dismounting, he spoke kindly to the sufferer, examined his wounds, anointed them with oil, bound them up, gave him of the wine he had with him, placed him upon his beast, and, regardless of trouble and expense, conveyed him to an inn, nursed him till the morning, and, when his business would not allow of his remaining longer, paid all the expenses, and gave his pledge to meet all subsequent charges, and then left him. Go thou and do for the drunkard what this Samaritan did for the man who fell among thieves. And what was this?

(1.) *He sacrificed his Wine.*—Some there are who would give up the stronger drinks, but would retain the lighter, or they would contribute of their means and sympathy towards relieving the drunkard or his family, but you must not ask them to give up their own beverage, whatever it may be. Of course, they will take it *moderately!* This is a very easy kind of temperance help, yea, it is the very thing that keeps the stream of intemperance flowing. I have not time now—I wish I had—to speak of the evils of this moderate drinking. I wish I had time to show you that every reeling inebriate was once a moderate drinker, with as little thought of becoming a slave to this vice as any of you have to-day. I wish I had time to show you how moderation can never cure intemperance, because it is the very cause of intemperance, and no cause of an evil can ever be its own remedy. I wish I had time to show you that excess is not, as some imagine and argue, the cause of intemperance, because *it is* intemperance itself, the effect and not the cause. I wish I had time to show you, my dear hearers, that not any of you are safe if you take intoxicating drinks at all. You need not tell me you have used them for years and no harm comes from it; that you take but very little; that you are educated, refined, cultivated, even Christian. Ah! let him that thinketh he standeth take heed lest he fall. I have already shown you that no station, profession, or pursuit is proof against his attacks if indulged in at all. Oh! the secrets locked in this breast of the temptations and struggles of some of the noblest men and women, who had placed themselves by the first glass within the power of the enemy. Dr. Albert Day, who has made a specialty of alcoholic inebriation for years, informed me yesterday that during the last fourteen years over four thousand inebriates have been placed under his care for reformation. Three-fourths of that number were men of position, education, and culture—senators judges, presidents' sons, professors in colleges, doctors of divinity, doctors of medicine, lawyers, authors, artists, and merchants. How the fine gold has become dim; the voice of the lute and the harp which delighted all been silenced! And who made these men drunkards? Where did men of education and refinement acquire the tippler's appetite? Where but at the elegantly furnished tables of moderate drinkers, many of them moderate-drinking religious professors! Why, then, think yourself safe? But apart from this, intemperance is a monster you cannot kill as long as you feed it. All the weapons on earth fall harmless at its feet as long as you give it food. You may as well try to arrest the lightning in its course as stop that mighty stream of intemperance which at this moment flows over this land, as long as you supply the spring from which it issues. And mark you, all who help supply the fountain are partakers of the guilt! Oh! what a large proportion of the respectable and Christian community are at this moment engaged in the spread of intemperance. The more respectable his position, the more religious his character, the more pernicious and extended the influence of the Christian who uses it. It is the countenance which the respectable religious moderate drinkers give that upholds the traffic and enables the dealer to sell to the drunkard. Who but the vilest of the vile would engage in a trade for which drunkards wee the only customers?

Again, how can you seek to reclaim the inebriate from his cups, and get him to abstain, while the bottle is in your closet or the decanter on your sideboard? But I pass to speak of the Samaritan who gave

(2.) *His money.*—He gave his oil and money. Compared with the rescue of a poor wounded traveller, what was money to him? I say it, and say it without fear of contradiction, I know of no cause to which the benevolent ought to contribute more liberally. It is short-sighted charity that aims at the alleviation of drunken poverty merely, and yet nine-tenths of our poverty is nothing else. A better service cannot be rendered the community in the present day than the promotion of the Temperance cause. But to its promotion money is required; and were the National Temperance Society, in whose behalf I this day plead, supplied with ample funds, the good accomplished might be indefinitely increased.

(3.) *This Samaritan sacrificed his time and labor.*—The Samaritan took the wounded man to an inn and watched over him. Now, to save the drunkard similar help is needed. Yea, to prevent the children and youth from becoming drunkards, time and labor are necessary. I rejoice to know that hundreds of young men and young women of this church are daily doing that very work. God bless them, and all associated with them, in their noble efforts. In one of our large cities, a fire broke out in a lofty dwelling. It was near midnight, and the flames had made headway before they were discovered. The fire companies rallied; the inmates escaped in affright; and the firemen worked with a will to subdue the flames. The smoke had become so thick that the outlines of the house were scarcely visible, and the fiery element was raging with fearful power, when a piercing cry thrilled all hearts, as they learned that there was one person yet unsaved within the building.

In a moment a ladder was swung through the flames, and planted against the heated walls, and a brave fireman rushed up its rounds to the rescue. Overcome by the smoke, and perhaps daunted by the hissing flames before him, he halted, and seemed to hesitate. It was an awful scene. A life hung in the balance, and each moment was an age. "Cheer him!" shouted a voice from the crowd; and a wild "Hurrah!" burst like a tempest from the beholding multitude. That cheer did the work; and the brave fireman went upward, amid smoke and flame, and in a moment descended with the rescued man in his arms. When you see those sons and daughters of temperance battling with temptation, struggling with the difficulties and circumstances they must encounter in their work —when, I say, you see them thus endeavoring to rescue the tempted and the fallen, and yet in an hour of weakness discouraged and about to retire from the work, then "cheer them!" Who knows but your words of sympathetic kindness may encourage fainting hearts, strengthen feeble knees, and fix the wavering purpose for nobler deeds?

So much, dear friends, as to what we should do for the drunkard. What shall we do with the

DRUNKARD-MAKERS?

In other words, How is the way of life to be made safe for travellers? If robbers on the highway, who strip their victim of his clothes and treasures, and leave him half-dead, are not guiltless, how can those who strip their victim not only of his clothes and treasures, but of character and manhood and all noble virtues—and who, when they bring their victims to the ground, leave them not half-dead merely, but twice dead—dead in body and in soul—be held guiltless? and if we would clear society of the one, why not of the other class? That the liquor stores are at the root of the evil, who doubts? Here is kept the food of drunkenness! Here is found the poison that initiates the temperate and finishes the intemperate. They are the schools of intemperance, and as long as they are permitted, the land will be infested with drunkenness. These are the Aceldamas of human blood, the shambles where thousands of lives are annually slaughtered, the licensed machinery which turns health into disease, decency into rags, love into hatred, young beauty into loathsomeness, mother's milk into poison, mother's hearts into stone, and the image of God into something baser than the brute. And can any one be engaged in this traffic and not know the mischief he is doing? Can he supply the lava which scorches the land and be innocent? Does he not know the effects of that in which he trades? Does he not know that of those who drink many will be drunken? and can he supply the cause, and detach himself from the effect? Can he hurl firebrands through the city and witness the conflagration, and claim exemption from blame? Can he spread contagion through your families, and, when he hears the dying groans and sees the funeral, tell you that he is innocent? He may tell you that he frowns upon intemperance, and sells not to the drunkard—so perhaps he may. He will sell till the wretch is made drunk, and then refuse him, till he is made *sober again.* But it is too late to talk about denying him now. *The man is ruined,* and the dealer puts the instrument in his hand with which he struck the blow. Do not sell to drunkards! Is it a less evil to make drunkards of sober men, or to kill drunkards? Ask that widowed mother *who* did her the greatest evil—the man who only put her drunken husband in the grave, thus freeing her of his cruelties, or the man who made a drunkard of her only son? Ask those orphan children who did them the greatest injury—the man who made their once sober, kind, and affectionate father a drunkard, and thus blasted all their hopes, and turned their sweet home into the emblem of hell; or the man who, after they had suffered for years the anguish, the indescribable anguish of the drunkard's children, and seen their heartbroken mother in danger of an untimely grave, only killed their father, and thus brought peace and quietness to their home, which of those two men brought upon the children the greatest evil? Can you doubt?

Now, what is to be done to close up these pest-houses—to seal up these fountains of desolation? Do? Why, persuade the keepers of them to leave their trade, we are told! Persuade them? Have you ever tried it? I have, and must confess with poor results. When you can arrest the lightning, still the thunder, and turn back the sea, then you may hope of success. *Persuade* men to give up their nefarious traffic! Why not endeavor to check the evils of lottery, gambling, and prostitution by appeals to the consciences of the keepers of lottery and gambling houses and dens of infamy? *Persuade men!* There are men—unprincipled men—so actuated by selfishness that they will sell till the iron grasp of the law seizes them and compels them to stop. Anxious neighbors may reason with them; wives in rags and tears may entreat them; barefooted, hunger-bitten children may appeal to them, and still they will sell. As long as money can be made by the traffic, there are men who would build their groggery in the crater of a volcano; they would sell rum amid the heavings of an earthquake; and as the drunkard steps down the bank and hangs, suspended by a single twig, over the bottomless pit, they would put between his chattering teeth the draught that would unnerve his arm and plunge him into an eternal abyss. And shall we talk of moral suasion to such men, and let them continue their damning work because they will not be persuaded?

What, then, would you do? Do with them as you would with every foe to society. If the traffickers in rum are engaged in a calling that is inimical to every interest of humanity and religion, then treat them as you would those similarly engaged. Suppose a class of men should advertise themselves as men who had for sale consumptions, and fevers, and palsies, and apoplexies, and deliriums, and death, what would the public say? What the Christian public? Yea, what would our authorities feel called upon to do? The public voice would call for punishment to be meted out to such foes of humanity; and the rulers that would not take speedy vengeance would be execrated and removed. Should a class of persons attempt to dig pitfalls in our public streets to ensnare passengers, or should they make use of bloodhounds to tear and devour our useful citizens, or hire a company of cut-throats to drag out our young men from their peaceful homes and murder them in our streets, what would our authorities do? Tell me where, in the eye of eternal justice, is the difference between him who strikes the blow of death and him who knowingly maddens the brain and tempts and fires the soul to strike it?

The very worst that has been said against the devil is, that he first tempts his victim, then betrays and punishes him through time and eternity. What better are our so-called Christian laws and the liquor-dealers in the traffic in drink? For money, they tempt and betray and punish the weakest of our race, and but too often send them to an eternity of woe! If we have no objections to passing laws against robbery, why object to passing laws against liquor-selling?

As long as these shops of temptation are open, who are safe? You, or your children? None! And what shall become of our weaker brother, whom we have reclaimed, when temptation tracks his steps, and drinking companions are on the alert to drag him into one or other of the numerous dram-shops open on every side to allure and destroy? No wonder so few reclaimed men are permanently saved.

Less than two years ago, there died in his early prime a minister of the Gospel, who was first the victim, and at last the conqueror, of drink. Some years ago, after a severe illness, he stimulated by medical advice. When he had fairly recovered from his sickness, he found himself in the coils of a serpent. It was the old story, alas! more than "twice told!" He fell, struggled to rise, stumbled, and fell again. He resolved, and resisted, prayed, and then in exhaustion yielded. At length, he was induced to enter an inebriate institution, where for a year he remained, beloved and respected by all the officers. When his cure was supposed to be complete, he left to accept a call to a vacant pulpit, his heart still yearning to be engaged in his Lord's work. On entering that church, he frankly told the people his weakness, and the terrible temptation to which he was subject, and threw himself upon their sympathies and their prayers. The people rallied round him and nobly worked with him. Immensely popular in the community, he labored with untiring zeal for the salvation of souls. His labors God richly blessed, but at the close of one year his strength gave way. Again was he tempted to stimulate and—resisted. By the help of divine grace and human sympathy, *he stood.* But he died—died a hero! for he conquered the foe which conquered Alexander the Great, and by which many strong men have been slain.

At his funeral, his wife seemed unusually composed. Wondering at this, the officiating clergyman enquired of her about her apparently happy feelings. "Oh!" said she, "HE'S SAFE! You don't know anything about what we have passed through. For years he and I have been standing on the brink of a precipice, trembling with apprehension that, at any time, he might go over. But *now he's safe!*"

"Safe, indeed," says one; "but what a danger is that from which death is the only escape and the grave the only refuge!" What an evil must that be which, when a man takes it into his bosom becomes a "slimy, gliding, writhing, biting, stinging adder, which winds itself around him, hisses its venom in his ear, and, when he hurls it from him and treads it under foot, pursues its fleeing victim to his death, and thrusts its forked tongue against the iron gateway of the sepulchre, until the loving wife exults to hear the clanging of death's gloomy doors, which none but Christ can open; and the anguish of widowhood is forgotten in the thought that the loved one is SAFE at last!

Brethren, if ever a cause demanded devotedness and sacrifice and energy, temperance is that cause. The interests at stake are the most momentous. Youthful hopes are at stake; female virtue is at stake; domestic happiness is at stake; the church's piety is at stake; the salvation of souls is at stake. And who is to do this work if not the lovers of God and humanity? Come, then, "to the help of the Lord—to the help of the Lord against the mighty!"

Self-Denial for the Promotion of Temperance

A DUTY AND A PLEASURE.

"If meat make my brother to offend, I will eat no flesh while the world standeth."—1 Cor. viii. 13.

SUCH is the noble sentiment of the noblest of men. Some of the Corinthian believers had been converted to Christianity from idolatry; others from Judaism. The Jews abhorred whatever had been offered in worship to an idol; but the Gentiles had not been thus educated. Some of the latter had eaten of the meat which had been offered to an idol, and having been instructed that an idol is nothing, thought it no harm to eat the sacrificial meat. But there were other Gentile converts who had not been so far enlightened, and, not knowing the superior education of their brethren, were in danger of being led astray by their example. St. Paul appeals to the former in behalf of the latter. He concedes that an idol is nothing; that meat offered thereto in worship is not thereby necessarily defiled; that to eat thereof was not sin *per se;* but because the eating thereof was a bad example, and tended to the spiritual injury of those for whom Christ died, he therefore appealed to them to desist from the practice. It was an appeal to Christian magnanimity, to philanthropy, to self-denial. Himself the example of self-denial to all, in the fulness of his own great soul he assures them, in the language of the text: "If meat make my brother to offend, I will eat no flesh while the world standeth."

This incident in apostolic history suggests the line of thought of the present discourse on the subject of temperance. I propose to appeal to the magnanimity of the better classes in society to discontinue the moderate use of wines and liquors, for the benefit of those who are in danger of becoming confirmed inebriates. And in making this appeal, I propose to make certain concessions; to consider the efficaciousness of this proposed self-denial; and then to enforce the duty by a variety of motives.

I. I think we may concede three things. First, that wines and liquors have their legitimate uses. I do not say that they are indispensable, and have no substitute; but it may be safely affirmed that they may be used beneficially. I am sure that every unbiassed man will feel with me bound to concede this much, and hence those ultra views, consigning wines and liquors to perdition, placing them under the ban of the Almighty and society, cannot find favor with calm and reflecting men. Had I time this morning, I could establish the fact beyond peradventure, beyond the shadow of a doubt, that there are two kinds of wine designated in the Bible. On some future occasion, it may be our happiness to discourse on this very thought, and thereby relieve the Lord Jesus Christ, by whose power

> "The modest water, awed by power divine,
> Confessed its God, and blushing turned to wine,"

and thereby relieve other persons whose history is recorded in the Bible, and relieve many passages of Scripture, from misapprehension, by showing the distinction between the good wine and bad, as recorded in the Bible. It is the utmost folly for any man to attempt to explain away certain passages of Scripture on any other hypothesis than the one just mentioned.

Secondly, we are bound to concede that the man who drinks wine and liquor moderately is not a drunkard as denounced in the Holy Scriptures. By no fair interpretation of language, by no proper use of ideas, can such a man be brought under the ban of drunkenness as described in that passage, "No drunkard shall enter the kingdom of heaven." Evidently Scriptural drunkenness implies a ruling passion, a degrading slavery, and a power that has gained the mastery, which is superior to the man himself.

In the next place, I think we are bound to concede that all moderate drinkers do not become confirmed inebriates. You and I can recall persons who, through a series of many years, have been moderate drinkers, and yet are not confirmed drunkards. The reason may be found in their physical organism, which is not susceptible to such influence in their case as in that of other persons. They may drink as much and even more per day than those who are more sensibly affected by the same or less quantity. One inhalation of chloroform will put this man to sleep, while the same quantity will set another man wild. The difference is found in the difference of organic susceptibility. Hence some men may drink and not become confirmed in habits of inebriation, because of the peculiarity of their organism. That they are not drunkards is no credit to them; it is to be placed to the credit of the Creator, for that which does not intoxicate them would and does intoxicate others. Therefore, no argument in favor of the free use of liquors can be drawn from those men who, in despite, as it were, of nature, thus practise moderate drinking through a long series of years. Let us, therefore, remove this old sophistry, and make this point plain and emphatic, and give the credit to God and not to man.

With these concessions freely admitted, let us now pass to consider the question: Were the better classes of society to discontinue the moderate use of wines and liquors, would that tend to diminish the habit and evils of intemperance? If so, how?

1. It would be the expression of apprehension that confirmed inebriety might follow. It would be the tocsin of alarm. It would imply danger ahead. It would be the reassertion of two facts, viz., that all confirmed drunkards were once moderate drinkers, and that all moderate drinkers may become confirmed inebriates. Hence comes the law that absolute safety is in total abstinence. There is safety in that for *all*. This would be an example and a warning.

2. It would render the trade in wines and liquors, including the manufacture and sale—wholesale and retail—of the same, less profitable, and lead to its abandonment. I suppose it is true that the larger profits of the trade are derived from the sale of such wines and liquors as are used by the higher classes of society; that the proprietors of our splendid saloons and hotel bar-rooms derive a larger profit from fancy drinks than from "whiskey straight." The logical effect of the discontinuance of the use of such drinks by such persons would be the closing up of nine-tenths of all our fancy saloons and hotel bar-

rooms. This, in turn, would affect the wholesale trade, and this the manufacturer; and cutting off the supply of drunkards from the ranks of moderate drinkers and rendering the article of intoxication itself scarce, the end would be gained, and intemperance would soon cease to exist. Many a man engages in the wholesale and retail busines of selling liquor not so much from the love of liquor as from his cupidity. And just as soon as these citizens find that their business has ceased to be profitable, they will abandon it and go into something else. If these are facts, are we not justified in the assertion that a grave responsibility for the evils of intemperance rests upon the moderate drinker and upon those who indulge in fancy drinks?

3. Were the higher classes of society to discontinue the moderate use of wines and liquors, the effect would be to render the custom of drinking unfashionable. Fashion is only another term for public sentiment. Acknowledged evils are tolerated by common consent. Public sentiment is the energy of law. There were laws against duelling prior to the duel between Hamilton and Burr, but for lack of public sentiment they were dead. The death of Hamilton, however, changed the public sentiment, and the duellist is now considered a barbarian. Fashion is at once a master and a monster: a master in the supremacy of power, a monster in the cruelties inflicted upon mankind. What and how we

eat, our style of dress, the construction of our dwellings, our modes of travel, are all governed by fashion. Fashions rarely come up. They almost always go down, till, in the last modified form, they touch the bottom of society. Extravagance in the rich begets extravagance in the poor. Many a clerk has ended his days in the penitentiary because he lived beyond his means. Many a daughter has forsaken the God of her youth, and gone with her whose ways take hold on death, because she coveted the pleasures of dress. What we want, therefore, is to render the custom of drinking unfashionable, so that those in the lower grades of life will not think that they are out of the world if they do not imbibe from the intoxicating cup. For the lower classes of society have just reason to complain that the custom has been set them in high places.

4. Then the plan I propose involves another thought. It would increase the power to persuade. Example is the inspiration of language. The life of Christ is of more value to the world than his teachings. Without his lofty, symmetrical character; without his life of unparalleled purity and benevolence, his most wise and most beautiful lessons would be to mankind "as sounding brass and a tinkling cymbal." Here is a father on whose dinner-table the wine sparkles; he seeks to reform an inebriated son. He pleads, he argues, he prays; but all his arguments are paralyzed by

his own moderate drinking. "Physician, heal thyself," is the son's withering reply. The wise must educate the ignorant; the strong must strengthen the weak; and only the pure can save the guilty. "What is good for the father is good for the son," is a satisfactory argument for the latter's use. The persuasive power of example is the greatest. The pledge, societies, asylums, and law are proper, but impotent without it.

But against this, our personal liberty may be urged as a valid objection. Personal liberty is a natural right, and the freedom to exercise it is one of the noblest achievements of the age. Each man has a right to himself; to the results of his mental and physical labors; to eat and drink and rest; to pursue happiness. All this should be conceded, and is. Yet there is not in all this universe absolute liberty. The highest form of personal liberty is bounded by the law of limitation. You can grow only so high. You can eat only so much. You can sleep only so long. Conceding this, may we not enquire whether there is not another law of limitation or a further limitation to this personal liberty—the law of Christian self-denial which has its formal expression in the Golden Rule, "Whatsoever ye would that men should do unto you, do ye even so to them: for this is the law and the prophets"? And the same thought is expressed in those words of Paul to the Romans: "Let not your good be evil spoken of." Doubtless, too much is often demanded of Christian men. The world is hawk-eyed. It is rigorously exacting. Yet it is better to suffer wrong than do wrong. There are many things innocent in themselves, but the true man prefers to sacrifice them—to deny himself of that which, though in itself innocent, may be abused by others, and innocent pleasures be converted into criminal passions. You and I have a fast horse; made for fleet ness; made by the Almighty—and the Almighty only can make a fast horse. We are on the same road, and try their speed, whatever it may be—2.50 or 2.20. There is nothing wrong in that *per se*. Those horses were made by the Creator for fleetness, and what is more delightful than to ride behind that noble creature? But young men observe us on the road; they propose to try their fast horses, and, in addition to the trial, bet a hundred dollars on the result. They transfer their habits from the road to the race-course. and we see before them the gambler's end. Self-denial, philanthropy, magnanimity, should induce us to forego our pleasure for the good of the others. The same thing is true in regard to games of chance. There is nothing wrong *per se* in our playing a game of cards. But the habit may become an example to others who will abuse it. Doubtless you and I could behold some tragedian or comedian on the stage in some of the grand creations of the Bard of Avon, and there would be no sin in it *per se*, for God made Shakespeare and gave him his marvellous genius; and may not the day come when men may behold these things without deleterious results? But take the associations of the drama; the associations of those connected with it, and their influence upon society, and the good man foregoes the pleasure that he may save others from consequences that may be traced to the drama. It is a higher pleasure to know that by our self-denial we have saved others from sin and death than to enjoy the pleasures of which we have denied ourselves. Perhaps the noblest question a man can put to himself is, "How may I suffer and thereby save others?" and he only has reached the true humanity who can answer that question by deeds of philanthropy and self-sacrifice.

II. But let us look at the motives which should induce you to this self-denial. Let us remember that nothing great or good is accomplished in any department of life without the practice of self denial. Enter yon college, where are two young men of equal endowments and equal promise. Impatient of college restraint, preferring the song, the dance, the race, one lags in his studies, and with difficulty receives his diploma. The other is rarely seen where wit sparkles, beauty glows, or fashion shines. Pale, thoughtful, studious, his clear eye is dreamy; visions of the future rise up before him. Charmed with the languages, he hopes one day to speak in other tongues, in which great men speak, in which great thoughts are found; or before him are long tables of figures, and he is now competing with the older mathematicians for the prize of honor. Or, like Bacon, he has marked out for himself a new course of scientific investigation. This is the difference between Bonaparte and Washington; between Frederick the Great and John Howard; between Chesterfield and Sir Philip Sidney. Our forefathers were British freemen. They could have lived in comparative ease and freedom, but they preferred to deny themselves wealth and ease that they might achieve for us a better civilization.

The Son of God enjoyed a glory with the Father before the world was. Enthroned in glory, worshipped by angels, the Ruler of the universe, he might have remained amid the beatitudes of Paradise. But he laid aside his crown; he withdrew from the society of angels; he came to earth "a man of sorrows and acquainted with grief," to save a lost world. "For ye know the grace of our Lord Jesus Christ, that though he was rich, yet, for your sakes, he became poor, that ye through his poverty might be rich." (2 Cor. viii. 9).

Take the whole history of the world from Adam to this day, and whatever has been attained that is beautiful in art, beneficent in science, salutary in law, noble in charity, God-like in religion, has been achieved by self-denial. Is the sparkling wine so sweet and the animating draught so fascinating that you cannot abandon them to save millions from the drunkard's woes? You should be prompted to this duty of self-denial by the safety of yourself and your family. Some of you may drink moderately through a long series of years and not become confirmed inebriates. You may be exceptional cases, but from your ranks will go the majorities to swell the vast army of drunkards.

The great massacre in Damascus, in 1860, in which hundreds were slain and millions of property destroyed, had its origin in the quarrel of two school-boys, one a Mohammedan, the other a Christian. The great fire which a few years since reduced to ashes the finest portion of Portland, had its origin in the careless discharge of a firecracker thrown from the hand of a boy. Total abstinence is the only safety of some—the sure safety of all. Every career of crime had its starting-point in some small offence, and then the career widened and lengthened like the Mississippi. Every drunkard can retrace his life of sin and shame back to THE FIRST GLASS.

According to Grecian mythology, Jupiter commanded Vulcan to make a beautiful woman, who was dressed by Minerva, adorned with charms by Venus, and endowed with a deceitful mind by Mercury. In her hand she held a casket, beautiful without, but within were all the miseries of mankind. When admitted among men she opened that fatal box, and forthwith stalked abroad, by day as well as by night, all the maladies and woes which now curse the human race. The first glass is Pandora's casket, beautiful to look upon, but within are health in ruins, hopes destroyed, affections crushed, prayer silenced, grief sitting on the vacant seats of paternal care, of filial piety, of brotherly love, of maternal devotion; crimes of every name and hue, from broken vows to ghastly murders; home deserted; prisons whose horrid doors open inward; poverty and vice, twin companions; shattered forms, tormented souls, a cheerless grave, a burning hell, a dishonored life, an offended God.

Where is woe? where is sorrow? where are contentions? where are babblings? where are wounds without cause? where is redness of eyes? In the FIRST GLASS! O parents! O children! touch not the first glass!

Be induced to this self-denial by the happiness which will accrue thereby to society at large. We shall infer the happiness by contemplating the misery. Shall we call to our aid the sublime science of numbers in forming our estimate of this misery? Statisticians, whose learning and research command our confidence, inform us that in the United States there are not less than 133,000 places licensed to sell intoxicating liquors, employing 390,000 persons. And if to this number we add those engaged in the manufacture and wholesale traffic, the total number will reach

570,000 persons, or one man to every 75 inhabi tants. But the whole number of clergymen and teachers in our land engaged in the benevolent work of religion and education is only 150,000, or about one-fourth the above number. It is esti mated that the total cost of intoxicating liquors used each year in our country is $700,000,000, to which must be added $40,000,000 for criminals, while the entire clergy of the country does not cost $30,000,000. It is estimated that every year intemperance sends to prison 100,000 persons, reduces 200,000 children to worse than orphanage, adds 600,000 to the long list of drunkards, and sends 60,000 citizens to premature graves. It is also estimated that while fewer women drink than men, yet a larger proportion of those who do drink become habitual drunkards. In New York, within the last ten years, out of 133,000 persons arrested for intoxication, 66,000 were women! Alas for a woman drunkard! How our thoughts are roused to pity and our words to complain when we think what might have been the result to us if *our* mother, *our* wife, *our* daughter, *our* sister had gone in the paths of intoxication! Could I speak to women high in social position to-day, and speak plainly, I would speak with earnest emphasis. To me it is absolutely appalling as I mingle in society, here and elsewhere, to see with what readiness those who are worthily called ladies—called so from their virtue, their intelligence, their education, their acknowledged refinement—drink the sparkling champagne when "it stirreth itself in the cup."

O women! will you not lift your hands to heaven to-day, and swear that never in the future shall the sparkling wine touch your lips; never again shall your example be against total abstinence?

Intemperance is the scourge of the world. There is no evil written in the long catalogue of moral and political woes attended with more harm to individuals or to society than inebriation. Profanity, larceny, lying, murder, are the offspring of intemperance. To substantiate this no elaborate argument is necessary; for the records of our penitentiaries, the inscription on the solitary prison wall written by the pen of time and the ink of tears, and the pauper's grave, are all proofs in support of the allegation. O inebriation! thou habit of folly, thou hast dimmed the brilliant genius of the legislator, philosopher, and orator, sealed the mouth of heaven-commissioned ambassadors, torn the royal diadem from the monarch's brow, and robbed the chieftain of his hard-won laurels.

But it would be more tolerable if the evils resulting from this pernicious habit were confined to the drunkard himself. Yet it is not so; for the lovely and intelligent women of our land are the victims of his misery. They drink in secret the cup of sorrow to its dregs· and, while we commiserate the condition of the unhappy man, let us lift the curtain and behold the disconsolate, weeping, heart-broken wife. Perhaps he won her in the morning of life, when the bloom of youth, health, and sobriety glowed upon his cheek, and the light of genius animated his bewitching countenance. They went to the altar with hearts of tenderness and love. Heaven smiled upon the union. The happiness of her coming years lay like an ocean of pearls and diamonds in the embrace of the future. Hope sat, like a bird of auspicious omen, high in the green leaves of fancy, and poured into her bosom the sweet harmony of a terrestrial elysium. But her husband, in an unsuspected hour, forgets his bridal pledge. The sparkling bowl of friendship steals upon the hours of domestic enjoyment; his noble nature yields to the bright eyes of the charmer; and, alas, he becomes, step by step, a daily drunkard. What scenes follow? Night after night finds him in the midst of his family brimful with spirits and passions; his wife meets him with a trembling hand, an aching heart, and a tearful eye; his dear children retreat from corner to corner as if an evil spirit had made its appearance; and even his faithful dog skulks away with the growl of anticipated blows. The little homestead becomes the theatre of family broils and angry blows, and neither his wife nor his children are secure from the fury of his drunken madness. Where the sacred anthem should bear aloft the sweet music of the family, the wild song of the drunkard is chanted to the impious orgies of vice. Where the grateful breath of prayer like incense should waft to heaven their wants and woes, he pours forth a torrent of curses upon their devoted heads. Where the holy Bible should spread its banquet of wisdom and love, he opens the tablets of a heart on which are written the history of wretchedness and woe.

Who does not shudder at this mournful picture of desolation and ruin? But mark the condition of his wife; the cries of her half-clad, starving children ring in her ears daily, and the hectic flush of premature death dries up her briny tears as they trickle down her cheeks; her heart is a little city of ruins—hope, pride, fortune, and happiness, all have departed; and even while she binds up his wounds, his gross ingratitude sends keenest pangs to her heart. While she sheds tears of sympathy over his wayward conduct, his cruel treatment freezes them into ice-drops before they reach his bosom. While she would entwine her affections around him as the virgin bowers enfolds the sturdy oak, his swelling anger and feverish passions snap the gentle cords and spurn her proffered tenderness. But still the doting wife grasps the hand that withers her hopes of earthly happiness, and leans tenderly upon that cheek that consumes the sweetness of her youth, her health, her beauty. But why are these things so? Why this self-ruin and self-degradation? Why this prodigality and penury?

Why this personal and domestic suffering and misery? I answer these interrogations calmly. Intemperance is supported and perpetuated by fashion and law. Fashion—criminal, nefarious, diabolical fashion—sanctions with its unknown power moderate drinking. In this cold world whatever is fashionable is right. No matter how injurious to health, corrupting to morals, or molesting to society the practice may be, if it is only fashionable, it is all right. It is fashionable to drink that social glass; hence, people think they must drink. But let the world remember that in our splendid saloons and fashionable circles the inebriate's career begins, and that Bacchus manufactures drunkards out of moderate drinkers.

This is but a mere outline of the picture of the great scourge, which picture, in the fulness of awful detail, God alone can paint. What, then, is the logical, philosophical conclusion, founded on truth and common sense? It is this: That the race can be saved from these woes by the self-denial of the higher classes of society; it is, that total abstinence is the safety of all; that, whilst some who moderately drink may escape inebriety, yet total abstinence will be the safeguard, not only of them, but the safeguard of all. Then, in sentiment with that glorious man, St. Paul, let us say, "If wine make my brother to offend, I will drink no wine while the world standeth." Doing this, you may be imitators of him who, though he was rich, became poor, that we through his poverty might be made rich.

It awaits your decision. Recall the self-denial of Christ for the benefit of mankind, then follow his example.

THE CHURCH AND TEMPERANCE.

BY JOHN W. MEARS, D.D.

TEXT—*Ecclesiastes* i. 15; *Revelation* xxi. 5.

"That which is crooked cannot be made straight: and that which is wanting cannot be numbered."

"And he that sat upon the throne said, Behold, I make all things new. And he said unto me, Write: for these words are true and faithful."

FOR a period very closely corresponding with that of the division of the Presbyterian Church in America, the struggle against intemperance upon the principle of total abstinence has been going forward. It was at Saratoga, in 1836, that the American Temperance Union took its stand upon that principle, and from that date we count the more than thirty years' war for national, social, legal, and ecclesiastical reform in the use of intoxicating drinks. In this era of church reunion, reconstruction, and revision, when the humble enquiry, "Lord, what wilt thou have me do?" is rising with fresh interest and earnestness from millions of reconsecrated souls, it seems proper to notice the coincidence of dates, and to glance at the relation of the Temperance cause to the church, and to enquire what may be our duty in this particular juncture, as officers and members of a branch of Christ's church, always among the most influential, but now assuming a position of eminence and responsibility before the public more exalted than ever. Besides, the fluctuations in the history of the Temperance reformation have been so great and so far from encouraging that just at this time there has arisen, in the minds of the great mass of persons favorable to the reform, the conviction that permanent success and a final triumph of its principles must be looked for from the active co-operation of the church of Christ alone. Out side organizations, Washingtonian movements, pledges, public meetings, restrictive legislation, the example of public men, the distribution of an appropriate literature, secret beneficial societies, have had their place, and have done their work with greater or less efficiency, and most of them still remain among the accredited agencies of the reform. But none of them, nor all of them together, have been found able, after a generation of experiment, to achieve the work for which they were put in operation. More than ten years ago, Temperance men acknowledged themselves to have suffered a "Waterloo defeat," and since the time of that utterance, especially during the war, the state of things became even worse; and now, although we have unquestionably made up some of the lost ground, have recovered from the panic, which we now see to have been rather discreditable, have infused financial strength into our national publishing operations, and are resuming our efforts at thorough legislative reform, and have secured the cordial and zealous co-operation or silent example of men in the highest political and military positions in the state and nation; yet the evil of intemperance is still so monstrous and so rampant; the reaction from the earlier advances of the cause is still so marked even in respectable society; the work to be done is so vast, that the minds of men are turning, in a kind of despair, in this direction for means of successfully carrying on the Temperance reform. The appeal is made with unusual emphasis to the church. More plainly than ever, it is felt that the fate of the Temperance reform is to be decided here. The great advocates of the movement knock at her doors, and wait in her courts to learn the doom of their cause.

"That which is crooked cannot be made straight: that which is wanting cannot be numbered." Coarse animal appetite, backed by covetousness and played upon by gambling politicians, is too strong for them. They turn to that kingdom which is not meat and drink, but righteousness and peace and joy in the Holy Ghost; they look to the society founded by the world's Redeemer, who maketh all things new; they recognize in the church those spritual and supernatural powers, by the side of which their pledges and orders and degrees and mysteries are the mere clap-trap of nature's journeymen, nine hundred and ninety-nine of whom cannot make or remake a man.

Hon. Henry Wilson, in a recent newspaper article, speaking of the importance of enlisting the American people more generally in the Temperance cause, says: "Can it be done? If so, how? In my judgment, there is but one way in which this great result can be reached. THE CHURCH MUST TAKE UP THE MATTER. It must become one of the living issues of the moral warfare in which it is engaged."

We believe this appeal is fairly taken. We believe the specific work and objects of the Temperance reform may be reckoned as among the legitimate concerns of the church in our day. We believe that there is a responsibility resting upon the church for the success of the Temperance cause which has been but partially met. We believe that the failure in carrying any great moral reform points naturally to the great instrumentality for man's good on the earth; and the appeal of men in despair of other means to the church is not more a compliment than a serious charge of dereliction in the actual performance of its duty; and while it is clear that in every stage of the Temperance movement the ministry, members, and newspaper organs of the church have been its most efficient allies, and that at all times the cause has depended upon these for whatever measure of success it has enjoyed, nevertheless, we believe the church is disposed at this time to reconsider the whole question; to take enlarged views of her own responsibilities; to acknowledge frankly her shortcomings; to gird herself anew for the work, and thus to respond to the appeal in this critical period of the cause.

In arguing, therefore, that the church should

maintain and advance upon her present position on Temperance, reckoning it more positively among the objects of her stated and regular activity, and not contenting herself with judicial deliverances or with occasional sermons, I maintain:

First. That the ground of the Temperance reform is that of the plain requirements of Scripture. It is not based upon results of the highest merely human wisdom. Its roots are not in the vague aspirations of the unrenewed heart. It does not belong to the brood of ideas generated in the brains of mere philosophers and social philanthropists, such as communism, abolition of capital punishment, and woman suffrage. It is a thoroughly Christian and Scriptural idea. The ground has long ago been cleared of misapprehension in the view of intelligent believers. We do not rest the Temperance reform on such arguments as are ascribed to it by one of the highest literary authorities in the country ("Appleton's Cyclopedia"): "The demand for prohibition, according to its advocates, logically rests on the assumption that alcohol is essentially poison—precisely as arsenic, opium, and nicotine are poisons—that the difference between wine and brandy, beer and gin, is one of degree merely, not of kind, at least so far as poison is concerned. They also argue in support of their positions that alcohol is a product of vegetable decay and dissolution, and hence necessarily hurtful; that there can be no temperate use of it as a beverage any more than there can be temperate theft, adultery, or murder; that if much strong drink does great harm; a little weak alcohol drink must do some harm; and that there can be no temperate use of such beverages but their total disuse."

That some temperance men regard these extreme positions as fundamental, we do not question. Nor do we intend to deny their correctness: we only express our strong doubt whether they can be maintained from the Word of God with such clearness as to put them among the axioms of Christian duty. The Christian church may not commit herself to them as established guides of her conduct. We cannot take the extreme position that the use of all intoxicating drinks as beverages would be, under all circumstances, and absolutely, a sin; or that the Scripture anywhere absolutely condemns all such use of them as a sin, or anywhere enjoins total abstinence from intoxicating drinks as a duty. We do not hold it necessary even to prove that the Bible nowhere allows the use of strong drink as a beverage. We do not think it indispensable to show, as has not unfrequently been attempted, that the score of passages in the Bible which seem to approve of the use of wine do not approve of it. There is more or less of what we might call exegetical finesse in these interpretations. They may be correct, but we cannot afford to put the whole stress of our cause upon them. Without doubt, the weight of the specific passages of Scripture on the subject is enormously on the side of total abstinence. And a careful and scholary enquiry may yet make it clear that "there is not a single passage in the Bible that contains an explicit approbation of intoxicating wine" (Ritchie: "Scripture Testimony," page 155). But there is no need of waiting for a final settlement of this point; not a whit more than in getting a Scriptural position against slavery, polygamy, or the dancing and worldly amusements of modern society.

The argument that touches the rock of duty and that remains immovable, whatever becomes of the others, is the grand and most Christian principle of self-sacrifice for the good of our neighbor, the law of Christian charity to the weak. It is Christ-like condescension to man, to society, in a state of great moral necessity. Paul, the great casuist of the new dispensation, has announced the principle in the fourteenth of Romans: "It is good neither to eat flesh nor to drink wine, nor anything whereby thy brother stumbleth, or is offended, or made weak;" and again, in 1 Cor. viii.: "If meat make my brother to offend, I will eat no flesh while the world standeth, lest I make my brother to offend."

The application of this rule to the evil of intemperance is perfectly easy and universal. Those who question or deny every other position taken by temperance men, must feel the force of this. Alcohol may or may not be poison. Any use of alcoholic drinks may or may not be sinful. But the enormous evils flowing from their use or misuse are among the everyday facts of our life. The weakness of the mass of men under the appetite for strong drink is a settled physiological principle. No matter, according to Paul, how strong we feel ourselves to be, and no matter how silly and weak our brother may appear in our eyes, we are bound for example's sake to deny ourselves of meat as well as drink, "while the world standeth," in order to avoid all responsibility for the fall and destruction of our brother, and to promote his welfare as a moral and spiritual being.

In the case mentioned by Paul, the offence arises from a morbid imagination and an oversensitive conscience. Eating meat offered to idols was altogether an artificial sin. But lest a weak brother should be led even into such a sin, Paul enjoined abstinence from the practice of eating meat offered to idols on the part of those who, like himself, knew that an idol is nothing in the world. But here is danger of a sinful excess of the worst sort. We are asked to practise and proclaim the Pauline principle of total abstinence, not to save a brother, as he proposed, from the evil results of a foible, but to rescue him from his downward path to a dishonored life, a grave of infamy, and a dreadful hell; to avert the doom of drunkenness from a rising generation; to bind up innumerable wounds and bruises and putrefying sores of the body politic, and to uphold the dominion of reason and of truth in the church and the world. The Bible, indeed, contains no explicit rule of total abstinence, simply because its law of charity is far wider than that laid down by the advocates of temperance alone. We must abstain from *everything* that can give serious offence. We must array the whole force of our example in the support of our weak and tempted brother; we must enter upon a life-long course of self-denial, if necessary to his substantial interests. Do not jeopardize the souls for whom Christ died for the sake of a little tickling of the palate or glow of the nerves. If we are not, in so many words, commanded to organize total abstinence societies and to establish the principle of total abstinence in social and church life, we certainly have a Scriptural charter covering the whole ground on which such movements stand. And we may rightly hold that the total abstinence movement of modern times is as truly a legitimate outgrowth of Christianity as the movement for the abolition of slavery, beginning with Clarkson and Wilberforce and ending in the proclamation of the Fifteenth Amendment to the Constitution of the United States, although no such phrase as "human rights" is found from one end to the other of the Bible.

There is an objection to the direct and active interest of the church, as such, in the temperance movement, which still has weight with not a few. It is supposed to conflict with the spiritual character and object of the church. We aim, it is argued, at the conversion of men; at the implanting of a wholly new principle of living through the power of the Holy Spirit. The Temperance reform, and, indeed, moral reform in general, treats only of specific sins, which are but symptoms of the real malady. Why distract the church in dealing with the malady itself, by your quackery about the symptoms? Do you not see that, if you once truly convert the man, you have morally reformed him, and that conversion is the only real and lasting moral reform after all?

We answer, that while the church on earth, in its supreme and final objects, is certainly spiritual in its character, it is not and cannot be a pure spiritual institution. It is partly human, partly divine. It is for man as he is, mind and body, belonging to time and to eternity. It is adapted to the facts of man's condition as a sinner, and as suffering for his sins. It contemplates sin as an evil and a curse as well as a crime. It pours out its Godlike sympathies and blessings on the suffering men and societies whom it does not specifically labor to convert. Surely it is safe for the church to mould its policy in accordance with the example of its divine Master. And how large a part of his recorded activity was directed to alleviating the woes of mankind! How he confronted sin as an evil with the majesty of his miracle-working power, often without even so much as hinting at his higher calling as the physician of the soul. And the prophetic description of the last judgment, with the Son of Man sitting on the throne of his glory, shows in a remarkable manner how closely he will hold his people accountable for a failure to carry out his own beneficent policy to a suffering world. And the church has never failed to recognize her duty of charity to the poor and suffering. It has not been held to be enough even that her elders and deacons should dispense the charitable contributions of the members. Organizations must be formed within and about the churches more effectually to meet these specific wants, and no one has found fault with them as inconsistent with the spiritual aims or internal completeness and sufficiency of the church for all its legitimate work.

What is the difference in principle between making a sewing society for the poor a part of the regular work of the church and establishing a weekly church Temperance meeting? If either of the two is shallow and remote from the profound idea of the church, it must be the effort for the relief of the poor; for the Temperance movement strikes at the root of three-fourths of the poverty to which your Dorcas societies are but salves and poultices that must be renewed every season at least. In fact, direct relief is the least satisfactory of all charity to the poor. It is often waste and mischief combined—money worse than thrown away. The true relief to an individual and a neighborhood is to raise their character, to remove their bad habits, to put them in the way of valuing and diligently using their opportunities of gaining a living. And almost the highest manifestation of the benevolent spirit of the Master towards the poor which the church in our day can give is to engage in active efforts to promote the Temperance reform.

But it is asked, Why should the church make a distinction among the evils and sins of the times? Are there not others abroad in the land equally demanding her zeal? Are not corruption and fraud practised on a gigantic scale, making a mockery of legislation, and converting business of almost every kind into mere gambling? Are they not "poisoning the very fountains of business morals in the metropolis of our country?" (Spalding's tract, "Rational Temperance"); and have not legislators almost ceased to blush at the imputation of bribery, or to deem it longer necessary to hide the hand that receives the price of their influence? We answer, that the sin and evil of fraud and corruption are too clear to need special denunciation. They are against the plainest statutes and letter of the moral code. The position of the church in regard to them has never been doubtful. Her testimony is explicit and unwavering. There is no question of Christian expediency here. It is one of the radical and open violations of known fundamental law. Besides, the sin and its results, although enormous, are comparatively subtle; they cannot easily be attacked by that class of personal efforts which we understand by moral reform. But intemperance is quickly followed by such a train of gross evils; it is so destructive of reason, so crippling to the right exercise of the faculties in the daily walk of life; it so ravages the bodily system, shattering the nerves, draining the vital force, arresting the natural processes, and exposing the system to every form of disease and to premature and disgraceful death; it so robs a man of the respect of himself and neighbors; it so quickly hurls him into poverty and disgrace; it opens the pores of his moral system so widely to every kind of criminal solicitation; it gives him such a pre-eminence—almost a monopoly—of our police and criminal courts, prisons, gallows, poor-houses, and lunatic asylums; it makes him such a vast charge upon our pockets in the shape of taxes; it makes him the centre of such pestilent, law-defying, Sabbath-breaking traffic; it bands him and his associates into such a powerful and dangerous element in politics, that it has become THE curse of our time, the demon that is to be cast out of modern society. And the church, which sees her relations to bribery and fraud in the light of the eighth commandment, must see her duty towards intemperance in the light of the law of charity, which covers all the commandments in the Second Table of the law. In a word, it is the use of a beverage which narcotizes the moral sensibilities and the intellect, and which stimulates the sensual brute nature of man, which dislodges him, for the time being, from his position as made a little lower than the angels, which removes and defaces the image of God in his soul, and turns the temple of the Holy Ghost into a lodging-place of demons; it is this enemy put into the mouth, which steals away brain and heart alike, that we may well summon the church of our day to aid in overthrowing, by special means and activities. We challenge every other specific form of vicious indulgence, or openly wrong practice, or accessible evil that afflicts the children of men, to match such a record as the following: "The annual amount of fermented and distilled liquors used in the United States would fill a canal four feet deep, fourteen feet wide, and one hundred and twenty miles long. The places where intoxicating drinks are made and sold in this country, if placed in direct lines, would make a street one hundred miles long. If all the victims of the rum traffic were gathered before our eyes, we should see a thousand funerals a week from their number. [Think of two-thirds of the city of Philadelphia furnishing one thousand funerals a week!] Placed in a procession five abreast, the drunkards of America would form an army one hundred miles long, with a suicide occurring in every mile. Every hour in the night the heavens are lighted with the incendiary torch of the drunkard. Every hour in the day the earth is stained with the blood of drunken assassins. See the great American army of inebriates, more than half a million strong, marching on to sure and swift destruction, filing off rapidly into the poorhouses and prisons and up to the scaffold, and yet the ranks are constantly recruited from the moderate drinkers! Who can compute the fortunes squandered, the hopes crushed, the hearts broken, the homes made desolate by drunkenness?"

If, again, it be objected that total abstinence and prohibition are extreme measures; that the temperance of the Bible is moderation, not abstention; that the misuse of an object is no good ground for setting it aside altogether; that the Christian is one who of all others has a right to rational enjoyment, and may expect divine aid in the moderate use of every good; in fine, that true reform, by divine grace, should make a man capable of manly self-control, and that little or nothing is gained for the character by abstaining from that which a man ought rather to be able to use in moderation, we can only answer by pointing to facts. Moderation has been tried long ago and found wanting. The fascination of strong drink is too great; the physiological effects of alcohol in creating a morbid thirst and craving, furious and insatiable as a wild beast, are too well ascertained. Whatever may have been the case in Bible lands and eras, whatever may be the case in other countries to-day, in America the downward way of the drinker from moderation to excess is too steep and slippery to allow the trifling of moderate indulgence. It is a whirlpool, which draws in swift and dreadful sweep from the outermost circle to the central abyss. The alcoholic drinks of our day are so far from being the genuine juice of the grape or the product of noble grains and fruits, that they might well have come from the caldron of Macbeth's witches. "Deacon Giles's Distillery" was a healthy place, and the scene of an honest traffic, compared with the enormities of fraud, adulteration, and poisoning now going on under the name of liquor manufacture, even among the vineyards of California and Ohio, as well as in cellars hidden under coffin warehouses in Brooklyn. A worse sort of devils than those which wrote "Death and Damnation" upon the drinks of forty years ago, are employed in producing the horrid mixtures of to-day, which find their way to our sick-chambers and even spread their unwholesome fumes around our communion tables. Do not talk of moderation in the use of these vile compounds; give us a tincture of arsenic at once, and call it by its right name of poison. Into the question of a moderate use of a possible pure alcoholic drink we cannot now enter. It is not before us. Such an article can hardly be said to have an ascertainable commercial existence. As well attempt to argue about the propriety of a Christian attending in moderation upon pure dramatic or operatic representations; such things do not exist in any degree sufficient to become a real element in a question of duty; and if they did—if pure liquors and dramatic entertainments were an appreciable item of traffic and amusement, they are so sure to become the snare and ruin of others that, even granting ourselves to be entirely clear of peril, it is our Christian duty, under the principle already referred to as laid down by Paul, to turn our backs upon theatre-going and wine-drinking, and to set the whole force of our example as total abstainers upon Christian principle against such perilous practices.

And if the objector persists in saying: There are terrible excesses and frauds in business, there is endless corruption in politics and legislation, there are wrongs of the sorest kind in the family relation —following in the line of total abstinence and prohibition, we must abolish business, shut up our legislative halls, and break up the family relations—we answer: The cases are in wholly different spheres, and not amenable to the same laws of procedure. Show us that we can dispense with business, law, and the family as readily as with a mere matter of indulgence; put, if you can, the fundamental, indispensable arrangements of society upon the same footing with just one of the thousand ways in which we may gratify appetite, and which, if denied, would leave nine hundred and ninety-nine others open to us; rank the use of intoxicating drinks as in dignity and importance comparable with business, with law, and with the family institution, and you may well imagine that you have put a barrier in the way of church action for its abolition, and raised a great argument for the effort simply to correct its abuses.

The argument is too idle, not to say wicked, to be put into shape. Yet we fear that there are those in and out of the church acting, or refusing to act, with a secret feeling that total abstinence and prohibition belong to revolutionary measures; and perhaps in the ministry there are those who would hold back the church from the charitable Pauline policy of total abstinence, pretty much as they would hold it back from an assault on the social structure itself to rid it of its abuses. What an amazing, unwarrantable, unscriptural exaggeration of the value of a single animal indulgence! Man's capacity of enjoyment through strong drink is to be reckoned among the sacred privileges of his being which the church dare not invade!

Just the reverse of all this is the true view of the case. In issuing her rule of total abstinence, the church would be acting in that well-recognized sphere of morals comprehended in keeping the body under. It is in this very region of appetite and indulgence that the Christian's first opportunities of self-denial and cross-bearing are found. So far from appetite and habit being privileged, we know that they are the strongholds of self and of sin; and if a monstrous, soul-destroying, and inevitable abuse is connected with some one appetite which can show no special reason for indulgence save the very universality that makes it so terrible, is not that just the very spot on which to lay the cross of absolute self-denial? Against that should not the church feel specially summoned to direct its most energetic and radical opposition? Do not Christian integrity and fidelity require the church to take the ground of total abstinence against so worldly, so selfish, so carnal, so perilous a course to one's self and others as the use of alcoholic drinks in any degree or form? May she not arm herself with the words of inspiration, and cry: "Look not thou upon the wine when it is red, when it giveth his color in the cup, when it moveth itself aright. At the last, it biteth like a serpent, and stingeth like an adder."

To give a more practical turn to our discourse, let us for a few moments enquire what there is that the church can do, more particularly at the present juncture, to promote the Temperance reformation. Not forgetting the great service it has already rendered, by sermons and addresses from the pulpit, and by the zeal of many of its members, and not doubting for a moment that the degree to which the principle of total abstinence has gained a lodgment in the moral convictions of the community is almost wholly due to the church, we are yet brought to a point where we may be conscious of grave omissions and of more serious responsibilities than ever. We have done much. We have lifted the ponderous pillar from the ground. Christian and moral persons in the community, joining their efforts, have nearly straightened it upon its base. The ropes seem to be taut; the last possible turn has been given to the windlass; yet the column slants and bears heavily upon its supports. Something remains to be done without which all our past efforts will be in vain. It may be just the simple act of *wetting the ropes* that is needed, and with that slight additional strain the work may be completed; the shaft may swing upright, and sink firmly into its place. Oh! that the dews of the Holy Spirit may fall upon all our Temperance machinery. It is for these that we wait. This will bring our work to a joyful completion. With diffidence, and in the way of mere suggestion, we propose such measures as the following:

1. Let the individual church constitute itself in some definite form a Temperance organization, so that its whole character, influence, and activity shall be publicly upon the side of total abstinence. Let regular Temperance meetings be held under the guidance of officers of the church, to which as much care shall be given as to any other weekly service. Let the reclamation of drunkards and

the conversion of moderate drinkers, and the pledging of the community to a policy of total abstinence, be recognized as regular parts of church work. My hearers are aware that this plan has been thoroughly tested in some quarters of our church, particularly in the largest church connected with our body, and the largest Presbyterian church in America—that of Lafayette Avenue, Brooklyn, Rev. Dr. Cuyler, pastor. Of this, Dr. Cuyler writes in a recent newspaper article:

"In this church (Lafayette Avenue, Brooklyn), we have had for several years a prosperous society, which is as fully recognized by the church as is its Sabbath-school. It numbers several hundreds of members, and affiliated with it is a Band of Hope among the Sabbath-school children. It has a very simple constitution and by-laws, a zealous president and secretary, a treasurer, and a dozen members of an executive committee. The only title to membership is a signature of the total abstinence pledge. Public meetings are held during the fall and winter in the church, and attractive *music* is always provided. Vast audiences have been addressed by such men as Mr. Beecher, Newman Hall, Mr. Greeley, Gov. Buckingham, Dr. John Hall, William E. Dodge, Mr. Gough, Mr. Barnum, Dr. Jewett, and many other powerful advocates of the reform. The expenses are met by a public collection at each meeting; and, with the exception of Mr. Gough's lectures, tickets are never sold at the door. At the close of each meeting the *pledge is circulated.* This is a vital feature in all effective Temperance work."

One of the best-appointed churches in the Fourth Presbytery (Buttonwood Street, Dr. Shepherd's) has carried on a similar movement, with entire success, for eighteen months past, having secured a thousand signers to the pledge in the first twelve months, including some most affecting instances of reformation. At the meeting, April 8, although the pastor and the elder who manage the meetings were both, for the second time, absent from sickness, the lecture-room was full, the services were deeply interesting, and a dozen or more new signatures to the pledge were obtained. Other churches in our own and other denominations are engaged in the work on the same general plan, and the results thus far warrant us in predicting the most extensive overturning that intemperance and the rum traffic have experienced since the early days of the Reformation, as a result of the general adoption of such a line of policy by the great body of the Evangelical churches.

2. The church might considerably clear its position and strengthen its influence on the subject, by banishing from the communion table the wretched article of commerce called wine; and, indeed, by refusing to employ anything but the pure unfermented juice of the grape at that most solemn service. It cannot be doubted that there are real perils to not a few persons connected with any use of alcoholic drinks, any and everywhere, including the Lord's table. Cases have

occurred, and are occurring, of reformed drinkers, whose appetite still lingers like a chained but chafing wild beast, which the first taste may set free in all its original wildness, and who dare scarcely smell the cup as it passes. We cannot see how any church, thoroughly pledged to the Temperance reform, can continue to subject them to this ordeal, or keep them away from the communion table. And if it is urged that our Saviour must have used a fermented article at the institution of the Eucharist, we reply, that in using leavened bread, the modern church has for mere convenience departed from the precise form of the original ordinance; why, then, for an object of far higher importance, refuse to make another change as little affecting the essence of the observance as in the other case? She does not hesitate to introduce leaven into the bread; why may she not withdraw the same principle from the wine? But, further, we think it quite unlikely that there was any fermented principle in either of the articles used by our Saviour at the Lord's Supper. That Supper is founded on the Jewish Passover, and the religious and rigid exclusion of ferment from the bread used on that occasion would naturally be extended to the wine, when that, in process of time, came to be added to the feast. It was, we should suppose, just as improper to use leaven, "the symbol of corruption," in drink, as in food. (Thayer.) At all events, the almost universal custom of modern Jews, as we read (Thayer), is to exclude fermented wine from their celebration of the Passover. And in the words of institution of the Lord's Supper it is noticeable that "wine" does not occur. The word "cup" appears in its place, and our Saviour speaks not of drinking wine, but of drinking the fruit of the vine, new in his Father's kingdom. The unfermented juice of the grape might well enough be designated by this general language. There is nothing, then, in the requirement of the original institution which would oblige the most rigid literalist to use fermented liquor at the Lord's Supper; why, then, make that blessed ordinance a possible occasion of stumbling to any, which ought to be one of the highest edification. In the strong language of Dr. Duffield: "Shall the cup of salvation become the cup of damnation —shall the cup of the Lord be made identical with that of devils?" Until the church guards effectually against the possibility of such a profanation, she fails in a most conspicuous manner to give her whole influence upon the side of Temperance.

Finally, the whole church of Christ should be recognized as a solid pledged body against the use of all that intoxicates. She alone is the true immortal order for the redemption of man, soul and body. Why should she hold a lower moral position than the human orders around her? She ought to point to man standing on the slippery places of appetite, the true path of entire self-denial. Crucified herself to the lusts of the flesh, purified from carnal and worldly compliance, with the light of a saintly heroism on her brow, she should stretch forth her hand to rescue the perishing. With a weary sense of the inefficiency of all merely human means of staying the misery, the woe, the wretchedness, the heaven-daring crime, and the frightful waste of intemperance, the orders and societies and public men and press of the land are turning to the church. With her is the residue of the Spirit. The dreadful hardness of men's hearts, the immeasurable power of their appetities, the cruel tyranny of custom, the insatiableness and uscrupulousness of avarice have defied all lesser assaults. The monster is abroad again, with half-a-million yearly victims in our own country alone in his train. The accursed traffic is thriving, melting the hard earnings of the poor into a lava-stream of desolation. The foundations of our political life are honeycombed by the sottishness of a large part of our wire-pulling and office-seeking politicians, who control the situation. Laws regulating the traffic are defied. Women are not merely claiming man's right to vote, but exercising what heretofore has been man's privilege—to drink to inebriety away from home. The very structure of society trembles. The church, God's chosen instrument for man's regeneration, must take order to meet the emergency. She is come to the kingdom for such a time as this. Woe unto her if help arises from another quarter, and if the unbelieving world can strengthen itself in the opinion that man can get rid of his worst evils in spite of the indifference or open opposition of a blind and conservative church! On the contrary, we believe that all Christian grace will be multiplied; all Christian life will be animated, joyful, and effective; and all converting influences will be granted, in those churches which throw themselves with generous enthusiasm into this wide and needy field of Christian effort.

THE ACTIVE PITY OF A QUEEN.*

(Reported for the Society by William Anderson.)

"For how can I endure to see the evil that shall come unto my people? or how can I endure to see the destruction of my people?"—ESTHER 8 : 6.

THE portion of God's Word to which, in connection with the subject of Christian temperance, I propose to call your attention this afternoon, is in the Book of Esther, the eighth chapter. We had better read from the fourth verse: "So Esther arose, and stood before the king, and said, If it please the king, and if I have found favor in his sight, and the thing seem right before the king, and I be pleasing in his eyes, let it be written to reverse the letters devised by Haman the son of Hammedatha the Agagite, which he wrote to destroy the Jews which are in all the king's provinces: for how can I endure to see the evil that shall come unto my people? or how can I endure to see the destruction of my kindred?"

In conversing with a brother minister, in Canada, during the summer, upon the subject of preaching on temperance, he mentioned this text to me as one upon which he had preached. It

* This sermon is printed from a very admirable report, and not from the preacher's manuscript, a circumstance which accounts for its colloquial style.
J. H.

has many times been present to my mind since then, and I gladly take the opportunity of being invited by our National Society to bring this matter before the people, to introduce the whole subject in connection with the sentiment of the verses that I have now read.

One cannot preach from this Book of Esther without glancing at some of the peculiarities of the book itself. The word-critics have been at work upon the book, applying to it the child's test of a proper Sunday book, and, not finding the name of God in it, they have been ready to question its inspiration. The fact that there has been such an imputation as this is sufficient reason for our ascertaining what can be said upon the subject. We should all of us know what is to be thought generally in relation to the authority of this book, because, although we may be a long way on this side of sheer unbelief, yet we may have such a feeble belief, accompanied by so many misgivings, that it shall have but little power in regulating our conduct; and we could not have very much confidence in speaking or in hearing words about the authority of which there is some doubt in the mind at the beginning.

When we look at this book in itself, it has certain peculiarities that attract the attention. It is, for example, a very faithful transcript of the general habit and character of Eastern rulers and of Persian courts; and, in this respect, it is thoroughly borne out by all that we know regarding those kings and courts from other sources. In so far it is confirmed in every detail that it touches by profane histo rians, and although the lights we have from history on this period are comparatively dim and obscure, yet, so far as they do shed any light, it is of such a kind as to increase our confidence in the statements of this book. The style of the book is substantially the same as that which we have in Ezra, the Chronicles, and other books written about the time which it purports to have been written. It has just sufficient flavor of the language of the Chaldee and Persian to suggest to us that the book was prepared in the region of Persia. If it be alleged that it was written by Mordecai, a Jew, away from Judea, and in the service of a monarch elsewhere, that is only in harmony with God's method in relation to other books, Ezra, Nehemiah, and Daniel—who were all in the service of foreign kings—having been employed by the Holy Spirit to leave written memoirs of the times and of the events in which they themselves had some share. On all these grounds it is obvious enough that the presumption is in favor of this book being historically true.

But we are not left to presumptions of this kind. Many of you are aware that there is a feast of Purim among the Hebrews, observed to this day, with very great care, over the world generally. Now, that feast, it is capable of proof, has been continuously observed from the time when this book purports to have been written. There is no authorization for that feast anywhere in the Bible but in the Book of Esther; and it seems to be impossible to explain the origin and continuous history of that feast among the people except upon the assumption that this book is historically true. We are told of the hissing, and spitting, and other indications of scorn, hatred, and contempt that are seen in some synagogues when this book is being read at the feast of Purim, showing clearly enough how real and historical the narrative is to them.

But, then, a book might be true and yet not be inspired. And so we have to look at that part of the question also. We know explicitly what constituted the Hebrew canon in our Lord's time, and he accepted that Hebrew canon as the Scriptures. He had occasion to find fault with the Hebrew people upon many a score, but he never did blame them as unfaithful custodians of the writings God had placed in their hands. We know they held this book in such high esteem that they placed it by the law; and there was a proverb among them that there might come a time when all the books would be lost but the law and the book of Esther. Now, if he put his seal upon it and endorsed it, we are constrained to receive it in precisely the same way as we receive other portions of the Old Testament record, as given us by the inspiration of God, and profitable for doctrine, correction, and instruction in righteousness, that the man of God might be perfect, thoroughly furnished unto every good work.

But if the name of God be not in the book —a circumstance which perhaps might be accounted for by the consideration that it was possibly written for the benefit of people outside of the Jewish kingdom, and that, therefore, it was thought wise to leave the being and attributes of the God of Israel rather to the inference of intelligent men than to explicit statement—it is impossible for any candid reader to deny that the hand of God is in the providences it records. It is a series of providential wonders from beginning to end; and I am not surprised that Dr. Carson, one of the ablest divines of the Baptist or any other church, when he wanted to write something about the particular providence of God, selected this Book of Esther to be the subject of commentary, statement and illustration at once of the truth he wished to present. It is strange enough that Vashti, by an assertion of her womanly independence, should have been driven from the throne; but it is stranger still that Esther, a young Jewish captive maiden, not much above the rank of a slave in the country, should have been raised to the place thus vacated; not, perhaps, to the place of first wife and equal, but to a place dignified by the name of queen. The won der grows when we find that her cousin Mordecai becomes so implicated in her history and in the history of the king, whose wife she has become, that he should be the detecter of the plot against the king's life; that he should be the means of saving the king's life from the conspirator: that he should be in such a relation to the queen as to be able to communicate freely with her when the time of danger came; that he should be, at the same time, the occasion of the scheme for the complete destruction of the Jewish people. All these things, surely, are matters of very great surprise. Then consider how many things have to combine in order to bring about the result. Had not the king been awake on one particular night; had not the reader turned to one particular portion of the Medo-Persian record; had not attention been called at the right time to Mordecai; had not Esther been in a position to influence the king—any one of these things being wanting must have affected the great result. I admit that one combination of these things might be a coincidence; but I submit, brethren, that here is an accumulation of coincidences which it is impossible to explain upon any other theory than that the hand of God is here. I would just as soon, by the laws of my own mind, believe that one of our ocean-going steamers had made itself and furnished itself for sea by a fortuitous concurrence of atoms, by an accidental coherence of all the parts that compose it, as to believe that the events that are recorded in this book have happened in any other way than by the designing, controlling, and infinite Mind that worketh all things according to the counsel of his own will; that uses all the complicated forces of human goodness and of human badness, of malice, ambition, pride, greed, and revenge, as well as patriotism and love of kind, for the accomplishment of his great purposes; that employs even the wickedness of the wicked, and yet that is not wicked, but is most holy, wise, and powerful to the end. We need not, therefore, brethren, have any kind of scruple or misgiving in our minds when considering a passage like that which falls under our consideration.

Esther herself is the central figure through this book, and a very interesting figure she is. Timid and gentle as a woman, enduring of the repression to which her sex is subject and has always been subject in the East, and yet with strong natural feeling, capable of exerting herself in a very high degree when a strain is put upon her nature, she is cool and calculating when necessity demands. There is everything about her to surround her with interest, and attract to her much of our sympathy. But, best of all, she is not unmindful of that source whence men and women alike have to receive strength, comfort, and guidance—that God of Israel who hears the prayers of his people, and who has taught us that, if any man lack wisdom, he is to ask of God.

I. Let us look at the calamity that was before her, in the contemplation of which she makes an appeal to the king, of which this text is a part: "How can I endure to see the evil that shall come unto my people? or how can I endure to see the destruction of my kindred?" Mordecai, a Jew, sitting in the gate of the king's palace, had been less subservient and respectful than was expected toward the prime minister of the king. Why he was so we are not told. It may have been that there still remained in his Jewish heart some of that hereditary scorn with which Hebrews were wont to look upon the Amalekites; but, however it was, his act aroused the malice and revenge, and perhaps also the greed and covetousness ultimately, of Haman, the prime minister of the king. He scorns to take revenge on one man; his burning wrath will be satisfied with nothing less than the sacrifice of a people. So he schemes and plans for the destruction of all the Jews that are captives and exiles in the land. It is no bad illustration, by contrast, of the blessings of our freedom; it is no bad illustration of the evils and powers of despotism that the order for this wholesale murder is given with such promptness by this reckless Eastern king, and that it is put with such promptness into the hands that are to execute it. Esther is made aware, through Mordecai, of what is impending, and she comprehends the whole situation. If she did not, the timely warning of her kinsman would have shown it to her. She adopts the requisite measures; she takes all the proper steps to enlist the co-operation of others; she enlists the religious feelings of her compatriots; she gives directions that all the Jews in and about the place shall fast, which was her way, and the way of the time, of supplicating Almighty God; she engages herself in all this work of calling upon the Lord: "I and my maidens will fast also." Besides, she takes proper means, after approaching the king, of influencing his mind, she elaborates with care and pains all the plans by which it may be confidently expected she will secure his approbation, and be enabled to counteract the devices of this wicked Haman. That she should have to adopt means like these, that it should be necessary to scheme and plan for getting the ear of her husband, that she should have to resort to these roundabout devices to conciliate his favor, may seem to us, with our brighter light and our happier Western home-life, strange and inexplicable; but there can be no doubt that, in doing all this, she was acting in perfect harmony with the arrangements of the court in which she lived, and adopting the means, strange and, in some respects, doubtful, as it would seem to us, that were best adapted to accomplish the result and to secure a favorable reception of her request on the part of the king, whose vassal she was.

And now, brethren, should we be able, any more than Esther, to contemplate the destruction of our people and our kindred—not threatening nor impending, but a destruction that is actually going on round about us every day and every year—should we be able to look on with unmoved hearts? It is a destruction, I admit, that has come in a very different way and by a very different set of agencies from that by which it came in this narrative. For the revenge and greed of Haman, substitute that love of gain that prompts men to embark in the liquor trade; for the usages of a reckless, oriental, dissipated court, substitute the common social customs of our time; for the destruction of those thousands, be the same more or less, of the Hebrew exiles in the domain of Persia, you may substitute the destruction of the multitudes of men and women, ay, and children, that is in progress continually round about us.

When a man tries to take in all the horrid situation at a glance, he is apt to fail altogether, from the very expanse of the dreariness that is before him. It is better, therefore, not to try to take in all the situation, but to fix one's attention upon a limited department of the great waste that is being made by intemperance over the world. Take our own city. We have here four hundred and seventy places in which worship of some kind or another is being addressed to the Almighty among our million of people. I am told—the statement is almost incredible—but I am told that we have seven thousand temples where Bacchus is worshipped with a homage quite as sincere as that we have in our churches, and far more costly to the community, for I am assured that two millions of dollars a year are paid as a simple tax in the first place upon the spirituous liquors that are consumed among us. What are the fruits of this widespread heathenish worship? They are to be found not in the thirty-four thousand people that are taken up in a year for drunkenness and disorderly conduct upon our streets—about one-half of all the arrests that are made by the police; they are to be found not simply in the eight thousand people that are being kept at the public expense in our prisons, asylums, and hospitals: but they are to be found, dear brethren, in the ruin and waste of life in many private dwellings, of which the police can take no cognizance; they are to be found in the blighting of so many hopes, in the ruin of so many prospects, in the untimely end of many lives all over the city, and all over the land, so widespread are the ramifications of the evil that has thus come to be established among us. There is a way of making this subject practical to you, dear brethren. How few circles are there into which some loss has not come through this prevalent sin! How few families there are in this church this afternoon that have not been touched more nearly or more remotely through this vice in some one of the circles in which they themselves move, if not, indeed, in their own immediate circle!

It is impossible for us, brethren, to exaggerate and overstate the evil and mischief that are being continually done in the ruin of men and women—their ruin in soul, body, and estate—through their indulgence in the sin of intemperance. In the case of Haman and his intended victims, if he had been able to accomplish his designs, the property and the lives of those thousands would have been sacrificed at a single blow. It would have been a sharp and severe blow; it would have been a thing done and done with. But that is not so with our social proscription that issues in the destruction of such multitudes. It is a long, wasting agony; it is a slow process. The victim dies by inches, so to speak; and not merely that, but he dies amid declining regard, lost self-respect, ruined means, weeping women, and sometimes degraded children. Fires burn themselves out; but this fire has the peculiarity of finding fuel for itself; for how often has it happened that the drunken wife has driven the husband to despair and to drunkenness, and how often has it happened that the drunken father and mother have communicated to the very physical nature of their children the diseased and self-destroying appetite!

How often has it happened that a family of social position and attractive manners has succeeded in inoculating a whole circle—perhaps a whole neighborhood—with a love of drink! How inevitably does it happen that, when a man has once embarked his means in the trade, his interest and his prosperity will grow with the growing love and passion for drink among his hapless neighbors round about him! Our fire does not consume itself for lack of fuel; it makes the fuel by which it is sustained and upon which it feeds. Brethren, if you think that I overstate the case, you can correct my estimate; but I do not well see how you can correct it, if you have been going through life with your eyes open to the actual facts that are continually transpiring around us. I think you will be compelled to admit that, looking at it in any point of view, not only in a social but in a spiritual point of view, this evil is so gigantic that our tongue gives no words that can overstate its wicked and atrocious characteristics.

Brethren, I am not speaking of some remote and distant era; I am not talking to you about the opium-eaters of China; I am speaking here, as Esther spoke before the king, of your own people and your own kindred. These drunkards that are round about, when they become paupers, you must support them; when they become criminals, you must detect their crimes, and then confine and punish them. And to what cost you are necessarily put in protecting yourself against them! As you take up the Monday morning papers, and glance over the crimes and casualties of the twenty-four hours that have gone before, and as you look at the poor, besotted, degraded, and animalized wretches that have been suddenly flung into eternity by the pistol or the knife of their assassin companions, you may get a momentary view of the horridness of this thing. But you see only a part of it there. You have to look at all its ramifications; you have to think how it affects homes; how it affects religion; how it affects relations to God; how it sears conscience; how it blinds human spirits to all the interests of time and of eternity—these you have to take into account in making a correct estimate of the magnitude and frightful character of the evils intemperance entails. No wonder that any good man, as he looks at this state of things, should say, "How can I endure to see the evil that shall come upon my people? How can I endure to see the destruction of my kindred?"

II. Pity is a sentiment. It is a fine sentiment. Sometimes it is a mere sentiment. Sometimes it evaporates in a little sigh; or it distils in a casual tear, and falls ineffectually to the ground. Pity of that kind is worthless; it is worse than worthless, it is mischievous. To have these pities that come to nothing does us harm—they weaken our character; they absolutely corrupt our nature, and they flatter us at the time that we are being good. That was not the pity of Esther; it was active pity; it was practical sympathy. I do not need to rehearse the steps that she took, and at which we have glanced already, which you can read for yourselves, if you take interest enough in the book to follow its successive incidents. It is enough to say that her aim and object, under God, were realized; it is enough to say that the tables were completely turned; it was Haman, and not Mordecai, that was hung on the gallows; Haman's kindred, and not her own, perished. The decree that he would have to go forth against the Jews was executed against his own people, with great severity I admit, but not with more severity than was natural and common in the times. The wicked was snared in the work of his own hands.

Now, my beloved brethren, from the example of this Jewish woman I would borrow a lesson for you and a lesson for myself. I would stir up in myself, and I would urge upon you, practical sympathy and active pity, like that exhibited by Esther. First of all, let us seek co-operation in the war that we would wage with this great vice. Strong evils, many times, can be best met by associated effort. The individual is weak, where the company or the multitude is often strong. There is strength in union, and there is a manifest advantage in Christian people being banded together in societies for dealing with this state of things. Information is collected, and then it is diffused; the weak are strengthened; the zealous, who have not always wisdom, are directed, and there is concentration given to the effort put forth. The human imagination—no small matter in a case of this kind—is impressed. I say, no small matter, for in a matter of this kind it is a great thing that a young man, for example, with principles unsettled, and too weak to stand straight up upon his own convictions, seeing these societies, their organization and results, should be able to say, "I see I can refuse drink and not be despicable. I see I can put away the glass and not be counted mean. There are most respectable men publicly banded together against this thing, and no man dare call them sneaks because they pursue this particular course of conduct."

It is something to have societies organized and maintained for the enunciation of right principles, and the organization and extension of effort in this reforming direction. Young men who are here do not despise the aid which these societies can give to you. If you think that you yourselves do not need them, recollect there are many other young men that do; recollect that there are many who have been wounded, and have fallen down, and they are trying to stand up again, and recover themselves, and they need a great deal of help. It is very hard for some of them to pass by the door of the "sample-room," the decoy that is cunningly arranged for those who have still left sufficient self-respect to keep them from going to a place that is palpably and indubitably for mere drink.

Young men! do not despise these agencies and societies, but go into them and help them along; and if it should seem to you that some of the agencies are not the best, that some of their arguments are feeble, why, do you find better agencies, and put into their mouths better arguments, and work this thing as it ought to be worked, for the benefit and recovery of your fellow-creatures. Men and brethren, strong men, do not you look lightly upon these organizations. You may say to yourselves, quite truly, "I have no need to be sheltered and protected in such ways as this." It is true, perhaps, of you, that your characters are formed, and your habits are made; your physical system is consolidated, so to speak; your heads are strong, and you can say to yourselves with perfect truth, and you sometimes do say to others, "I can take this thing or leave it; I can do with it or without it." Then, my brethren, if you can do with it or without; if your minds and tastes are in this state of equilibrium in relation to it, do without it for the sake of those who are in danger through the means of it.

Fathers! do without it for the sake of your young sons, if for no other reason. How can you tell but that their youthful steps may trip to that destruction on this side of which your slower feet have been able to halt? Think of them; pity them; care for them. I do not say, deny yourselves, for you say there is no self-denial in the matter. Then, for their sakes, put that thing away which you cannot but see is the slope down which such multitudes run swiftly into the sea and are drowned.

I make my appeal to Christian women, to mothers and sisters. Mothers and sisters! whom our love and devotion have crowned queens in our homes, whose influence and whose tastes do so much to form our habits and to determine the character of our lives, to whom all manly gallantry accords at least the show of respect and of devotion, I make my appeal to you. Mothers, your sons may not be in any danger, you fondly think; but there are others with hearts as tender as yours, and they are being broken, slowly broken, by the ruin of their sons.

Sisters! it seems to you as if those proud and manly brothers of yours never could be seduced to ruin; but there are other brothers as brave and as manly as yours; and to-day, while I am preaching in this church, they are in haunts of unnamable vice, and they are crushing out the lives of their sisters, because they have thus been lured to ruin. I make my appeal to you, mothers and sisters; if these poor shattered remains of humanity could be arranged in rows before you, how would you like to stand up in the presence of their mothers and sisters, and say, "I helped to produce these results. I put the wine-glass to their lips. I made it fashionable and manly for them to drink. I urged them to the beginning of their course, of which this is—God forgive me!—the melancholy and miserable result"? Nor do I plead with you simply on man's account. Mothers and sisters! this is not a man's sin only; for, as I see it, this is a woman's sin too, and in far greater measure than many people are ready to suspect. I dare not trust myself to describe the things I have seen with women, young and tender, and sometimes beautiful, upon whose more impressible temperament and finer organization the destroyer had taken firmer hold, and with women no longer young, but whose soul and sense were dead long before their eyes were closed. For woman's sake, for your own sister's sake, I make my appeal to you. Mothers and sisters, discourage and discountenance the usages that make it so easy to learn to depend upon the excitement that is given by the kindly glass of wine; and, when you see that wine resorted to to give lost fires to the eye, to give lustre to the cheek, and to give fluency to the tongue, let me beseech you to see in these things unconscious prophecies of the time that shall come when destructive fires shall be kindled in the soul, when the hectic of disease shall burn upon the cheek, and when the incoherent mumblings shall indicate the confirmed and helpless drunkard; and, thinking of these things, I bespeak your pity, your sympathy, your active pity, your practical sympathy. "How can you endure to see the destruction that comes upon your kindred?"

Let not the church turn away from this thing; let not any one say to himself, "This is a mere platform theme. It is a sore upon the body politic, but it is a sore that ought to be handled only by professional men, and not rudely put before us." Do not say that, dear brethren, when the ruin is so obvious and so dreadful. When men are robbed, and wounded, and stripped in their helplessness in your way, do not make your model the priest or the Levite, but the good Samaritan. Stop, my brethren; come down; do what you can to lift that robbed and wounded man who is still your brother, and do what you can in all proper ways to break the power and to scatter the influences that culminate in results such as now claim your pity. How shall the church act about this thing? Had Esther stood still in the safe elevation of a Persian palace, in unthinking indifference about the destruction of her kindred, who would not condemn such base heartlessness? And how is it to be with the church of Christ, his spotless spouse, herself reclaimed and won and saved, and lifted up to sit together in heavenly places in Christ—how shall it be with her if she has no eye to pity and no heart that yearns to save, and no hand to stretch forth relief, when such sin, misery, and wholesale destruction are before her everywhere? So I make my appeal to you, my brethren of the Church.

There are queens of society; would that I could make my appeal to those queens of society all over these United States! I would say to them, Catch the spirit and copy as far as you can the active sympathy and pity of this Hebrew woman—this patriot of the olden time. When two weeks bring round the genial Thanksgiving Day, and when the young and old gather round the family board, ye queens of society, ye queens in our homes, do not put the wine-glass in their hands, do not put the poisonous beverage to their lips. In that clear crystal of pure water, believe me, is better far than the wine, rosy though it be; for at last it biteth like a serpent, and stingeth like an adder. And when the New Year's Day comes round, and when your friends are gathered in your parlors, let there be the freest interchange of all kindly good-will; let there be unhindered flow of soul; but, O woman! do not, I beseech you, tempt man again by putting the forbidden fruit to his lips. It may be good-nature and kindliness in you, but, oh! recollect it may be death to him.

I can hardly think of any one of the causes that we are in the habit of pleading from our pulpits, the arguments for which have not some application to the case of the intemperate. I can hardly think of an argument for foreign or home missions that has not some appropriateness in the connection in which I now speak to you. I would have you look with interest upon these temperance organizations, and help them. Do not trouble yourself about certain differences of opinion among those who are intent upon reform in this direction. Perhaps from some constitutional incapacity to follow it, I am conscious of a kind of impatience of minute argumentation on subjects where broad and sufficient and unquestioned views exist on which we are all agreed that we ought to act. It is here precisely as it is among men who are seeking political reform. Good men have said to themselves, and I hope will continue to say it to the end, "Why, this is not a question as between one party and another party; it is a question between men of whom we hope the best, and men who are evidently and undeniably bad." One man has one view of the method in which this thing ought to be antagonized, and another has a somewhat modified view; but, brethren, there is substantial agreement among us that the thing is bad, "only evil, and that continually." Let us, with such light, views, and convictions as we have, contend against it, until the causes of the waste and destruction of so many of our people and our kindred be swept utterly away.

If there is any people on the face of the earth that ought to be in earnest about this thing, it is the American people. If there is a land upon the face of the earth that ought to be intent upon having things right in society, in law, and in fact upon this matter, it is this. Only think, with our universal suffrage, your property, your liberty, and, with our elective judiciary, your very lives, may be bought and sold for rum. In view of the things that have transpired within these years past, I should not have wondered any day if I had seen an indignant and injured community spring to its feet, and say, in the presence of the nation, to these tools of corruption: "When our fathers decided upon manhood suffrage, they meant the ballot for *men*, not for imbruted, not for ignorant men, not for savages, but for MEN.. And we must take care in future that this dreadful power for good or for evil be kept only in the hands of men." But there is no use in plying with an argument like this these tools of corruption themselves. It is from a sphere to which they do not rise; it has to do with interests of which they take no cognizance. Men who are lost to all sense of what they owe to God and to man are not likely to care about great political principles: they are above their pursuits and above their perceptions.

I leave this with you, Christian people, for, after all, you must bear the great burden and weight of this great work in the world. You know the value of immortal souls, for Christ has saved you; you know the deceitfulness of sin, for you are continually on your guard against the destroyer. Divine grace has reached you and redeemed you; divine pity awoke its echoes in your soul, and led you to trust and love Almighty God. Under the influence of that kind of pity, you, Christians, must look upon your suffering fellow-creatures; and, having a clear and distinct perception of all the issues in time and eternity, you can say with an intelligence that others do not feel, "How can I endure to see the destruction of my kindred?" May God help all of us to be faithful in our place, and to exhibit always that active pity and practical sympathy of which the text gives us such a beautiful example!

TEMPERANCE AND THE PULPIT.

BY REV. C. D. FOSS, D.D

"If the watchman see the sword come, and blow not the trumpet, and the people be not warned; if the sword come, and take any person from among them, he is taken away in his iniquity; but his blood will I require at the watchman's hand"—EZEKIEL xxxiii. 6.

I PURPOSE to preach, this evening, a sermon on the subject of temperance; not on temperance, in the general sense of the word, as referring to all the appetites and passions of our complex nature. I use the word in that restricted sense which custom has put upon it, and the fact that the word has become specific emphatically indicates that the chief of the foes with which this victim has to contend is not avarice, nor gluttony nor amusement, but the intoxicating cup.

There are reasons, very numerous and very weighty, for which this theme should be urged on the attention of men from the pulpit. The statement of some of these reasons will serve, I trust, to give to the doctrine of total abstinence the grip of a moral obligation on the consciences of my Christian auditors, and especially of the young men of the congregation, whom I shall more directly address at the close of this discourse. I dwell on this point, not at all by way of apology for the presentation of this theme. The cause of temperance is the cause of suffering humanity and of God. Those men, therefore, ought pre-eminently to be its advocates who are specially set apart to advance the glory of God by preaching good tidings to fallen man. If I felt that I needed any vindication for making temperance the theme of frequent discourse from the pulpit, I might find it in the fact that I belong to a church which has a total abstinence Discipline, and to a Conference of ministers, numbering two hundred and seventy, which years ago resolved itself into a total abstinence society, without a single dissenting voice, and which has repeatedly enjoined on all its ministers the duty of preaching specifically on this subject. Among the things forbidden by the "General Rules" of the Methodist Episcopal Church, immediately after profanity and Sabbath-breaking, we find these words: "Drunkenness, buying or selling spirituous liquors, or drinking them, unless in cases of extreme necessity."

My object in showing you the intimate relations of this theme to the Christian pulpit is to intensify your conviction that it has imperative claims on the attention and sympathy of every philanthropic man. If it is my duty to help forward this chief among the moral reforms of the age, it is your duty also. That it is my duty, and the duty of every pastor, who can doubt? If drink, accursed drink, be not a devouring "sword," by which many a wretched, self-destroyed victim "is taken away in his iniquity," then let "the watchman" "blow not the trumpet"; but if it be the arch-destroyer of men, even of the strongest, more fatal than the sword of Alexander or Napoleon, then let the trumpet everywhere lift up its note of alarm, and nowhere "give an uncertain sound."

I. *The pulpit should set itself against the sin of intemperance and the causes of intemperance, because of the unnumbered and incomputable evils which flow from it.* I will not shock your sensibilities by a protracted recital of these evils, and, alas! I need not. They are so widespread as to be well-nigh omnipresent; they thrust themselves before all our eyes, and strain almost all our heart-strings. There are but few families which have not been befouled by the slime of this serpent and pierced by the sting of this adder. If not in the immediate circle of the home, then in the next larger circle of near relationship, the curse has fallen. How many times, in the discharge of my pastoral functions, have I visited homes in which there has been an ominous silence concerning some one member of the family—perhaps a husband, a brother, or a father! By-and-by, without any inquiry, the sad truth which I feared has come to my knowledge. He is a drunkard—a voluntary victim of that accursed appetite which has wrought more various and blasting evils among men than any other of those "fleshly lusts which war against the soul."

Lord Bacon says: "All the crimes on earth do not destroy so many of the human race nor alienate so much property as drunkenness." Take the bald and terrible fact that every year 60,000 human wrecks are buried in drunkards' graves in the United States alone; 1,200 polluted souls go howling forth into a drunkard's hell every week; 170 per day.

This annual contribution comes from the ranks of an army of drunkards 600,000 strong. But the death of so many inebriates is the least of all the evils of intemperance to the community at large. To the victims themselves, it is indeed the sum of inconceivable woes, the fulfilment of that divine warning often sounded in their ears: "At the last it biteth like a serpent, and stingeth like an adder"; but to the community their exit is a gain. Their loathsome bodies and ruined intellects and corrupted souls were an offence to men, and the hopeless agony of broken-hearted love had long wished them gone. The loss to the community dated back long before the final catastrophe, to the time when the hand began to tremble, and the brain began to be clouded, and the freeman began to be a slave.

Take the facts, that intemperance in this nation has actually cost it more money than all its schools, colleges, and churches, and all the expenses of the government before the war; and that of all the murders, robberies, and other crimes, four out of five are directly chargeable to drink. In Potter County, Pa., where no liquor was sold in 1865, not a single case was brought forward for trial at the autumn session of the court.

But you must not look simply at drunkards. Intemperance begins long before the point of visible inebriation. Drunkenness is only the sign which intemperance hangs out to the world in its later stages. Many of its worst evils are produced before a stranger would surmise anything wrong. That heroic man who delivered such telling blows against this sin when he stood almost alone, Lyman Beecher, put before the people, more than forty years ago, these memorable words: "A multitude of persons, who are not accounted drunkards, create disease and shorten their days by what they denominate a 'prudent use of ardent spirits.' Let it therefore be engraven on the heart of every man THAT THE DAILY USE OF ARDENT SPIRITS, IN ANY FORM OR IN ANY DEGREE, IS INTEMPERANCE. Its effects are certain and deeply injurious, though its results may be slow, and never be ascribed to their real cause. No person probably ever did, or ever will, receive ardent spirits into his system once a day, and fortify his constitution against its deleterious effects." Dr. Beecher also speaks, in the same connection, of that well-known "state of experience when the empire of reason is invaded, and weakness and folly bear rule; prompting to garrulity or sullen silence; inspiring petulance or anger, or insipid good-humor and silly conversation; pouring out oaths and curses, or opening the storehouse of secrets, their own and others." It is now a well-established fact that, long before the goal of drunkenness is reached, real intoxication occurs; and there are incomputable evils of intemperance before the tongue begins to falter or the feet to trip.

Add to the manifest and disgusting effects of drunkenness, which we must see wherever we turn our eyes, this immensely larger catalogue of the evils which flow from intemperance in its earlier stages; remember that the ministers of religion are called to imitate the example and carry forward the work of him whose biography is written in these five words, "who went about doing good," and that his doing good consisted in overcoming evil, and then tell me whether the pulpit has or has not a mission against the greatest aggregation of evils under which Christendom groans.

II. The pulpit should make war on rum, *because rum makes war on the pulpit. Intemperance is one of the hugest obstacles in the way of the Gospel.* The reign of King Jesus and the reign of King Alcohol are always in inverse ratio. Wherever rum-shops are the great centres of attraction, there churches are deserted. The assertion of Paul is proved true: "Ye cannot drink the cup of the Lord and the cup of devils." If the tables of drunken revelry are numerously surrounded, the sacramental table is neglected. Satan has no more efficient batteries planted over against our citadels of virtue, our homes and school-houses and churches, than those temples of his where the incense of XXX ales and wines and liquors perpetually fills the air. He has no better infantry and cavalry than the multiform drinking customs of society.

As a Christian minister, I oppose drink, because it opposes me. The work I try to do, it undoes. My charge against it at this point is single and simple: it is an obstacle to the spread of the Gospel; nay, it is an enemy which assails the Gospel, and whose complete success would drive the Gospel from the earth. The chains it forges are the strongest and most galling ever fastened on the human body or the human soul. There is not a sinner on the face of the earth so unlikely to be savingly affected by the influences of the Gospel as the habitual drunkard. He may be a man of delicate sensibility, of lofty purpose, and of towering intellect; he may have qualities which, untainted by alcohol, would adorn any character; but, if he is addicted to his cups, his destination is almost inevitably the bottomless pit. The salvation of a thorough drunkard is one of the mightiest miracles of Almighty grace. I know men who are frequently convicted of their need of experimental religion, but who are held back from a single step towards it by the charms of rum. All other fetters would be as gossamer in the way of their urgent longing; this holds them. Many a poor, broken-hearted wretch has staggered up to the altar for prayer, and cried earnestly for mercy, and reeled away again to drown his sorrows in the bowl which caused them, and which will aggravate them, until they culminate amid unquenchable flames.

So far as the probability of success in the proclamation of my message is concerned, let me go to the brazen blasphemer of the name most dear to my heart; let me go to the forger, who for long years has been using satanic cunning to defraud his fellow-men; let me go to the murderer, who lies in felon's chains awaiting the execution of the law's supreme penalty; but send me not to the pitiable object in human shape, whose spirit is beclouded, and whose flesh is reeking with the fumes of rum. And why? Because his will is enthralled by the direst bondage conceivable. His manhood is in the dust, and a demon sits on the chariot of the soul, lashing the fiery steeds of passion. No possible motive, or combination of motives, can be urged upon him which will stand a moment before the infernal clamorings of his appetite. One of these unfortunate beings (for I know not but they are to be pitied as much as blamed) once said that, if he were placed in one corner of a room, with a jug of rum in the opposite corner, and a cannon firing balls across the room every instant, he should start for the rum. No other habit has such power. It is not so with the swearer or the forger or the murderer. The Gospel can be presented to either of them from a more advantageous standpoint.

The truth here insisted on stands out with fearful vividness, if you compare a drunkard's death-bed with that of other sinners. Take the case of one who escapes death by his own hand or by accident (a multitude of them are carried off in these ways), but who stands on the verge of a dishonored grave, brought there by his own excesses. It seems as though the good influences which linger round all other death-beds, as long as life remains in the body, have deserted him. You need not repeat in his ear the fearful assurance that "no drunkard shall inherit the kingdom of God." He feels it in his inmost soul. "Hell from beneath is moved to meet him" at his coming. The devils are so sure of him that they cannot wait for the spirit to leave the body. They come up and fill the room. His eyes see them just as distinctly as they see the terror-stricken relatives that stand around his bed.

Listen to a brief account of this dreadful condition, extracted from the writings of one who has experienced it, and has since become an eloquent advocate of temperance:

"Who can tell the horrors of that horrible malady, aggravated as it is by the almost ever-abiding consciousness that it is self-sought? . . . Hideous faces appeared on the walls and on the ceiling and on the floors; foul things crept along the bed clothes, and glaring eyes peered into mine. I was at one time surrounded by myriads of monstrous spiders, which crawled slowly, slowly, over every limb, whilst the beaded drops of perspiration would start to my brow, and my limbs would shiver until the bed rattled again. Strange lights would dance before my eyes, and then suddenly the very blackness of darkness would appall me by its dense gloom. All at once, whilst gazing at a frightful creation of my distempered mind, I seemed to be struck with sudden blindness. I knew a candle was burning in the room, but I could not see it—all was so pitchy dark. I lost the sense of feeling, too, for I endeavored to grasp my arm in one hand, but consciousness was gone. I put my hand to my side, my head, but felt nothing, and still I knew my limbs, my frame, were there. And then the scene would change. I was falling—falling swiftly as an arrow—far down into some terrible abyss; and so like reality was it that, as I fell, I could see the rocky sides of the horrible shaft, where mocking, gibing, fiend-like forms were perched, and I could feel the air rushing past me, making the sweat stream out by the force of the unwholesome blast. Then the paroxysm sometimes ceased for a few moments, and I would sink back on my pallet drenched with perspiration, utterly exhausted, and feeling a dreadful certainty of the renewal of my torments."

Now, with what prospect of success could the minister go to the bedside of such a fiend-haunted man, to pour into his ears the consolations of the Gospel? Far be it from me to say that the occupant of such a bed cannot possibly pass from it to Abraham's bosom. I am ready to preach Jesus to any man as long as the blood courses his veins, but I will say I am utterly unable to conceive a case more hopeless.

It is not surprising that the great apostle of temperance, who had twice suffered all the horrors above described, should breathe forth, as I have heard him, with thrilling effect, the following prayer: "Almighty God, if it be thy will that man should suffer, whatever seemeth good in thy sight impose on me. Let the bread of affliction be given me to eat. Take from me the friends of my confidence. Let the cold hut of poverty be my dwelling-place, and the wasting hand of disease inflict its painful torments. Let me sow in the whirlwind and reap in the storm. Let those have me in derision who are younger than I. Let the passing away of my welfare be like the fleeting of a cloud, and the shouts of my enemies be like the rushing of waters. When I anticipate good, let evil annoy me; when I look for light, let darkness come upon me. Let the terrors of death be ever before me. . . . Do all this, but save me, merciful God, save me from the fate of a drunkard."

Now, shall the pulpit, or shall it not, utter its emphatic and reiterated protest against men's needless haste in rushing into evils so enormous? Shall it or shall it not warn the young against those threads of gossamer, which are scarcely felt until they grow into chains of steel, unbearable and unbreakable? Shall it or shall it not jealously guard itself against the assaults of this wily foe? For there is no other temptation which has been so destructive to the character of Christian ministers. God's command to Aaron and his sons was, "Do not drink wine nor strong drink . . . lest ye die." If all their successors had heeded this warning, religion would have been spared many a severe reproach. What a proof it is of the insidious and awful power of this temptation, that any minister of Christ should be lured on by it to destruction, in spite of all the seemingly resistless motives which cry out against the monstrous folly and sin! His position, his reputation, his family, his church, his Bible, his Saviour, all protest; but the enchanting cup meets him at every turn, and down he goes. Oh! what a fall—from the pulpit into hell!

III. There is another thought, which makes me feel that this theme should be earnestly and plainly discoursed upon from the pulpit. *It is manifestly God's order that the church should take the lead in every great moral reform.*

Slavery was not abolished, and never could have been, by any band of voluntary reformers, following in the wake of infidels and open revilers of Christ and his church. I once heard from the lips of that silver-tongued orator, whom I never hear without coveting him for Jesus, this declaration: "If all the churches in this country had been sunk through the earth forty years ago, the cause of human freedom would have been further forward." Over against such insane folly put the words of that great, good man who guided the ship of state into the port of universal freedom, and whom posterity will call not only patriot, but sage: "The government has been nobly sustained by all the churches; God bless the churches; and blessed be God, who, in this our great trial, giveth us the churches." The mightiest of human forces is the aroused conscience of a great people, and the chief quickener and educator of the conscience is the pulpit. Therefore,

"I say the pulpit, in the sober use
Of its legitimate, peculiar power,
Must stand acknowledged, while the world shall stand,
The most important and effectual guard,
Support, and ornament of virtue's cause."

One great error of the Washingtonian movement was, that it did not ally itself with religion, but often threw contempt upon the church. A popular and eloquent temperance speaker, during that campaign, said, as he arose to speak at a meeting which had been opened with prayer, "I never can bear to be prayed over when I am going to talk temperance." Gough has no objection to being prayed over, nor Dodge, nor Colfax. One of the most hopeful features of the great reform is, that it is at length chiefly in the hands of religious men, and that its promoters feel the urgent need of enlisting the hearty co-operation of the ministry and the church.

'Christmas Evans, the great Welsh preacher, met with much trouble in his temperance efforts from his brother ministers who were not willing to make the entire sacrifice of their cups. One in particular, Mr. W——, of A——, was obstinately opposed. Evans prepared to meet him. He polished an arrow, and put it in his quiver. On one occasion he was appointed to preach, and, as usual, there were gatherings from far and near to hear him. Mr. W——, of A——, was there also; but, as in anticipation of an attack, he at first said he should not be present while Evans preached; yet such was the fascination that he could not stay away. By-and-by he crept up into the gallery, where the preacher's eye—for he had but one—which had been long searching for him, at length discovered him. All went on as usual until the time came when the arrow might be drawn, which was done slyly and unperceived. "I had a strange dream the other night," said the preacher. "I dreamed that I was in Pandemonium, the council-chamber of Hades. How I got there I know not, but there I was. I had not been there long before there came a thundering rap to the gate. 'Beelzebub, Beelzebub, you must come to earth directly.' 'Why, what is the matter now?' 'They are sending out missionaries to preach to the heathen.' 'Are they? Bad news this. I'll be there presently.' Beelzebub came, and hastened to the place of embarkation, where he saw the missionaries, their wives, and a few boxes of Bibles and tracts, but, on turning round, he saw rows of casks, piled up, and labelled 'gin,' 'rum,' 'brandy,' etc. 'That will do,' said he; 'no fear yet. These casks will do more harm than the boxes can do good.' So saying, he stretched his wings for hell again. After a time came another loud call: 'Beelzebub, they are forming Bible Societies.' 'Are they? Then I must go.' He went, and found two ladies going from house to house, distributing the Word of God. 'This won't do,' thought he, 'but I will watch the result.' The ladies visited an aged female, who received a Bible with much reverence and many thanks. Satan loitered about, and, when the ladies were gone, saw the old woman come to the door and look around to assure herself that she was unobserved. She then put on her bonnet, and with a small parcel under her apron, hastened to the next public-house, where she pawned the new Bible for a bottle of gin. 'That will do,' said Beelzebub, 'no fear yet'; and back again he flew to his own place. Again came a loud knock and hasty summons, 'They are forming Temperance Societies.' 'Temperance Societies! what's that? I'll come and see.' He came and saw, and flew back muttering, 'This won't do much harm to me or my people, they are forbidding the use of ardent spirits; but they have left my poor people all the ale and porter, and the rich all the wines; no fear yet.' Again came a louder rap, and a more and more urgent call, 'Beelzebub! you must come now, or all is lost; they are forming teetotal societies.' 'Teetotal! what in the name of all my imps is that?' 'To drink no intoxicating liquors whatever. The sole beverage is water.' 'Indeed; that is bad news! I must see after this.' And he did, but went back again to satisfy the anxious inquiries of his legions, who were all *qui vive* about the matter. 'Oh!' said he, 'don't be alarmed. True, it's an awkward affair, but it won't spread much yet, for all the parsons are against it, and Mr. W——, of A—— (sending up an eagle glance of his eye at him), is at the head of them.'" "But I won't be at the head of them any longer," cried out Mr. W——, and walking calmly down to the table-pew, signed the pledge amid loud cheers.'

It remains only to ask what is the general plan of resistance to be employed against this stupendous evil?

I am persuaded the youth before me would be glad to know what they ought now to do, and what they ought to plan for the future against an evil which the most strenuous exertions of our generation will not suffice utterly to abate. I know the heart of a young man. I know his jealousy of any influence which can interfere with the fullest and most symmetrical development of his mind and heart. I know his generous impulses to reclaim the erring and inspire them with the same noble sentiments which thrill his own breast. And with regard to this pitiable weakness and shameful sin of intemperance (for it is both), I now say to every young man before me, "Do thyself no harm," and "Love thy neighbor as thyself."

Many of the most intelligent, philanthropic, and religious men in the world have been giving earnest attention to this subject for ages, and especially during the last thirty or forty years. I submit that their deliberate judgments are entitled to great respect. There have been and are among them men of profound scientific attainments, chemists, physiologists, physicians, able lawyers and judges, governors and senators, philanthropists, scholars, divines. They have met and consulted. They have brought to their aid all the discoveries of science, all the principles of human action, all the power of prayer. They have framed their theories, and put them to the test of experience and public criticism, and then have improved them. They have done all this under the solemn pressure of an abiding conviction that the chief foe to our social happiness and national security is strong drink. The conclusions they have reached are that, first of all, nothing but sleepless activity can carry forward this noble reform or save it from disgraceful and disastrous wreck. They assert the need of contributions of influence from the purse, the pen, the tongue, and the conscience —the four powers which control society. The evil they seek to overthrow is founded on those two mighty forces of evil, appetite and avarice, and has for its chief body-guard social usages and political corruption.

The advocates of the temperance reformation are thoroughly agreed in another thing, viz., that *the chief hope and indispensable condition of the success of this movement lies in total abstinence.* Up to this point, I think it likely no person present has dissented from any position I have taken. Grant me now a candid hearing while I attempt, in a few words, to vindicate this vital principle. I desire to place it on a foundation where you can all stand firmly with me. So I neither affirm nor deny anything concerning several positions which are confidently held by many able advocates of total abstinence. I do not assert that all intoxicating beverages are essentially poisonous, though this is cogently argued by many learned physicians and chemists; and though it is generally conceded that they have no nourishment in them, but are simply excitants. I do not say that they are in every instance positively injurious. I do not say it is a sin for any man, under any circumstances, to drink a glass of wine. Let the twofold basis on which I now rest the argument for total abstinence be distinctly understood:

1. *It is the only personal security.*
2. *It is the only effective example.*

Hence every young man should adopt it as one of the rules of his life, and make it like a "law of the Medes and Persians, which altereth not."

Bear in mind the truth already announced, that the sore evils of intemperance begin far back of the point of visible inebriation. The simple item of exposure to disease will serve as an illustration. In Albany, in 1832, there were 396 cases of cholera; all but 16 terminated fatally. Of these, 140 were drunkards; 38 free drinkers; 131 moderate drinkers; and 5 total abstainers. In St. Louis, in 1849, out of a population of 75,000, there were about 10,000 deaths by cholera—13 per cent. Among the victims, there were only 10 out of the 2,000 Sons of Temperance there—one-half of one per cent. So total abstinence had the advantage, 26 to 1.

But I will not dwell on secondary matters. I declare my conviction that total abstinence is the only complete security against the disgrace and the doom of drunkenness. I know how hard it is for any man to realize this for himself. I know how prompt the almost indignant response: "I have too much self-respect to admit the insinuation of such weakness; I can stand." I confess to no little sympathy with such feelings. But let such overweening self-confidence be sobered by facts. Who of all the sixty thousand whom drink tumbles into the most dishonored of graves in this country every year ever expected to go there when the cruel habit began? Who of them all did not say, as you and I are ready to say to-night: "I know my strength; I have too much manhood in me to become a slave"? Ah! there comes a voice from the grave of many a brilliant son of genius—many a once holy minister of the Gospel—saying to you, young man, and to me: "Let him that thinketh he standeth take heed lest he fall."

I do not hesitate to say that a personal religious experience is no sufficient safeguard against the demon of drink, unless it be girt about with the bulwark of total abstinence. If a Christian plays with a serpent, he may be bitten to death. God promises no miracles. The Sunday-school is one of the safest havens on earth; yet from its sacred precincts thousands of teachers and scholars have been swept into ruin by this fell destroyer. The Rev. Dr. Guthrie, in his book on "The City, its Sins and Sorrows," cites many facts, which almost pass belief. I give a few specimens. Among the prisoners tried at the Glasgow assizes in September, 1848, sixty-two had been connected with Sunday-schools; and of these, fifty-nine admitted that drinking and public-house company had led them away from the Sunday-school, and into crime. At Launceston, out of one hundred boys in a Sunday-school, forty were overcome by drink. "At Ipswich, out of fifteen young men professing piety, and teachers in the Sabbath-school, nine were ruined through drink." Such frightful statements would be instantly rejected if they came on any inferior authority. They only show the power of the rum-fiend where the temperance reformation has but little foothold. Religious youth! listen to me. I appeal to you to say whether if, in the face of such facts, any man plays with this adder, and is stung to death, his ruin is not deserved?

I have one more argument. It is one which addresses itself to every noble sentiment and generous impulse of our natures. "It is good neither to eat flesh [offered to idols], nor to drink wine, nor anything whereby thy brother stumbleth, or is offended, or is made weak." O that stumbling brother, that stumbling brother! What can I do to save him? I must not pass him by. I am my brother's keeper. It was the first deist and murderer who denied this plainest maxim at once of social ethics and of religion. "No man liveth unto himself." We are each in a network of influence, and our every movement affects others. We are bound to recognize this fact; and we must share the responsibility of the results of our action. It will not do to say, "If I drink only one glass of wine at a party, my neighbor ought not to be led by my example to drink five, and go home drunk." Very likely he will be. You know he may be; and if he is, what will you answer at the judgment-bar?

The principle is that things not wrong *per se* are to be given up if our use of them hurts others. This principle made Paul the man he was. It was the key-note of his sublime career. He was ever ready to surrender anything personal for the good of men. "I am made all things to all men, so that by all means I might save some." "I could wish myself accursed from Christ for my brethren." "The love of Christ constraineth me, because I thus judge that if he died for all, then were all dead; and that he died for all that they which live should not henceforth live unto themselves." The same spirit of self-sacrifice for others' good gave Christ his fame. "He humbled himself and became obedient unto death; . . . wherefore God hath highly exalted him, and given him a name that is above every name."

Oh! if this grand principle of self-sacrificing love to men for Jesus' sake could become universally operative in the church, what magnificent results it would achieve! It would set ever-narrowing bounds to the tide of drunkenness, and throttle the demon of drink; it would untie the purse-strings of many a rich man, and move him to lay all his net income and half his estate on the altar of God; it would loose many a tongue that now finds no words to plead Christ's cause with the perishing; it would make every disciple an unceasing laborer together with God; it would bring in the millennium in our lifetime; it would soon present this world a spotless jewel unto Christ.

THE EVILS OF INTEMPERANCE.

"Who hath woe? who hath sorrow? who hath contentions? who hath babbling? who hath wounds without cause? who hath redness of eyes? They that tarry long at the wine; they that go to seek mixed wine. Look not thou upon the wine when it is red, when it giveth his color in the cup, when it moveth itself aright. At the last it biteth like a serpent, and stingeth like an adder. Thine eyes shall behold strange women, and thine heart shall utter perverse things. Yea, thou shalt be as he that lieth down in the midst of the sea, or as he that lieth upon the top of a mast. They have stricken me, shalt thou say, and I was not sick; they have beaten me, and I felt it not: when shall I awake? I will seek it yet again."—PROVERBS xxiii. 29-35.

NEVER in the history of this commonwealth was there an hour when the subject of intemperance needed a more serious and thorough consideration than the present. During the last forty years light has been poured upon it such as it never had before. Science, experience, reason, philanthropy, religion; all the powers of the wise and good have combined in the work of examining and exposing the enormous crime and ruin which attend the use of intoxicating drinks. The "former times" may have been, in some respects, "the times of ignorance," which God comparatively "winked at." But now that darkness is all past. The true light shineth. No intelligent man needs to take, or has a right to take, any dubious or half-way views upon this subject. There is no reasonable doubt in regard to the crime and curse of intemperance. Its immorality, its history, its influences, could be made no clearer if written by an "angel standing in the sun." We come to you with no faltering faith or ambiguous words in regard to this matter. We do not say: "We *think*"—"we *believe*"—"we *suppose*" that the matter stands so-and-so. We KNOW, we ARE SURE, that intemperance is one of the most tremendous crimes and curses that man ever felt or Satan ever gloried in.

Probably intemperance never raged in our country more than now. The devil has availed himself of the present wretched state of things, as a sort of truce, in which to build up his fortresses and enlarge his forces with immeasurable industry and success. Political legislation has generally been in the interest of strong drink. Some reformers have grown weary of the struggle. Men who have stood beside the graves of drunken fathers, or brothers, or sons, still take no interest in the temperance cause. In the meantime, the great commander-in-chief of drunkenness has erected immense fortifications of brewery, distillery, and warehouse on many a hilltop and wharf, and has lined every city street, and every country roadside, with rifle-pits of bar-room and saloon. Never did any other chieftain so skilfully arrange his forces to sweep every neighborhood in all the country from end to end.

And what is the community doing all this time?

More than one-half of them are sleeping or indifferent, while tens of thousands are continually being captured or destroyed. Among those tens of thousands is an appalling multitude of the young. The cry comes up to us on every side that the young are becoming drunkards. You can see it everywhere for yourself. In the barroom, in the restaurant, by the beer fount, on the steamboat, in the car, you can see young men drinking, or manifesting too plainly the effects of drink. A few years ago, it was accounted a deep disgrace, and was practised only in secret. Now, it is done openly, as a thing of bravery and glory—the glory of their shame.

This state of things calls upon every generous and virtuous young man to take a proper and decided stand upon this subject. If you are radically wrong here, there is tremendous danger that you will come out wrong everywhere.

I shall confine myself at this time to one single department of the subject, namely, *The evils of intemperance.* This is the great basis on which we build our opposition. Our antagonism to strong drink is not a mere sentiment or theory; it is based on dark, dreadful, unquestionable facts—the actual evils of intemperance.

It is to these evils, you will observe, that those sentences of Solomon refer which I have read to you; and what a picture is that! Look at it again. It was taken nearly three thousand years ago; but what a perfect photograph is it of the drunkard still! His woe — his babbling — his wounds—his redness of eyes—the biting serpent —the strange women—the reeling—the stupidity —the insatiate thirst. Why, it is perfectly life-like! It has a thousand counterparts every day.

I shall divide the evils of intemperance into three classes—namely, *Personal, Social,* and *Civil.*

I. In attempting to speak of the *personal* evils, a formidable multitude appears before me, from which I can select only here and there a repulsive cluster. Let me allude first to

(a) The *physical* evils of intemperance. Alcohol is a poison. Who says so? Science. It is no bugbear of temperance men, as such. Chemical tests, and the witness of men of the highest scientific character, put it high on the list of vegetable poisons. Upon this subject, any number of names and testimonies could be given. Let me give a sample or two:

One physician says: "We have incontrovertible proof that spirit is a poison of the same nature as prussic acid, producing the same effects, killing by the same means, paralyzing the muscles of respiration, and so preventing the necessary change of black into vermilion blood."

The name of Sir Astley Cooper is a lofty one in medical science, and this is his testimony: "No man can have a greater hostility to dram-drinking than myself, insomuch that I never suffer any ardent spirits in my house, thinking them evil spirits. And if the poor could witness the white livers, the dropsies, the shattered nervous systems which I have seen, as the consequences of drinking, they would be aware that spirits and poisons are synonymous terms."

Another physician says of the drunkard's corpse: "Every tissue proclaims but too distinctly the injury it has received. There are no marks of weakness or decrepitude, as the result of natural decay and advancing age; but all the organs, in accents awfully impressive, speak of poison, of madness, of self-immolation. The anatomist turns away in horror."

Such are simply samples of the testimony which men of science give upon the subject. All that is needed to produce death in the case of alcohol as of any other poison, is that one takes sufficient quantity. It is possible, in a single draught, to take enough to kill a man at once; and this has been done. Its effects upon brute animals are similar to those on the human species. Dr. Percy, a British physician, tried the experiment of injecting two and a half ounces of alcohol (about one-third of an ordinary tumblerful) into the stomach of a dog, and the animal dropped down dead very much as if he had been struck with a club.

You may tell me that some persons *do* use spirituous liquors many years, and yet they live. But does that prove that they are not poisonous?

In Germany, it is quite customary, in some places, for the ladies to take a mild solution of arsenic to improve their complexions; and the men sometimes take small quantities pure as tonics, and think they cannot do without it; and these persons may live many years. But is not arsenic a poison for all that? And do not physicians testify that such persons' lives are shortened by such habits?

Nature does indeed fight bravely and long to resist and repair the damage of some of the poisons forced upon it, whether by arsenic, or opium, or alcohol; but the poison *is* there nevertheless, and it does shorten even the longest life, while it cuts the most of its victims down in the very beginning of their race.

In all this, I have spoken only of the real nature and legitimate effects of *genuine* alcoholic liquors. But if these things are so with the genuine articles, how much more deadly must be the poison of those vile compounds, colored, and flavored, and sold all over the land under the fictitious names of "brandy," "gin," and "champagne"? Oil of vitriol, oil of almonds, oil of turpentine, lime-water, sub-acetate of lead, sulphate of lead, strychnine, logwood, tannin, fusel oil, and cockroaches—such are some of the delicious elements which help to make up more than nine-tenths of the delightful beverages which young men, and fashionable men, and poor men, and rich men, and all kinds of drinking men, claim as their privilege and joy to use. What fine elixirs of life, in which friend may pledge the health of friend!

The late Dr. Nott said: "I had a friend who had been once a wine-dealer, and, having read the startling statements made public in relation to the compounding of wines and the adulteration of other liquors generally, I enquired of that friend as to the verity of those statements. His reply was: 'God forgive what has passed in my own cellar, but the statements made are true, and all true, I assure you.'"

Professor Draper, of New York, two or three years ago made an examination of the brandy at some of the principal hotels on Broadway, where it was retailed at fifty cents a glass, and in every instance it was a mere compound of villanous poison. I knew a landlord whose "brandy" was discovered to have cost him thirty-seven cents a gallon. I knew a druggist who paid two hundred dollars for a recipe to make these liquors. The liquor inspector of Cincinnati, a few years ago, after a careful examination, declared that he did not think there were twenty gallons of pure brandy in the whole city.

If you choose to turn from brandy to beer, I can only commend you to the testimony given in the city of Albany, in the famous trial of Taylor against Delavan—a testimony of facts in regard to the manufacture of beer in that day too loathsome to bear a repetition in the pulpit.

Is it not, then, most amazing that we must plead,

and so often plead in vain, to prevent men from pouring such disgusting poison into their vitals? Do you wonder that the habitual drinkers of these things should put on such dreadful tokens of disease? Do you wonder at the bloodshot eye, the burning skin, the horrid breath, the bloated form, the unquenchable thirst, the staggering pace, the delirium, the death?

(*b*) We pass now to the *mental* evils which proceed from the use of alcoholic drinks.

The immediate and inevitable effect of these things is to stimulate the brain. The brain being the great instrument of the mind, whatever affects the brain injuriously must affect the mind in a similar way. In some cases, the stimulus creates an increased brilliancy at first, but it is a temporary and suicidal flash, only burning out swiftly into the ashes of an utter ruin. I need not repeat to you here the names of men, once renowned for intellectual magnificence, but afterward degraded by strong drink to the stupidity and loathsomeness of a sot. Every year has its sad wrecks from this cause, in which the state, the ranks of literature, the legal and medical professions, and the pulpit mourn, in sadness and shame, the loss of some of their brightest ornaments. The Senate of the United States has no loftier names upon its roll than those of some who in after-years went down to their graves beclouded or utterly ruined by intemperance. The medical profession has seen, in its own ranks, how powerless are the finest genius and most accurate knowledge of disease to prevent men from yielding to that beastly habit, whose inevitable end is the foulest disease and the meanest death. The Gospel ministry has blushed for shame as it witnessed some of its most distinguished preachers degraded from their high office by the drunkard's curse. It has even mourned an instance, only a very few years old, when one of its most gifted and tender messengers of grace was seduced, by the demon of the wine-cup, to exchange the sacred desk for a seat on the curb-stone, with a drunkard's tongue belching forth obscenity and oaths.

Oh! how unspeakably painful and disgusting is this brutal degradation of godlike intellects What is more horrible in any human being than the vacant stare, the babbling, the nonsensical muttering, the wild and profane yells of the inebriate? What an outrage on a being once created in his Maker's image! Devils are the synonym of every moral evil, but devils never become drunkards. With all their depravity of heart, they keep the intellect clear. This vile disgrace is peculiar to humanity alone.

(*c*) I now proceed to speak of the *moral* evils of intemperance. Vice loves to grow in clusters. But there is no other vice around which such gigantic clusters grow as intemperance. There is not a commandment of the Decalogue to the violation of which intemperance does not naturally lead. Try them, one by one, beginning with the first table of duties to God. How is it in regard to the true love and worship of God—the honor of his name—the observance of his Sabbath? Does not intemperance break this table of the law into ten thousand pieces every week? Then apply it to the second table of duties to man, and is it not notoriously the most infamous patron of disrespect to parents, of murder, of impurity, of dishonesty, of lying, of covetousness? Is it not accursed by every law on the statute books, both of God and man—by the whole history of human crime?

Statistics gathered through several years, both in this country and elsewhere, show that not far from six-sevenths of the crimes committed and brought to trial can be traced to the use of intoxicating drinks. This does not include that vast world of hidden immorality which reeks with the fumes of drunkenness, but is not brought out to public view. Go to your grand-jury rooms, go to criminal courts, go to county jails and state prisons, go to brothels, go to gibbets, and everywhere you will be confronted with the awful fact that intemperance and crime go hand in hand.

I need not carry our discussion of this matter up to the higher plane of Christianity. It is idle to speak of Jesus and his Gospel to one who is wedded to his cups. You might as well preach to a maniac as to a drunkard as long as he yields to his appetite. No man can possibly become a

Christian until he first becomes a sober man. A drunken Christian is as great an anomaly as a swearing Christian or a thievish Christian.

In speaking of the personal evils of intemperance, we have now noticed the physical, mental, and moral aspects of the case. There is yet another view more terrible than all. It is:

(*d*) The *eternal* evils of intemperance. Beyond all the degradation and woes of the present does this dark curse cling to its victim. Not even when the bloated and burned-out body staggers into the grave has the end come. The drunkard's curse lives throughout a dark and hopeless eternity. "Be not deceived," says the Apostle Paul, "no drunkard shall inherit the kingdom of God;" and in saying so, he classifies drunkards along with idolaters, and adulterers, and thieves, and other classes of guilt and shame (1 Cor. vi. 9, 10). It is a noticeable truth that the Holy Scriptures do not speak of drunkenness with that mild and sentimental sympathy which is manifest so often nowadays. Modern humanitarians are teaching the world only to pity crime, not to punish it. In like manner, drunkenness is regarded by this class as almost exclusively a weakness, not a sin. But the Word of God uses very different language. There it is regarded only as a crime, which, if unrepented of and unforsaken, will inevitably debar the soul from the blessedness of everlasting life. It is one of the abominations and defilements with which no man can enter through the gate into the heavenly city.

A more brief consideration shall now be given to:

II. The *social* evils of intemperance.

If any of you were asked to name that evil which, more than any other, or even more than all others combined, had destroyed the happiness of families; had broken the hearts of loving wives; had blasted the affections, characters, and prospects of childhood; had turned homes of cheerfulness and comfort into prisons of despair; had substituted rags for garments of taste; and had brought every conceivable amount of cruelty on beings of innocence and love—what would you name? How long could you doubt? Would not every man, woman, and child be compelled to say that, of all the curses ever inflicted on families and communities, there is nothing so unmitigatedly hellish as intemperance? It has turned the once faithful husband into a compound of beast and fiend; it has nerved the hand that once gave the wedding-ring to deal the deadly blow; it has inspired the lips that once spoke only of love to belch forth the foulest curses of the pit; it has made children fly from a father's approach as they would from a devouring monster.

One of the most horrid sights that God looks down upon is a drunkard's home, and one of the most pitiable objects in all his universe is a drunkard's wife. I know not what language to use to express the deep wretchedness of her lot. The most terrible punishment spoken of in antiquity was that devised by Mezentius, who sometimes put a person to death by chaining to him a corpse face to face, whose putrefaction should gradually kill the living man. I can only think of the drunkard's wife as chained in this way to a loathsome horror; chained for months and years; chained with no hopes of release, save that which the grave may bring to one or the other, or to both.

Nor is even that hope unmixed with the saddest fears; for that foul corruption dies not with the wretched forms in which it first arose. The drunkard is the embodiment not only of a crime, but also of a *disease;* and that disease is *hereditary.* The most careful investigation has confirmed this fact. Physicians testify that "diseases from drinking spirituous or fermented liquors are liable to become hereditary to the third generation, gradually increasing, if the cause be continued, until the family becomes extinct." Children of drunkards come into the world with the disease of intemperance in their blood, and the marks of it on their vitals. They have been subjected to the most careful examination after death. Dissection and the microscope have revealed precisely the same marks of disease in them as in the confirmed inebriate. Dr. Riggs, of London, once stated that "one-half of the deaths among children in that city was produced by hereditary inebriety."

And what is the case of the children who do not die? Their physical systems are in the same morbid state as that of a reformed drunkard. They may grow up and get along well enough if they entirely abstain. But let them beware how they touch the first drop! There is a latent appetite in them, like the love of blood in the young lion, which the first sip will make ravenous. This explains why so often the children of inebriates become inebriates themselves, and that so suddenly. It is not merely the force of example, but the development of hereditary thirst, which only awaited the occasion of a beginning to spring at once into a full-grown habit.

Nor is it only in this form that the disease is transmitted from parent to child, but the delirium tremens, or mental decay, or even temporary intoxication of the parent, often leads to the insanity or idiocy of the child. It is said that this cause produces forty per cent. of all insanity, and fifty per cent. of all idiocy.

What a heritage is this to transmit from generation to generation; sometimes overleaping the one immediately succeeding and striking on the third! What a demon of the blood and of the brain must intemperance be, thus to poison the sweet current of life both in the body and the soul! How emphatic the inspired declaration: "Wine is a mocker, strong drink is raging, and whosoever is deceived thereby is not wise."

III. I promised to say something of the evils of intemperance in its *civil* relations, or the evils which it inflicts on the state.

In no other form of government ought the purity of the state to be a matter of such anxious interest as in a republic like ours. Whatever touches the honesty of the ballot-box or the moral integrity of our halls of legislation ought to be watched by every patriot as the brave and sleepless sentinel watches the slightest token of an enemy's approach. Each of these should be regarded by freemen as almost as sacred as the Sanctuary of the Most High. Yet how has the demon of intemperance disgraced the legislative halls of our land, both state and national! What deeds of shame have gathered round our ballot-boxes! The fearful testimony which comes to us from every quarter is that intoxicating liquors, in the interest of their manufacture, traffic, and use, and in the legislation which they seek, are among the most powerful controllers of our elections. The result of all this is that the great majority of our public men are not sincere friends of total abstinence. Some of them are as far from that

"As from the centre thrice to the utmost pole."

Jefferson is reported to have said that "no man

ought to be trusted with office who drank." If that rule were strictly applied to many a legislative body, there would not be a quorum left.

The matter of *taxes* comes up sometimes for discussion in connection with the subject of intoxicating drinks. Various tables of statistics, compiled before the war, agreed in the general fact that about two-thirds of ordinary county taxes went for pauperism and crime, and of that pauperism and crime six-sevenths were produced by intemperance. This would show that about four-sevenths of ordinary taxes, before the war, were exacted by alcoholic drinks. These tables of statistics are, of course, not absolutely exact. With the utmost care, they can only be approximations to the truth. Yet, gathered as they were in different years, and in places far remote from each other, they present a very significant agreement in the result to which they come. We need, however, no precise details. We need only look at our poor-houses, and court-houses, and jails—at the long list of officials, from policeman to judge, whose chief concern is the prevention and punishment of crimes growing out of intemperance, to satisfy even the most incredulous how outrageous is the extortion which strong drink is exacting from the taxpayers of the land.

But I am not willing to dwell upon this aspect of the case. The great question before us rises infinitely above the measurement of dollars and cents in our tax bills. So far as the state is concerned, even if there were no taxes connected with this vice; if it was a source of princely revenue; if every drunkard's corpse could be transmuted into solid gold, and every dram-shop was a public mint; if the whole cost of liquor in the United States (six hundred millions of dollars a year) could be poured directly into the national Treasury to pay the public debt—even then the state could not afford to encourage habits of intoxication. No amount of gold and silver can be weighed against the loss of public virtue. The question of morals, of happiness, of present and eternal welfare, cannot be ciphered out in tables of currency or coin. No state can possibly become so rich but that, if intemperance generally prevails among its citizens and rulers, every true patriot may well repeat, with anxious heart, the dying words of the great William of Orange: "God have mercy on my poor country!"

In the course which I have taken to-day, you perceive I have limited your view to a single feature of the subject of intemperance, viz., its evils. I have endeavored to give you, as far as I could, reliable facts and statements. I have felt that such a course was necessary for every one who desired to know on what basis a strong, reasonable, and Christian opposition against intemperance may be impregnably established.

And now I feel warranted in asking you, every man, woman, and child:

Is it right, or is it wrong, to be the patron of intoxicating drink as a beverage?

Is it right, or is it wrong, to encourage the traffic in it?

Is it right, or is it wrong, to put the bottle to a neighbor's lips?

Is it right, or is it wrong, to set an example, even in a "moderate" or fashionable way, by which a weaker brother or a child may be ensnared and ultimately ruined?

These are questions of practical morals which I imagine not a single judgment or conscience now present will have any difficulty in answering.

Now, on the other hand, let me ask a few questions of general fact. How does the community practically regard this thing? Is it not under the ban of public opinion? Does not the law crush it? Does not philanthropy exterminate it? Do not young and old fly from it? Is it not quarantined like a ship loaded with pestilence? Do not men walk far away around it as they do from a yellow-fever district?

What is the answer to these questions? The answer is that the horrible monster is caressed and pampered to an extent like this: "There is a sufficient quantity of fermented and distilled liquor used in the United States to fill a canal four feet deep, fourteen feet wide, and one hundred and twenty miles in length" (*Nat. Temp. Almanac*, 1870). The National Beer Congress, at its session in Newark, N. J., June, 1869, estimated the amount of beer manufactured in the United States at over five and a half millions of barrels, and the capital employed, directly and indirectly, at one hundred and five millions of dollars ($105,000,000). The lowest estimate of actual cost of spirituous and fermented liquors consumed in the United States annually is six hundred millions of dollars ($600,000,000). This is an annual expenditure equal to one-quarter the amount of our present national debt, or nearly two millions per day. Some of this, we know, is used for chemical and mechanical purposes, but the greater part is the deadly drink of infatuated human beings.

And what is the fruit of all this? What a harvest of drunkenness and death! It is estimated that sixty thousand go down to drunkards' graves every year. These represent a quarter of a million of wives and mothers, and sisters and children, overwhelmed with shame, sorrow, and often poverty, by the untimely ruin of husbands, fathers, brothers, and sons.

But where, my young friends, does this vast evil begin? Always in the first glass. Always in the "moderate use." Always in the hollow sophistry that temperance does not mean total abstinence. Always in the vain confidence of being able to control the appetite and to stop just at the proper time. Of the sixty thousand drunkards who die every year, probably not one expected to come to that end. But the mighty deceitfulness of that deadly appetite sweeps its victim into helplessness and ruin before he is aware. It was only in the past week that we read the telegram of three men who were drawn into the rapids of Niagara. They expected, of course, to cross the stream in safety, but the current soon became too strong. Their oars were too feeble for the tide. Their boat was tossed and broken in the rapids. Two of the men sank quickly. The third, being an expert swimmer, tried to reach a little island in the stream. He came within six feet of it, but the rushing waters swept him past. In despair, he threw his arms upward and sank. It is the picture of daily scenes on the mad stream of intemperance. So they venture out; so they are swept away; so the most of them sink in speedy ruin; so here and there a resolute one makes a desperate effort to save himself, and almost succeeds; but the infernal tide is more than a match for his exhausted powers; he abandons the effort in despair, and sinks into eternal death. Your safety, my young friends, is to let that dangerous indulgence alone. What is fashion to you? What the bantering of reckless comrades? What even the invitation of female beauty, if it would entice you into the drunkard's path? In that sparkling wine-glass there is an adder, and, if you trifle with it, it will sting you unto death even as it has stung millions. Then, when the hopes and promises of your life shall all have been blasted, your habits ruined, your character destroyed—when we shall have carried your poor, besotted corpse to the grave, what will it then avail that once foolish companions encouraged you?—once even thoughtless woman asked you to indulge the demon which every day makes ten thousand broken-hearted women weep?

God grant you grace, my young friends, whenever tempted to taste the intoxicating beverage, to say: In the name of health—in the name of wealth—in the name of friends—in the name of honor—in the name of virtue—in the name of example—in the name of everything I hold dear in this world—in the name of my immortal soul—in the name of heaven—in the name of God—No!

LIBERTY AND LOVE.

I MUST express my great sorrow that there is so large a division of sentiment on the subject of temperance, and that this division of sentiment is inclined, in many parts of our land, to take on so acrimonious a form as it does. There are hundreds and thousands of men who not only are themselves temperate, but are anxious to spread temperance principles and practices throughout the community; but they differ as to the measures which it is best to employ.

Some men differ as to the number of elements that are to be included. There be many who say that all alcoholic and distilled liquors should be excluded, but that vinous and fermented liquors should not. There are others who say that these last should be included in the exclusion. But there are still others who say that tobacco ought to be excluded. And there are others yet who say that you ought to exclude all intoxicating drinks and narcotic stimulants—tea and coffee as well as the others. Still others say that you ought to go on to vegetable diet strictly, and not take away the life of any creature. It is held by some that there can be no true temperance until men become farinaceous. I do not propose to discuss any of these questions.

Then, there is a division of men in respect to the measures which should be taken to promote temperance. Some people think that the cause ought to be carried forward by the churches alone, and that there should be no temperance societies. Others think that the work ought to be done by temperance societies simply. Others again think that there ought to be temperance laws—license laws. Still others think that there ought to be laws which should preclude the manufacture and sale of intoxicating drinks. Besides these, there are thousands who think that moral suasion is the only influence that should be resorted to in this matter. There is a great conflict of judgment among men on this subject.

Now, in regard to it all, it is a great misfortune that there should be this division of opinion; and it is a still greater misfortune that this division of opinion should lead to uncharitable judgments, and to the want of faith of man in man. A high-toned temperance man—a man who, as it is said, "goes the whole figure," and wants to sweep away by legislation the evils of intemperance—is apt to look with contempt upon the man who, although he is abstinent, says: "I think we had better be moderate, and not undertake any more than we can carry out, doing what we can for temperance by quietly talking in our own neighborhood." And I see that in an adjoining State there is a painful feeling of acrimony existing among men who are avowed friends of the temperance cause.

I affirm the right of a man to form his own judgment about these things, and to stand by that judgment without detriment or harm. You have no right to take away a man's reputation for temperance principles simply because he does not come on to your platform, nor adopt your measures. You have a right to your views, and you have a right to advocate them; and nobody has a right to take away your peace, or comfort, or good name because you do not agree with him.

Discord of views prevails also as to the use of distilled and fermented drinks. First, I affirm and defend the liberty of men to form their own judgments, and thereby their own consciences, as to what is right and expedient in this particular. If a man says: "I have carefully read every treatise, and I have considered deliberately all the arguments for and against absolute temperance, and it is my sober judgment that the use of mild wines is especially favorable to health and to temperance, I say two things to him: "First, I differ with you; but, secondly, I recognize your right to form your judgment on that ground as much as I recognize my own right to form my judgment on that ground. I am not of your way of thinking, and I wish that you did not think as you do; but you are an honest man, and I defend your liberty of judgment and your liberty of conscience." You have a right to judge his conclusions; but you have no right to judge his conscience. You have a right, as much as you please, to multiply arguments, and views, and statements, so as to induce him, if possible, to change his judgment; but so long as his judgment is not changed, he must be allowed to stand upon it; and he must be counted no less honorable in standing on his judgment than you are in standing on yours. Are not these men who differ from you as honest as you are? Are they not as sincere as you are? Are they not as conscientious as you are? *Who art thou, then, that judgest another man's servant? To his own master he shall stand or fall.*

But now, on the other hand, while I boldly and clearly affirm the liberty of men on this subject, I have a right, most solemnly and earnestly, to appeal to all right-thinking men as to whether they use their liberty charitably or not. The Apostle puts this argument very distinctly: *Use your liberty charitably, amiably, according to the law of love.* Your rights are yours; but they are not yours for a selfish purpose. Your personal right or liberty is to be administered under the great charter of love. And I have a right to ask every man to consider attentively this whole matter of temperance in the community in which he lives, and in the day in which he lives.

I ask, first, Is there any other single source from which comes so much danger or so much distress as from the drinking habits of society? Is not intemperance the paramount mischief, as well as the fountain of almost all the other mischiefs which exist among us? Does it not stimulate the worst part of men? Does it not lead to an immense variety of vices? Your own observation of what is taking place in society at large, and the vast accumulation of statistics and facts such as we ordinarily find in temperance documents, must, it seems to me, have convinced you that the evils with which we have to contend in the community may be mainly traced to this cause. I ask every young man here, and every man of any considerable experience, if he does not know thousands, or if not thousands hundreds, or if not hundreds scores, certainly, of cases of overtaxed business men in our large cities, who have run themselves into absolute ruin by the habit of using intoxicating drinks to keep up their strength and their fire? Has there not been a vein of mischief of this sort running through the business community? Have you not seen it? Have you not known men that were discouraged, and badgered, and pressed in their business, who, for the sake of abating their suffering, have taken away the keen vitality of their life by resorting to the cup? And has not the habit thus formed finally led to their downfall? Is not this going on all the time? Are there not hundreds and thousands of cases, almost in our very midst, of persons who have in some such way become victims of this terrible scourge?

If a ship comes into the harbor with cases of yellow fever on board, there is a great clamor, and we expect that the ship will be stopped, and that the quarantine officers will do their duty, and prevent the infection from spreading to the adjacent shores. And if through any neglect on the part of these officers there are cases on shore, everybody in the city is up in arms about it.

Now, I tell you that there are, to-day, hundreds and thousands of persons in our midst who are infected with this terrific fever of drink. Their neighbors know it; their partners know it; you and I know it. It is a matter of common observation. Almost any one of us could put down the names of scores of these men. The habit of indulging in intoxicating drinks is eating out the lives of multitudes of otherwise worthy and most desirable citizens. Especially is this the case in New York, where this evil is aggravated by the conformation of the city. The island being long and narrow, men's business is thrown far from their residences, and they are compelled to resort to restaurants for their noon meal. And here they are brought under bewitching temptations to drink. I think the restaurant system may have laid to its credit more temptation to drink than any other circumstance. Men go into restaurants where liquor is kept for sale. One man opens a bottle of claret, and another man thinks he must. If one is invited by a friend to drink, he does not like to refuse, and he feels under obligation to return the compliment. And the scruple which he has against drinking gradually wears off. He does not know how, but little by little he slides into the habit of drinking. At length he loses the repulsion from it which he experienced at first. And, finally, he finds himself regularly indulging, from day to day, in drinking—not as medicine, but as a matter of luxury or enjoyment. And how many men, beginning so, find, after months or years, that the necessity of indulgence has grown on them, or that a latent tendency in that direction has been fired in them, so that they cannot get over it! How many are thus led to pursue the drinking customs of society through the influence of restaurants in New York! Myriads of young men who are full of blood, and full of fire, and full of imitation, are led into intemperance by the example which is set before them in these places by their elders.

I have been informed that there is an immense increase in the drinking habits of what are called respectable young men in these cities. I am told that, quite generally, when an enterprise is taken in hand, they step out to drink; that when they have a fortunate stroke of business, they step out to drink; that they drink when they are going over to business, and drink when they are coming back. There is undoubtedly a great deal more drinking than there used to be. And it means business. It is not altogether drinking from courtesy, or from compliance: it is drinking deep and drinking often for a purpose. And this excessive drinking is accompanied by manifest and growing effects upon these young men. And, from excitability, from compliance with social customs, from the example of the fashionable classes, from the facility with which men are enabled by this means to reach the feelings of their fellow-men, and from a hundred other considerations, the drinking tendencies of society are increasing. And there is no other thing that so takes down the health, and blunts the conscience, and deadens the sensibility, and prematurely prepares the young for disease and suffering and disgraceful death, carrying terrible blight to the household, and immeasurable woe to many souls, as this very practice of drinking for luxury and for diet.

Now, I appeal to Christian men, I appeal to moral, right-thinking citizens, is there any just end to be gained that should lead you to persist in drinking? Have I not said that, abstractly considered, you have a right to form your own judgment in this matter? And now, having guarded your liberty, I ask you, was there ever a case where a man might better bring his liberty to the altar of love and humanity? Was there ever a case which more strongly appealed to a man in this direction than this very one? Was there ever an instance in which a man might more appropriately say: *If meat and drink make my brother to offend, I will eat no flesh and drink no wine while the world standeth?*

Have you a right, for the sake of the indulgence of your own pleasure, which is momentary and transient, to set such an example, and to lend the whole force of your personal influence in such a way as will lead young men into a habit which will be to them damnation? Though you may be cold and conservative, and though you may be so far advanced in life that you can indulge moderately in the use of intoxicating drinks without being drawn into excessive indulgence, have you any right, either for pleasure or profit, to throw the pall of your example over young men, and solicit them, and ratify their erratic desires? I appeal to you because, though you have a right to your own opinions in this matter, and though I accord to you that right, I believe that you have at heart the welfare of the young, and that if it were made plain to you that a little sacrifice of personal indulgence on your part would be the salvation of scores and hundreds of men, you would make the sacrifice. And was there ever a case where a man might use his liberty for the welfare of others, if this be not one?

I appeal to all men to avoid setting an example of drinking at public dinners or in any public places. You may say: "If am going to drink at all, I will drink openly." No, no, no! That is not right. If your physician says you must drink, I say about drinking as the Apostle said about faith—"Have it to thyself." And when you attend a New England dinner, or a Historical Society dinner, or a Geographical Society dinner, or any great dinner, do not drink. There are very few men who could sit at the head of the table on such an occasion, as I saw one of the chief and most honored poets of America sit, and press away the glasses, and say to the servants as they came round: "*None, none.*" That venerable man, as he sat there, quiet and unostentatious, was reading a lesson which, I am afraid, but few understood. As I recollect it, it was a noble testimony and a noble example. And I would say to every man who will allow himself to be influenced by my persuasion: I beg of you, in hotels, in restaurants, at public dinners, in public places everywhere, even if you think you have impunity in the matter of drinking yourself, *forbear.* Do something for the good cause. Do something that will help men. We need an example; and you do not know how many eyes may be looking upon you. You do not know how many men, if you lift your hand with the cup, will lift theirs, and perish.

May I not urge parents to consider the effect upon their children of the use at home, as a luxury, of intoxicating drinks? I do not say that a parent shall never drink wine; but it does seem to me that it is wise to have an emphatic understanding in the household on this subject. It seems to me that parents, bringing up their children in the midst of the perils of this day and community, might emphasize their example on the subject of temperance at their tables. I have known good men to pour out wine and give it to their boys, because, as they said, they would not take anything that their boys might not take. That is a reason why you should not take wine yourself, but it is not a reason why you should give it to them. And for the sake of the sanctity of the household in this day and in this country, I beseech you to think well about this matter. And if with your conscience you have gone over the ground, may I not ask you to go over it again? May I not ask you, as in the presence of God and with the solemnities of the eternal sphere upon you, to carefully consider the subject once more, and ask yourself whether you ought not to exclude wine from your board? May I not say to every one who calls in his friends, and hospitably spreads his table, and opens his saloons: You may be able to stand; but is your conscience or your strength to neglect the weak, the tempted, and the temptable? Ought you not to have a consideration for those whose consciences come under your influence?

There is nothing more painful to me than to see how beauty, and politeness, and courtesy seduce. A young man comes to the city from the country. It is a great thing for a young man who has been brought up in a village to come to New York. He is occupying a humble position as clerk in a store. He is a young man of promise; and this fact does not escape his employer's attention. He has been there two years, and has improved in many respects. He is dressing better; he has dropped off his uncouth manners; he has many marks of courtesy about him; he has *savoir faire*, and many other virtues, and his employer is pleased with him; and on going home some night he says to his wife: "I think Thomas is very promising; he is turning out finely. And I do not know as it would do any hurt, now that we are going to have these little parties, and as our girls would like some beaux, to ask him over. I believe there is the making of a man in him, and nobody can tell what may happen."

He *is* asked over, and he feels that it is a great compliment. When he came to the city he did not know what was before him, but fortune seems to have smiled upon him. He has had pretty hard work, but he has browbeaten and overcome a great many difficulties, and things are now going more smoothly with him. And in his exultation he says: "I have got it in me, and I am going to succeed." And then comes this sweet invitation from his employer—one of the first men in the community—a man who stands among the very highest in business circles. And this young man who has been brought up with a religious horror of drinking, and who has been able to resist all the temptation which has been brought to bear upon him in restaurants, in drinking-saloons, and among his companions, goes to the hospitable mansion of his employer, and there in a side-room is a bowl of champagne punch (I believe that is what they call it), or something of the kind; and all the other young men go in there to brace themselves up and get ready to be brilliant. It is the custom of the house, and his companions say: "You are not going to take on airs in this way. Besides, you are not going to insult the man in his own house, and tell him that he had no business to put that bowl there." And in an ill-advised moment this heretofore religiously temperate young man yields, and drinks the first cup.

Now, I do not say that that first cup is going to destroy him; but I do say that he has been grievously wounded. That cup may be of little consequence; but if a young man consents to do what his conscience tells him he has no business to do, he has taken the first of a series of steps downward. When a man begins to act contrary to his moral convictions, his power to follow those convictions in the midst of temptation is materially weakened. And when you, by your example in the household or elsewhere, lead a man to do that which his conscience condemns, you have done him an injury from which he can never wholly recover. So take care that you do not destroy men by your example.

I beseech of you who are looking forward to the approaching festive season of the holidays—Christmas and New Year's Day—to take high ground on this subject of temperance. I make my annual solemn and affectionate appeal to every young man in this congregation, to maintain a conscience void of offence. If your conscience says that drinking is bad, and ought not to be allowed, stand by your principles, no matter if you be tempted by an angel of light, with a devil in him.

I make my appeal, also, to every young woman. Since drunkenness comes first and hardest upon woman, since it is to her what a swine is to a garden, rooting up every sweet blossom, and destroying every fruit, and making a wilderness of the garden of the Lord, I have a right to say to every young woman: By your look, by your word, and by your act, bear testimony and exert your influence against intemperance. Let not your fair hand, that yet one day shall go out in pledge, convey to another that cup which shall desolate and destroy the household. If there be one thing that woman should stand for, it is temperance.

I beseech of you who are hospitably disposed, whatever have been your old customs, your Old World customs, or your old country customs, think this matter over again. Men, brethren, fathers, you who have never thought of taking this ground, am I unreasonable? Have I not put your liberty on the right ground, and defended it? and am I wrong in begging you to use that liberty so as not to destroy men with it? May I not beg of you now, many of you, before you leave this house, to say: "By the help of God I will use my reason, I will use my conscience, I will use my money, I will use my house, I will use my table, so as to make sure that no man shall stumble upon my example and end in destruction"?

THE WINE OF THE WORD,

AND

THE WORD CONCERNING WINE.

"All things indeed are pure; but it is evil for that man who eateth with offence."—ROM. xiv. 20.

ONE of the questions of the hour is the wine question. On its settlement hangs the use or disuse of all light alcoholic stimulants; and whether these shall be banished from the side-board, the dining-table, and the circles of social and festive life, will go far to settle the *status* of the temperance cause, and its success in staying the monster evils that come from indulgence in the more fiery liquors. It will go far to settle the temporal and eternal welfare of tens of thousands, many of whom are growing up in Christian homes and in attendance upon the church of God. If the Christian conscience cannot be secured on the side of abstinence, we must despair of securing the worldly conscience. If over the wine-cup and other intoxicants men stumble to perdition, and the practice of God's people is nevertheless in favor of the wine-cup, then men will continue to stumble to the end of time. With a drinking church behind us, we can do little or nothing with a drinking world before us. The ruin from intemperate drinking can scarcely be overestimated. There is no such other one source of woe and crime in the world as the excessive indulgence in alcoholic drink. And this excess of indulgence comes in a vast majority of cases from indulgence in moderation. There is that in the very nature of alcohol which tends to excite thirst for deeper draughts of it. If we stop the moderation, therefore, we are sure of arresting a large amount of the excess. If we lend our influence and example to moderation, effort to prevent excess will be largely spent in vain. There are thousands upon thousands who are weak, of excitable temperament, easily tempted, strong passioned, and to whom moderation in the use of alcoholic stimulant as a beverage would almost inevitably lead to dissipation and ruin. These ought to abstain entirely, all will concede. But do not those who love Jesus Christ, and who profess to be actuated by the Gospel law of love, owe a duty to them that are weak? Are we not bound to help them to abstain both by our precept and by our example? Should example and, therefore, approval be given to a practice that, though possibly not sinful in itself, is known the world over to be a stumbling-block and an occasion to fall for multitudes? And if so given, will not the multitudes keep on perishing? Surely, therefore, this wine question is of incalculable consequence. And the right settlement of it must begin at the house of God. What is the great law by which God's people should be governed in this matter of wine-drinking?

Some assert their Christian liberty, and say, "There is no sin in drinking a glass of wine. It is of no personal harm. It is lawful, therefore I will drink it." Now, the apostle distinctly recognizes, in the fourteenth chapter of his Epistle to the Romans, this law of liberty. And in view of it he makes some frank and manly concessions. He says Christian liberty may be freely exercised with reference to all those things that, in themselves considered, have no permanent moral ground for their prohibition; in other words, things that are not in their essential character either right or wrong. Speaking of meats and drinks, and holydays and ceremonies, his noble avowal is, "I know and am persuaded of the Lord Jesus there is nothing unclean in itself," *i.e.*, there is no essential moral pollution in any of these things. Participation could be had in them without contamination. To touch them is not necessarily to besmear ourselves with the pitch of sin.

But, he adds, take heed how you use your liberty. There is a higher law of love which limits the law of liberty, and this law of love has a law's obligations just as binding as those of any law on God's statute-book. Under this law, a thing in itself lawful becomes not only not expedient, but it ceases to be lawful, and becomes a sin—a double sin—a sin against a brother, and a sin against Christ. The law of love as laid down by the apostle demands "that no man put a stumbling-block or an occasion to fall in his brother's way." It is not right, he says, to eat flesh or to drink wine, or to do anything whereby a brother stumbleth. All things indeed are pure, but it is evil (κακόν, not merely hurtful, but *wrong*, evil in a moral sense, sin) for that man who eateth with offence, *i.e.*, so as to be an occasion for a brother's fall. Liberty to do that God never gave any man. It is not, therefore, by the unauthorized dictum of a church court, or by the unreasoning zeal of an enthusiast in temperance reform, that the liberty of Christ's people is sought to be restrained. God himself, by his unmistakable Word, undertakes to restrain it. Hence, if there be any impeachment of the divine wisdom in this matter, as has been charged, it is by those who advocate a liberty which God has expressly denied.

Now, there are those who recognize and acknowledge the sinfulness of so using our liberty of action as to injure our fellow-men, yet whose reasoning on this wine question seems to be in favor of the largest liberty. They argue that the Scriptures authorize the use of wine and other fermented drinks, provided they be used within the limits of strict sobriety. And they say these are the limits allowed of God, and this is the liberty given to every man. It is asked, "If God permits a man to use alcoholic drinks temperately, who will dare take upon himself to say that he shall not do so?" And it is argued that to press the obligations of law here is to take away that liberty which God has given whereby every man to his own master standeth or falleth.

This seems like putting the whole grand doctrine of Christian expediency within the domain of a divinely allowed liberty, which is simply to take wholly away from the law of love its grip of oughtness, and to sink it to the level of a thing indifferent—"of his duty in respect to which every one must judge for himself." But in this matter God has taken judgment out of our hands. He says the violation of this law, or the imperilling a weak brother in the exercise of our liberty, is a *sin*. When it comes to that, no man has a right to judge for himself. His drinking wine, then, is *not* "a simple question of expediency." He is brought face to face with "an offence against Christ," and what liberty has he for that? Not any, it certainly would be fair to conclude, that any Christian man would care to maintain.

This, then, is the great law. A thing pure is evil for that man whose indulgence is an injury to others. It is morally wrong to put an occasion to fall in a brother's way—a Christian sins against his Lord when he so uses his liberty that it becomes a stumbling-block to them that are weak. Thus every man is clinched with a moral obligation—bound by an imperative "ought." It is not a matter of liberty at all. It is a matter of law and a law's obligations. Because the law pertains to a thing indifferent—*i.e.*, neither right nor wrong *per se*—*obedience to the law* is not a thing indifferent, but a clear and demanded duty.

Now, on the supposition that wine-drinking is not wrong in itself, does this law of love bind us to let the wine-glass alone? Is abstinence from all alcoholic beverage a Christian duty? By some it is emphatically answered, "No! God has clearly and repeatedly, from end to end of his Holy Word, by precept and example, authorized, approved, and sometimes even enjoined, the use of intoxicating wine and strong drink as a beverage." Through column after column of our public prints, men have recently labored to prove this—to prove that such wine is the only wine of Scripture; that God directed the Jews to indulge in its use at their religious festivals; that Christ made this intoxicant in large quantity at a marriage feast; that he freely drank it on various occasions. And all this tremendous sweep of argument and wholesale Scriptural endorsement of wine-drinking has been accompanied and modified by only this mild disclaimer: "It *may* be one's duty, notwithstanding the truths here set forth, to abstain in given circumstances from all use of wine and strong drinks." This is certainly very softly put, as if even this were a doubtful matter. And doubtful it is if the above Scriptural argument be true.

Doubtful it is if God has so often, and so publicly, and in such variety of circumstances, sanctioned the use of the intoxicating cup. Once admit the argument, and the mild disclaimer is swept to the winds.

"It may be one's duty in certain circumstances to abstain!" In what circumstances? Try to conceive of any that could call for abstinence more imperatively and bindingly than those in which the fearful woe was pronounced upon Ephraim for drunkenness, and when all Judah "erred through strong drink," and priests and prophets "were swallowed up of wine." Such a state of things has no parallel even in this day of dissipation and excess. But it was not only then that men stumbled so fearfully by wine. From the time that Noah drank of the wine and was drunken, the brink of the wine-cup has been the brink of ruin. Hundreds of thousands have been swept to perdition by the alcohol of the cup. It is not by any means a desolating and dreadful ruin peculiar to our own day and land. The woe and the curse of this thing scarred Israel all along her history, and the record of Israel's folly is heavy with the sounding retributions of God for it. Drunkenness was a common sin in the time of Christ. So he warned his disciples, saying: "Take heed lest at any time your hearts be overcharged with drunkenness." And at the wedding in Cana, the governor of the feast, speaking of the general custom of such feasts, said: "Every man at the beginning doth set forth good wine, and when men have *well drunk*"—drunk freely, to inebriation—"then that which is worse." Here is proof of the *habit of excess* at feasts, whether true at Cana or not. So "drunkenness and revellings" are among the works of the flesh named by Paul, and he enjoins the saints at Rome not to walk "in rioting and drunkenness." He counsels the Corinthians to avoid the company of the drunkard, *though he be called a brother.* Among gross offenders he names drunkards, adding, "Such were some of you." In almost every letter he wrote, he sounded out some warning against the sin of drunkenness. And Peter, too, recognizes the prevalence of the evil, and speaks of the saints to whom he wrote as having in the time past of their life "walked in excess of wine, revellings, and banquetings." These passages certainly prove the commonness of intoxication in the East in the time of Christ. And as distilled liquors were unknown, the intoxication must have been largely from wine.

Now, we are asked to believe that God gave his sanction to the use of alcoholic wine and strong drink *in all these circumstances*—that his personal divine warrant for drinking intoxicating liquors was given publicly, repeatedly, at various times and in various conditions—given to a people who were swept to the fearfullest excesses of intoxication, so that the Word of God says even their priests and prophets reeled and staggered through strong drink, erring in vision and stumbling in judgment. And it was not a divine permission simply because of the hardness of their hearts; but it was a clear and repeated divine sanction, God approving the use of alcoholic wine and directly enjoining it, and this, too, when *the same terrible excesses accompanied its use as now!* We are asked to believe, also, that the Saviour made the intoxicating beverage on a public festive occasion, and drank it and sanctioned its use, when it would be known all over Judea and all over the world that he did it—made it for guests who had already indulged freely, and who were "well drunk" (whether to satiety or to inebriation, it matters not)—made a deceiver, and placed it before men for their free use, knowing it to be a constant and fatal lurer to ruin, having in its very nature as an intoxicant the element that gives it its deceitful power, and which God had therefore solemnly called "a mocker."

If this be all true, where, then, are the circumstances in which abstinence for the sake of others may be one's duty? I say it, fearless of sustainable contradiction, they are not conceivable. Here is a liberty given again and again of God, *in the very circumstances in which it is said we ought not to exercise it!* But surely, if God approved and enjoined the use of the fermented juice of the grape, and told his people to drink it openly and publicly within the limits of sobriety, notwithstanding the frequent and sometimes awful prevalence of intemperance among them, and even though the consecrated stewards of religion tripped and stumbled and were swallowed up of wine, we need not be afraid to go and do likewise. If Christ used alcoholic wine and gave it to others to drink, we need not be afraid to follow his example. So will reason every wine-drinker in the land. So, I grieve to say it, they *do* reason. They welcome and applaud the efforts made to prove that the Bible sanctions the use of alcoholic wine and strong drink, and that there is no ground for the division of the wines of Scripture into intoxicating and non-intoxicating. They placard their saloons with "the wine of expediency," and they quote the Biblical endorsements with an ill-concealed gratification. They say, and they have a right to say, "If this be true, the divine warrant and the divine example in the recorded Scriptural instances leave us at full liberty to use wine in any circumstances, little or much, habitually or occasionally, provided we use it within temperate limits." They laugh at the talk of possible circumstances calling for abstinence. Panoplied about with the Scriptural argument, they are bomb-proof. They are fortified and upheld in their moderate drinking by all such logic, and all the "grip" of obligation is utterly gone from the Christian doctrine of expediency in its application to the wine question.

But rather than lose the clinch of this great law of love, where, certainly, if anywhere in the wide world, and concerning any one thing, application should be made of it and men's consciences should be bound by it, let us see if something cannot be said in favor of the division of the wines of Scripture into intoxicating and unintoxicating. We are told that "the reasoning by which such a division is sought to be established is *perfectly absurd.*" Let us hazard the absurdity. The point is worth the risk.

"Wine is a mocker." This is God's word. No one doubts that the reference here is to intoxicating wine. Why is it called of God a mocker? Surely not because when used to excess it is hurtful. Beef is hurtful when used to excess. Is beef a mocker? We must all be agreed, I think, that wine is a mocker *because of its inherent quality—a something in the wine itself*, by which its users are lured into excess. A thousand other things are occasionally used to excess, but the use of intoxicating wine, frequently, naturally, and, alas! often fatally, *leads* to excess: the *tendency is that way.* Somehow the *current sets* in the direction of over-indulgence, and so seductive and subtle is this tendency that some of the noblest and the best of men trip and stumble before they are aware. This is the mocker power of wine—this power of deceit—which is in the very nature of alcoholic wine as an essential element. It gradually wakens desire in a man as indulgence goes on, until he and the desire change places, and he is no longer the master of the desire, but the desire is master of him.

Therefore, of this mocker it is said, "Whosoever is deceived thereby is not wise." So it deceived Noah when he drank of the wine and was drunken. So it deceived Ephraim and Judah, priest and prophet, when they were swallowed up of wine. Hence the Scriptural injunction, "It is not for kings to drink wine, nor for princes strong drink, *lest* they drink, and forget the law, and pervert judgment"—words that mark and prove a liability, a proneness, a natural tendency. Hence, also, the command, "Look not upon the wine"—when? "When it is red, when it giveth its eye and goeth down smoothly." The very quality is here described that gives to wine its deceitful power. These are signs of the presence of alcohol. No one doubts that alcoholic wine is here referred to; and it is *this kind of wine* that we are solemnly commanded not to look upon, for this kind is a mocker. The insidious subtlety and venomous guile of the "serpent" are in the mixture, and at the last it giveth the serpent's "bite."

Now, is this the wine used to symbolize the feast prepared by divine wisdom, and to which the Son of God invites the church, saying, "Eat, O friends, drink, yea, drink abundantly, O beloved"? A wine that deceived and disgraced Noah, that swept a whole nation, including its holy men of God, into the sin of intemperance, that kings and princes are forbidden to drink lest they pervert judgment—is this what Christ summons us in figure to drink "abundantly"—a mocker, a deceiver in its essential nature, and because of the intoxicating element in it? Is this the kind of wine that the Jews were enjoined to drink freely as an act of worship before the Lord in the temple? Is this what Jesus made and gave freely to others—the very same wine so minutely described by the Word of God as giving its eye and moving itself aright, a mocker, with the bite of a serpent and the sting of an adder? Surely the proof must be overwhelming, and there must be no alternative consistent with the Word of God, before we can believe that. It is not a question, you see, as to the use of wine *as an emblem*, whether of mercy or of wrath. The gravelling difficulty is, Would God call a thing a mocker, and then press the mocker to men's lips? Would he tell men not to look upon it, and then give it to them to drink? I grant this is yet only presumptive and inferential as to two kinds of wine. But what might there is in it! How naturally and inevitably, in the absence of proof either way, the presumption and the inference carry both our judgments and our hearts. Who that loves Christ does not desire that this may be true?

Now, what if there is another kind of wine spoken of in the Word of God *that cannot possibly be intoxicating*—where fermentation and the consequent presence of alcohol are out of the question—what then? Why, is it not reasonable and consistent, the demand alike of common sense and common conscience, to regard *this* as the wine commended in Scripture as a blessing, making glad the heart of man? To the law and the testimony.

God, threatening Moab with desolation, said (Isaiah xvi. 10): "In the vineyards there shall be no singing and shouting: the treaders shall tread out no *wine* in their presses. I have made their vintage shouting to cease." And again (Jeremiah xlviii. 33): "I have caused *wine* to fail from the wine-presses; none shall tread with shouting." Again: Gedaliah, made governor by the King of Babylon over the cities of Judah, thus commanded the Jews (Jeremiah xl. 10): "Gather ye *wine* and summer fruits and oil, and put them in your vessels." And the record is, "They gathered wine and summer fruits very much." The Bible also speaks of "presses bursting with new *wine*;" of *wine* found in the cluster;" and it says of this wine, and of this only, and in this very connection, "A blessing is in it." Here, then, is frequent reference to the pure, unfermented juice of the grape, just trodden out of the presses, just gathered for the vintage, even found in the cluster. And here *this grape-juice is repeatedly, and by the Jews themselves in their own Scriptures, called* WINE, *both yayin and tirosh.*

Now, by no possible device of reason or fetch of logic can this be made the wine that is "a mocker." Wine fresh from the cluster or the press mocks or deceives no man. The guile of the serpent has not yet entered it, for alcohol requires time and a process for its formation. It is the simple, unfermented juice of the grape, just as cider, right out of the press, is the simple, unfermented juice of the apple; and as such, God says a blessing is in it. Here, then, is the Scriptural distinction between wine and wine. It is not made to suit a modern exigency. God's Word makes it. Is it only "a hair-breadth" distinction? Is there nothing more than that between "a blessing" and "a mocker"? Each was called wine by the Jews, because wine (*yayin*) is a generic word applied to the juice of the grape in all conditions, whether sour or sweet, old or new, fermented or unfermented. But it is still held that "the *word* wine, unless used figuratively or qualified by some other word or phrase, always means the *fermented* juice of the grape." How do we know that? There are, indeed, passages where the case is clear, the context plainly showing that the wine spoken of is intoxicating. There are other passages, such as those quoted above, where the case is equally clear, the context plainly showing that the wine spoken of is unintoxicating. There are still other passages where God approves of wine and sanctions its use, with no proof whatever that the wine is intoxicating *but the bare word.* What else than "perfectly absurd" reasoning is it that would carry all these passages bodily over to the side of fermented wine? Why must we hold that intoxicating wine is necessarily meant in all such cases? Without the shadow of a shade of proof, must God's approval be tied, *nolens volens*, to the *intoxicating meaning of a doubtful word?* Common sense is affronted at the suggestion of any such reasonless necessity. The origin and, therefore, the original meaning of *yayin* is in dispute. Philologists are not agreed as to its derivation. Some half-dozen possible roots are assigned it. Parkhurst, in his old Lexicon, says it is from a Hebrew word signifying "to press, squeeze; as being *the expressed juice of grapes*." Dr. Ralph Wardlaw says the word is from a verb signifying to *press* or *squeeze*. Webster gives a similar derivation. There is not one philological reason, therefore, why we should hold that the word *yayin* means an *intoxicating* wine unless it is otherwise stated. There are abundant moral reasons why we should not so hold. The word is certainly applied to unintoxicating wine, was so applied by the Jews, and the proof of it is the Word of God. To such wine, unmistakably such as shown by the context, divine commendation is expressly given. When the same word is used elsewhere, coupled with the same divine sanction, *we are bound to believe the same wine is meant* unless it is otherwise stated.

Let one thing more be now proved, and the whole case is too clear for question. Were the ancients in the habit of using the unfermented juice of the grape, which they called wine, and did they understand the art of preserving it free from fermentation? The admissions of those who, nevertheless, claim a Scriptural endorsement for the use of intoxicating wine, are sufficient and conclusive answer. The article in Smith's "Bible Dictionary" on wine says: "Sometimes it" (*wine*) "was preserved in its unfermented state, and drank as must." . . . "It may be at once conceded that the Hebrew terms translated 'wine' refer occasionally to an unfermented liquor; but, inasmuch as there are frequent allusions to intoxication in the Bible, it is clear that fermented liquors were *also* in common use." Dr. Maclean, in the *Repertory* for 1841, says: "That, in treating of wines, these" (classical) "writers have mentioned modes of preserving the juice of the grape other than by fermenting it, we without the least hesitation admit; and that this unfermented juice, whether inspissated or not, *was sometimes used as a drink*, we do not question." Rev. Henry Holmes, missionary at Constantinople, says ("Bibliotheca Sacra," May, 1848) of the boiled juice of the grape, which he kept for two years without its undergoing any change: "Here is a cooling grape liquor which is not intoxicating, and which, in the manner of making and preserving it, seems to correspond with the recipes and descriptions of certain drinks *included by some of the ancients under the appellation of wine.*" Dr. Laurie, in the "Bibliotheca Sacra," while contending that all the wines mentioned in Scripture were fermented, nevertheless admits we *can* "find traces of an *unfermented wine* in a few classical writers."

Now, some of these concessions are perfectly clear with reference to the preservation and use of the unfermented juice of the grape among the ancients, and others are just as clear with reference to the application of the word *wine* to this unfermented liquor. Taken together, therefore, they constitute the very best evidence of the only point that remained to be established, viz.: Did the ancients preserve and use unfermented grape-juice, and call it wine? For they are admissions forced by classical and historic record for those who stoutly controvert the position that there are two kinds of wine, intoxicating and non-intoxicating, mentioned in the Word of God. And how could these concessions be honestly avoided in the face of the following, among other, evidences of ancient usage?

Aristotle says of sweet wine that "it is a wine *in name*, but not in fact—*it does not intoxicate.*" It had the *name*, therefore, even in his day. Josephus, the Jewish historian, paraphrasing the dream of Pharaoh's butler, who dreamed that he took clusters of grapes, and pressed them into Pharaoh's cup, and gave the cup to Pharaoh, repeatedly calls this grape-juice *wine.* Bishop Lowth, 1778, in his "Commentary" (Isaiah v. 2), says, "The fresh juice pressed from the grape" was by Herodotus styled *oinos ampelinos*, *i.e.*, wine of the vine.

The ancient custom of squeezing the juice of grapes into a cup has had corrobation in a figure of Bacchus exhumed at Pompeii, represented as thus engaged.

Pliny, book xiv., speaking of a wine called Aigleuces, always sweet, gives this method of producing it: "They plunge the casks immediately after they are filled for the vat into water until winter has passed away, and the wine has acquired the habit of being cold." Columella says, book xii., "That your must may always be sweet, thus proceed," and he then gives the process of putting it into a new amphora, carefully excluding the air, and placing it in cold water for a month or six weeks, when it will remain sweet for a year. Athenæus says, vol. i., book i.: "They often used boiled wines." Virgil, in his Georgic, book i., refers to this boiling process, the object of which was to concentrate the wine by evaporation, and so prevent fermentation. Alexander translates this line in Virgil: "Or with the fire boils away the moisture of the sweet wine." But why multiply proof of a position which Anthon, in his "Dictionary of Greek and Roman Antiquities," Archbishop Potter, in his "Grecian Antiquities," Smith, in his "Dictionary of the Bible," and many other scholars of acknowledged competency, confirm and support? Moses Stuart, that prince of philologists, says: "Facts show that the ancients not only preserved their wine unfermented, but regarded it as of a higher flavor and finer quality than fermented wine."

There were, therefore, two kinds of wine in

ancient use. The one was sweet, pleasant, refreshing, unfermented. The other was exciting, inflaming, intoxicating. Each was called *wine.* How natural, now, to say of the one, A blessing is in it, and it maketh glad the heart! How natural to say of the other, Woe and sorrow are the fruit of it—it is a mocker! There is no difficulty now in the reconciliation of Scripture with Scripture. The Bible is *not* a wholesale endorsement of the use of the intoxicating cup. It puts no weapon into the hands of the wine-drinkers. And the binding obligations of the law of love in its application to the wine question may be pressed home upon the conscience and the heart, unweakened by any opposing plea of divine precept or example.

I do not believe that the drinking of wine is a sin *per se.* I do not believe that a church court should make it a matter of discipline. But I do believe that the Christian who is known by precept or practice to be an advocate of the use of the cup takes upon himself a fearful responsibility. The effect of such precept or example is felt far beyond the circle of those with whom such Christian comes in contact. The higher the position of the man, the wider will be the influence of his word or deed. *And influence and responsibility go together.* Wherever he is known as an advocate of the use of wine and strong drink, his influence is felt as such. And who is gifted with the power to see and say whether, among the thousands yearly swept to ruin by alcohol, there may not be those to whom his example has been a stumbling-block, on account of which and over which they have gone to perdition? It is not needful that we proffer the wine-glass, directly or personally, with our own right hand, to some one that is weak in order to be the occasion of that brother's fall. Before God we are responsible for our *influence*, whether it extend to those whose palms we touch in the grasp of friendship, or to those into whose eyes we have never looked. Destroy not him with thy wine for whom Christ died. It is not right—it is *wrong*—it is *sin—sin against a brother*, and *sin against Christ*—to put a stumbling-block or an occasion to fall in another's way. Does it not become every Christian, therefore, in view of the conceded perils of wine-drinking—in view of the awful record of lost souls connected with the use of the cup, and in view of the obligations of God's Gospel law of love, to let the wine-glass alone? Why this stout assertion of *lawfulness*—this vigorous and vehement defence of liberty? As if liberty were endangered! As if any possible evil could by any possibility result from the self-imposed restraint of total abstinence, that could for one moment be compared with the sad and woeful evil of being the occasion by indulgence of a brother's fall! Oh! let us have a care that our good be not evil spoken of—that our liberty be not vindicated at the expense of charity. Certainly love is a diviner, more Christ-like thing than lawfulness. Self-sacrifice for the sake of others is a far higher level of spiritual life than the mere doing right. And to fortify a custom so indissolubly connected with evil consequence as wine-drinking, by building Scriptural bulwarks about it, is certainly to impair and fatally weaken any pressure of the claims of Christian benevolence alone. We may win from the chief patrons of the intoxicating cup hearty applause for such building work, but we shall not be making straight paths for the stumblers.

God speed the time when Scriptural arguments in behalf of wine drinking shall be buried in a grave as deep as that where now lie the arguments by which the Word of God was once marshalled to the support of slavery! God speed the time when alcoholic wines and strong drinks shall be swept from every Christian sideboard, and table, and social feast; every member of every Christian church in all our land, in the spirit of a pervasive, abounding, all-embracing charity, saying, "*Wine maketh my brother to offend; stumblers by the alcoholic cup are on every side of me: therefore I will drink no wine while the world standeth.*"

STRANGE CHILDREN.

"Rid me, and deliver me from the hand of strange children, whose mouth speaketh vanity, and their right hand *is* a right hand of falsehood: that our sons *may be* as plants grown up in their youth; *that* our daughters *may be* as corner-stones, polished *after* the similitude of a palace."—PSALM cxliv. 11, 12.

THE strange children in David's time were the idolatrous heathen. Their influence upon the chosen people was most pernicious. Not only was their conversation vapid, but their actions were deceitful. In token of friendship they stretched forth the right hand, but the salutation was insincere and the heart treacherous.

To turn from such a deceptive race was a duty solemnly enjoined upon those in covenant with Jehovah. To avoid them would be the first impulse of wisdom, for their influence could not but prove baneful, especially on the susceptible minds of the young and unwary. And while, in accordance with divine command and human reason, the king was endeavoring to exterminate these strange and wicked heathen, it was highly proper for him to direct his prayer to the Almighty, and entreat him to afford the much-desired deliverance.

Could this result be accomplished—could these unhallowed children of Satan be removed, and their corrupt influences stayed, what a happy people would Israel be with Jehovah for their God! Not only would they be blest with full and plenty, but their sons would be "as plants grown up in their youth"—springing up numerously and coming to early and beautiful maturity—the support of the land; and their daughters would be "as corner-stones polished after the similitude of a palace"—like the caryatides, or columns representing female figures, elegantly sculptured, and placed on the corners of noble edifices by Egyptian architects, the pride and glory as well as the support of the temple of state.

Time has wrought great changes since David sat on the throne of Israel. The Holy Land has long been desecrated by the tread and rule of infidelity and heathenism; and the once holy people, having rejected Messiah, have lost the divine favor, and, scattered over the wide world, have become a hissing and a by-word to their fellow-men. They in turn are now the strange children—strange in their stubborn rejection of holy truth and in their alienation from the God of their fathers.

The partition wall once excluding the Gentiles is now demolished, and "the chosen of the Lord" may be found in every land and among every people. And where are they congregated in greater number and influence than here? Rescued from foreign oppression and domestic treason; a free and independent people, with wise rulers and an equitable government; better than all beside, having in our custody the oracles of God, the institutions of the church, and enjoying the influences of the Spirit and all the means of grace in great profusion—certainly we people of these United States, while we do not claim the exclusive blessing, may regard ourselves as among the most favored, and believe that God speaks to us from his high abode, saying, "This people have I formed for myself; they shall show forth my praise."

I need not tell you there are among us also "*strange children*"—"*men of Belial*;" "*whose mouth speaketh vanity, and whose right hand is a right hand of falsehood*"; who are corrupt themselves, and secretly conveying their vile influence into the minds of our youth, thereby undermining the foundations of holy truth, and threatening us with general demoralization and material ruin. Against every such endeavor we should contend with all our might; and, while we labor, we should appeal to our God, and cry out earnestly, "*Rid and deliver us.*" This is the duty of patriotism, philanthropy, and religion. It is more: it is the dictate of self-interest, if not self-preservation. Upon this watchfulness, effort, and prayer depends not only the welfare of the community and republic, but also the character, condition, and future prospects of our children, and, as a consequence, our own comfort, the glory of God, and the good of countless souls.

Concerning the corrupt politicians of both parties, the gamblers, the profane swearers, the swindlers, and many other strange children who infest our land, we may not now particularly speak. But there is one monster sin, alarmingly prevalent, to which we wish to call your attention. *Intemperance* is spreading desolation everywhere. There is hardly a community or a family free from its terrible ravages. Like the horse-leech, it drives its fangs into the flesh of every victim it can reach, and with insatiate thirst cries out more greedily than ever, "Give! give!" More than any other vice it impedes the progress of piety. It opens the way to every species of crime, and leads down to infamy and death.

This is an old and threadbare subject, yet it constantly presents new phases and illustrations, and is, therefore, fearfully interesting as well as vitally important. There is just one thing for us to do with this evil. We must fight it, as we do that old deceiver, Satan, to the bitter end. We must contend with the demon of the bottle in every form, giving him no quarter, and driving him absolutely from our coasts. Nor can we admit this is only a social or a political evil, and, therefore, should be corrected only by the press or the platform or the ballot. It is a sin. Drunkenness, and whatever leads to it, is a sin. They who become intoxicated commit a crime against God and the state, and it requires no profound argument to prove to any reasonable person that they who, in any way, by example, or persuasion, or traffic, induce others to indulge their wicked appetites, are also guilty.

Just look at the folly and criminality of some people who claim to be models of morality and piety. They know the tendency of appetite. They behold how the love for strong drink usually increases until the occasional sip becomes a regular beverage, and the small glass is exchanged for the large goblet; until the taste becomes a draught, and the draught a flood; until the tippler is transformed into a toper, and the toper into a sot. They see the poor victim little by little drawn into the net of the destroyer. They stand upon the shore of this Niagara with folded arms, watching the boatman gliding down the current, pulling away lustily at the oars. And thus they gaze until at length, with demon yells, he cries out, "Too late! too late! my soul is lost," and then leaps over the cataract into the yawning abyss. And yet, strange to say, while this fearful tragedy is repeated in this country two hundred times every day and oftentimes happens before their eyes, there are peole who apologize for the custom of drinking; who claim it is a good thing, and should be perpetuated; who battle the advocates of total abstinence as if they were either knaves or fools; who go on drinking and selling, risking their own souls and the souls of their children and friends, and helping by their influence, directly or indirectly, to fill earth with drunkenness and hell with victims.

Ancestral education may influence these "strange children"; but appetite and covetousness have more weight with them. The love of spirituous liquor and the craving for money, these are the potent causes of intemperance, and never did the devil discover better agencies than these for the accomplishment of his diabolical purposes.

What can be done to arrest this evil and prevent its future ravages? This is a great question, which we propose to consider and, if possible, answer. He is a skilful practitioner who can make a good diagnosis; but he does better who prescribes a successful remedy.

Much has been said and much been done in regard to this matter in the ages past, and especially within the last thirty or forty years. The friends of temperance should not be discouraged, or for a moment slacken their efforts. Their labors have not been in vain.

Yet it is evident we have made but little headway. With all our preaching and lecturing; in connection with all our organizations, local and national; by our moral suasion and our legislation, what have we accomplished? The most we can say is, we have stayed the flood, and prevented it from overwhelming us. We have not as yet been able to turn the tide up-stream, and force the flood backward. While we have been working, the enemy has not been idle. Satan has been more cunning and ardent than ever. He has stirred up opposition where it should never have been manifested. He has arrayed against this movement to save men from drunkenness a part of the church, and put his false arguments in the mouths of those who love Jesus. He has produced controversies and divisions and diversions in the temperance ranks. He has inflamed the lovers of strong drink with an increased appetite, and he has stimulated the guilty vendors to a greater thirst for gain. He has taught his willing and skilful agents how to drug their liquors, so as to cheat their silly customers out of their money and sobriety in the quickest manner possible, and send them most directly and rapidly down to infamy and ruin. And when sober, thoughtful people have ventured to dispute his influence, he has met them with intrigue and ridicule and falsehood and threats. Temperance reformers and advocates have been obliged to contend against prejudice, appetite, moneyed interest, and all this backed up by diabolical machination. What wonder they have succeeded no better!

It is a matter of surprise and congratulation that they have stood their ground so well, and accomplished so much. Had it not been for their zealous efforts, instead of an army of 600,000 drunkards which now reel around our streets, no doubt the victims of intemperance might be counted in this country by millions. The cause has had some degree of success.

But we believe a brighter day is dawning upon us. The legions of the enemy have been kept in abeyance; but now comes the cry of victory. Already we hail the final triumph of truth and righteousness, although it may be afar off. God's people are coming to the rescue, and like Cromwell's troops they go into the battle with the Word of God in their hands and the voice of prayer upon their lips. We shall prevail, for God is our Leader, and the success of our cause is promotive of his glory.

But, fellow-workmen, we must toil on, and from our past defeats learn useful lessons. One grand mistake which has been made by temperance reformers is, they have attempted to breast the river at its mouth, rather than at its source. In preaching and lecturing, they have addressed themselves almost exclusively to inebriates and moderate drinkers of mature minds and fixed habits. Would it not be better to begin with the children, who are easily influenced, and educate them to total abstinence principles? A speaker once asked a company of boys whether they had ever thought, if they never tasted intoxicating liquors, they could never become drunkards. One little fellow, in the simplicity of his heart, replied, "*No.*" And it really seems as if the mass of well-meaning, Christian people are like that child—they do not recognize the plain truth, that if their children never taste the poison, they can never be ruined by it.

Temperance friends, we need not retrace our footsteps. Our path is in the right direction. It is not required that we change our tactics. They are reasonable and effective. It is only requisite that we add to our plans and efforts. The vilest sot is still a man, our fellow-man; and while there is breath in his foul body, we should labor and pray to reclaim him to sobriety and holiness. The man or woman who indulges only moderately in the dangerous drink, we should warn, persuade, and by every proper influence try to save from destruction. Let inebriate asylums be multiplied. God be praised for what has been accomplished by medical treatment and careful nursing! Let philanthropy do her best to ameliorate the sin and suffering which exist on account of indulgence in strong drink. Let us enforce the laws now on the statute-book with reference to this unhallowed traffic, and increase their stringency. Let us steadily, judiciously work for a prohibitory law. The poor drunkard himself clamors for it when he is in his sober senses. It is puerile to say it is unconstitutional and unreasonable. As well say a law against arson or burglary, or the free sale of strychnine or laudanum, is unconstitutional. With equal reason it might be argued that a law prohibiting the location of a powder-mill in the very heart of this city is unconstitutional. One thing is certain, it is unconstitutional for the inebriate to drink, *very unconstitutional*, and it ought to be unconstitutional for any one to put the bottle to his mouth, or even permit him in his weakness to take what he knows to be for his injury. I believe in prohibition, that it is both feasible and equitable; and have no doubt that the lawlessness and political corruption which grow out of the free use of intoxicants, and which are fearfully on the increase in our large cities, will drive the mass of law-abiding and law-loving citizens to the same conclusion ere long. We cannot afford the free sale of impure and drugged liquors, and this is about the result of a license law which provides a community of 10,000 inhabitants with fifty drinking places—one for every 200 people.

But there is another method of reaching the source and cutting off the supply of drunkenness. If we would, like the prophet of old, put salt in the spring, and thus heal the impure waters of Jericho, we must operate on the minds of the children. Let there be a general and efficient movement in this direction, and it will tell upon the coming generation. Our eyes will not behold so many filthy spectacles as now appear on every hand; and our feet will not be compelled to follow to the grave so many persons who, on account of wicked indulgence, have not lived out half of their days.

Do we wish our sons to escape the influence of

the strange children, who would entice them to ruin, and become as plants grown up in their youth? Look at the gardener. He watches the sprig as it emerges from the ground. He keeps the weeds from choking it and stealing its nourishment from the soil. He sees it is not so surrounded with trees and foliage that it is deprived of the warm sunbeams. He waters it, and manures it, and prunes it, and drives the bugs from it, and thus he brings it to a quick and healthy maturity. We must do this with our children. Can we expect, when so many adverse influences are at work, that our sons will grow up to be strong, virtuous, holy men, if we neglect them in their infancy and childhood? Do you imagine, intelligent parents, if you permit your boys to form their own habits, or permit Satan to fill their minds with evil thoughts and lead them in sinful paths, you can, after they attain manhood, and perhaps have gone astray, influence them to become sober and godly men? Surely you could not reasonably expect such a result from such a course of treatment. If, after your neglect and indifference, they should do well, it would be almost a miracle, for which you might well praise God.

Do we wish our daughters to be as corner-stones, polished after the similitude of a palace? We should remember the stone-cutter does not produce his beautiful columns by one stroke of his chisel or hammer. He applies water to soften the hard material. He nicks and nicks, and rubs and rubs, early and late, to present the smooth surface and the graceful carving to the eye. He is active and earnest, prompt and persevering, and this makes him successful. We must be like him. We must be diligent. We must cut off all the rough edges of nature. We must carefully and constantly rub down the coarse surface of sin. And we have this advantage over the stone-cutter. We can begin our work before the stones are hard. When these precious blocks of marble come to our hand, they are quite soft and pliable, and we are very foolish workmen if we wait to operate upon them until they become repulsive to impression.

The command of God and the dictate of reason is, "Train up a *child* in the way he should go," and the promise given us for our encouragement is, "When he is old, he will not depart from it." Why not consider that these words apply as well to the subject of temperance as to any other? If we could raise some heart-broken parents from their graves, and by a magic touch put them, and others who still live to mourn over their children destroyed and hopes wrecked, back a generation; if, retaining their bitter experience, they could retrace their steps, and have their innocent offspring again to train—how early would they listen to the voice of wisdom, and not put off until to-morrow the work which should be done to-day!

Do you see that drunkard reeling through the street or rolling in the gutter? He is in tatters. His eyes are bloodshot. His features are distorted. His breath is hot and pestilential. His touch is pollution. From him the brutes turn in loathing and disgust. Parents, that forlorn remnant of mortality was once a sweet and pretty child. He was as fair and lovely as the infant you left to-night sleeping in his cradle. His mother washed, and dressed, and nursed, and kissed him, and played with him, and hung over him with maternal affection when he lay in placid sleep, just as mothers do now. His father took him in his arms, and with pride and hope folded him to his bosom. Friends came to that pleasant home and petted the child, and congratulated the happy parents on their promising boy. Who then thought he would come to this? Who for a moment fancied he could ever be in such a plight as that in which we now see him? And yet this is the history of hundreds of thousands now cursing our land, filling our asylums and prisons, mortifying and impoverishing their friends, and ruining themselves for both worlds.

Can you not learn the lesson? If you would not witness your children transformed into such loathsome objects; if you would have them grow up like thrifty plants, and stand as symmetrical, polished, substantial columns in the temple of state and the sanctuary of God, you cannot begin too early to instruct and influence them.

You must educate them to be sober men and women.

Do you ask how this work, the education of the dear children to habits of temperance, is to be performed?

We reply, first of all, parents, teachers, and friends should give to the young the benefit of their *example.* We will suppose that a man in mature life can withstand temptation, and cannot by any intrigue be drawn into the devouring whirlpool (which is, as you well know, an hypothesis not always realized). Do you think, with the cup to his lips frequently or even occasionally, he can deter his children from a like indulgence? Exceptions there are to the rule; but the swearing father may expect to have swearing boys; the lazy mother will usually have lazy girls; the careless instructor will be surrounded as a general thing with careless pupils. And so, if you will drink intoxicating liquors, my friends, you may reasonably expect to be imitated in this as in other habits. You perpetuate if you do not create the fashion. The sparkling young eyes are upon you when, it may be with a gusto, you imbibe your glass of wine at dinner, or smack your lips over your beer with a friend who happens to come in to spend the evening. Very naturally, the young people conclude what is good for the parent is good for the child, and that such a grand old custom, so promotive of sociability and good cheer, should be kept in the family and handed down from generation to generation.

If, then, you sincerely wish the rising race, and especially those dear youth under your care and influence, to be sober and thrifty men and women, you should give them the benefit of your example. Is this a hard thing? Not half so hard as many things you willingly and cheerfully do, kind parents, for the benefit of your offspring. No harder than to spend sleepless nights and painful days with your sick ones. No harder than to tug and toil in order to obtain a competency for the support and education and outfit of your children. Not so hard by a hundredfold as it may be in after years to watch your sons and daughters drinking to excess; to witness them the slaves of appetite; to hear their reproaches heaped on your heads, and to follow them to the drunkard's grave. You may be paying very dearly for your occasional glass, my friend. Pause and consider!

Next to a good example is *the positive influence* in favor of temperance. You may find it difficult to operate upon the minds of those who are advanced in life. People are as a general thing very fearful of reforms. They pride themselves on their conservatism, on their individual force of character, on their genteel habits. It requires a miracle to move some, and nothing short of the millennium will influence others who are set in their way. They are like a conceited old wine-cask, determined to be nothing but a wine-cask, and which at length, full of emptiness and vanity, falls to pieces from advanced age and decay.

But the young are usually pliable. They are easily reached and easily influenced. What shall we do to interest them in this cause, thereby saving them from dissipation and ruin, and securing their co-operation with us in efforts to save others?

An excellent thing is the family pledge. Many years ago, when total abstinence was in its infancy, a Christian minister called together his household, and explained to them the dangers of intemperance, and proposed that parents and children should then and there agree to abstain from all that will intoxicate. The proposal was agreed to. The parents signed their names. The older children followed. And one little boy, too young to write his own name, was enrolled by his father. Forty years have passed away since that occurrence, and that boy who understood the subject well, but was not old enough to sign his name, stands before you now to recommend the family pledge.

Children's temperance societies may be made very effective. The Band of Hope is very popular, and this very properly pledges the youth against the low and wicked habit of profanity and the use of tobacco as well as indulgence in intoxicants. Juvenile societies are often connected with Sabbath-schools, meetings being held on week evenings once a week or once a month, at which dialogues are spoken, addresses delivered, songs sung, and the pledge circulated.

By these efforts thousands of children have been kept from the paths of the destroyer, and if Christian parents and teachers entered more generally and heartily into the work, much larger results would be accomplished. In the year 1847, a Sabbath-school teacher visited a city jail. In one ward he found seventeen young convicts, and to his astonishment learned that fifteen of the number had been Sabbath-school boys. One of them said, alluding to his early instruction, "If I had remembered what I learned, and kept from drink, I should not be here." The question was asked, "Did not your teacher, with other good advice, urge you to abstain from intoxicating drinks?" The reply was, "No"—and this was the testimony of the others. Upon reviewing his own Sabbath-school work, this teacher felt condemned for his negligence in this particular, and standing in the cell of that prison, he made a solemn mental promise that no child should in the future come under his care without being warned against the dangers of intemperance, and advised to a course of total abstinence.

Christians, you are all interested in the children. Then come and join us in our efforts to save the coming generation from the experience of the past. Help us in trying to reach the outcast youth, who in a few years will be besotted and desperate characters, destroying the peace of the community, and filling our houses of refuge and penitentiaries, unless we bring them under a wholesome influence. It is in vain to talk of saving the soul when the body and the habits of the mind are neglected. If the demon intemperance once gets hold of the rising race, it will be useless to tell them of a Saviour and try to woo them into his kingdom. It will probably be *too late—too late*. Thousands now near will be beyond the reach of your voice, and in infamy they will go down to premature death and eternal anguish.

We shudder at the thought. Are our children in danger? Are the most likely youth of our age liable to fall? Is it almost certain that the many children who have drinking parents and unhallowed homes will grow up to be pests in society, and die in sin and shame? Merciful God, have compassion on us! Rouse, fellow-Christians, and help! Fathers, mothers, philanthropists, patriots, come to the rescue! The country calls you. Humanity calls, God calls. Jesus, who died to save sinners, bids you enlist in this cause, because it is auxiliary to the great work of redemption. We plead for the soul; for, remember, the Bible declares no drunkard shall inherit the kingdom of God.

We have great encouragement in engaging in this great work. If we go forth as Christians, with earnestness and faith, we may find to our rejoicing, as the seventy disciples of old did, the very devils subject to us. We may behold Satan fall like lightning from heaven. Perhaps we will have given unto us power to tread on serpents and scorpions. We believe our cause is of the Lord, and he will help us. And therefore we labor in hope, and, applying the lever of prayer to the fulcrum of divine truth, we cry out, "Rid and deliver us from the hand of strange children, whose mouth speaketh vanity, and their right hand is a right hand of falsehood; that our sons may be as plants grown up in their youth; that our daughters may be as corner-stones, polished after the similitude of a palace."

THE

IMPEACHMENT AND PUNISHMENT

OF

ALCOHOL.

"LOOK not thou upon the wine when it is red, when it giveth his color in the cup, when it moveth itself aright. At the last it biteth like a serpent, and stingeth like an adder."—PROV. xxiii. 31, 32.

WE are here to confront the great enemy of our time; to handle the greatest living question. This monster has "the world" for a home, "the flesh" for a mother, and "the devil" for a father. He stands erect, a monster of fabulous proportions. He has no head, and cannot think. He has no heart, and cannot feel. He has no eyes, and cannot see. He has no ears, and cannot hear. He has only an instinct by which to plan, a passion by which to allure, a coil by which to bind, a fang with which to sting, and an infinite maw in which to consume his victims.

I impeach this monster, and arraign him before the bar of the public judgment, and demand his condemnation in the name of industry robbed and beggared; of the public peace disturbed and broken; of private safety gagged and garroted; of common justice violated and trampled; of the popular conscience debauched and prostituted; of royal manhood wrecked and ruined; and of helpless innocence waylaid and assassinated.

In examining this case, we shall appropriate whatever we can find of service in the labors of chemists, jurists compilers, scholars, in every branch of the subject.

We now approach to-night the most difficult part of this subject—The Correction of the Evil. Even a child may accurately determine when it is sick, while the most skilful practitioner may utterly fail in his prescription. Your stable-boy may know that your horse has been stolen, though Pinkerton and all his band may not recover him. The public mind has only to glance at this criminal to be certain of his guilt. For he goes about armed with all malignity, concealed behind all craftiness, seeking with infinite cunning to entrap the unwary and destroy the feeble. Like a blood-hound, he scents his victims afar off, tracking them with patient and infallible instinct across fiery sand-fields and over the barren rock-waste. Once on a young man's track, with one sniff of his heel, nothing but the running stream of living water can check his pursuit and give the fugitive rest. In dark rooms and dingy cellars, in secret conclave, he devises his plans and mixes his drugs. By night and by day he draws out the catalogues of crime. With hands polluted with blood, and locks that wriggle and crawl and hiss; with purpose fixed for slaughter, and with heart unpitying and unrelenting, he presses his infernal work. With the gold his crimes have brought him, he seeks to secure friends in the halls of legislation; to put his judges upon the bench, his advocates at the bar, his witnesses on the stand, and, to make surety doubly sure, his views in the public mind. He would control, if he could, not only our almshouses and prisons, but also our legislative halls and our public presses. He would fill not only our cells and graveyards, but also our judgment-seats and our police commissions. This is our foe—cunning as a fox, wise as a serpent, strong as an ox, bold as a lion, merciless as a tiger, remorseless as a hyena, fierce as the pestilence, deadly as the plague. To condemn and correct such a criminal is not the pastime of an hour, but *the manly, hero-born, martyr-bred work of a lifetime.*

The Legislature of Illinois has given us a law with which we can handle this monster. I will read the distinguishing features:

SECTION 1. *Be it enacted by the People of the State of Illinois, represented in the General Assembly,* That it shall be unlawful for any person or persons, by agent or otherwise, without first having obtained a license to keep a grocery, to sell in any quantity, intoxicating liquors, to be drunk in, upon, or about the building or premises where sold, or to sell such intoxicating liquors to be drunk in any adjoining room, building, or premises, or other place of public resort connected with said building: *Provided,* That no person shall be granted a license to sell or give away intoxicating liquors, without first giving a bond to the municipality or authority authorized by law to grant licenses; which bond shall run in the name of "The People of the State of Illinois," and be in the penal sum of three thousand dollars, with at least two good and sufficient securities, who shall be freeholders, conditioned that they will pay all damages to any person or persons which may be inflicted upon them, either in person or property, or means of support, by reason of the person so obtaining a license selling or giving away intoxicating liquors ; and such bond may be sued and recovered upon for the use of any person or persons, or their legal representatives, who may be injured by reason of the selling intoxicating liquors by the person or his agent so obtaining the license.

SEC. 5. Every husband, wife, child, parent, guardian, employee, or other person, who shall be injured in person or property, or means of support, by any intoxicated person, or in consequence of the intoxication, habitual or otherwise, of any person, shall have a right of action in his or her own name, severally or jointly, against any person or persons who shall, by selling or giving intoxicating liquors, have caused the intoxication, in whole or in part, of such person or persons.

SEC. 8. For the payment of all fines, costs, and damages, assessed against any person or persons, in consequence of the sale of intoxicating liquors, as provided in section five of this act, the real estate and personal property of such person or persons, of every kind, except such as may be exempt under the homestead laws of this State, or such as may be exempt from levy and sale upon judgment and execution, shall be liable, and such fines, costs, and damages shall be a lien upon such real estate until paid ; and in case any person or persons shall rent or lease to another or others any building or premises to be used or occupied, in whole or in part, for the sale of intoxicating liquors, or shall permit the same to be so used or occupied, such building or premises so used or occupied shall be held liable for and may be sold to pay all fines, costs, and damages assessed against any person or persons occupying such building or premises.

SEC. 10. In all prosecutions under this act, by indictment or otherwise, it shall not be necessary to state the kind of liquor sold, or to describe the place where sold.

We urge the maintenance of this law *because it is the only available system that will reach the case.*

I can see but *five possible* courses of action, one of which must be followed. The first and easiest in seeming, but not in fact, is *to sit still—the do nothing policy*. I need not argue this case. It is not admissible. Indeed, it is not long possible. We cannot sit still if we would. We are on the crusted crater of *Vesuvius*. Its eruption is only a question of time. Soon it will belch, and we shall find such a grave that no future antiquarian will more than dream of our existence. The tiger is at our throat. Sit still and we are dead. *We must act; we must move*. All that sin ever wants is to be let alone. The thief has his hand in your pocket, and asks you to hold still. If you move, you may put him to more trouble or disappoint him of his gains. The assassin is in your chamber, stealing, with clinched dagger, up to the crib where your child slumbers. All he wants is time. The work of reform is always aggressive, and wearisome, and dangerous. It must have its convictions from above, be in league with God, move by a command so supreme that no human veto is heard. It can have no fellowship with conservatism. Cautious it may be, but never cowardly. It takes bold and strong strokes to liberate an angel from a block of marble. Every advance is fatal to the old forms. Even the serpent's worn-out skin creaks and rustles when the inhabitant moves out. Like cinders, it is crisp and crotchety while it lasts. God sent his Son into the world not to bring peace, but a sword. It is an old war against an aggressor—sin. He must be *driven* out of the world, and this means conflict, and struggle, and woe. The sooner we settle down to the conviction that we are to endure hardness like good soldiers, the better it will be for us.

Another line of action that has been presented, tried, and exploded, is just now practically brought forward as an amendment to this law—to except wine and beer. It is the *substitution of wines, lighter drinks, in the place of alcohol or strong spirituous liquors.* To pave the way, it is stated by Ex-Governor Andrew, of Massachusetts, in his pamphlet for which he received $10,000 from the Liquor Ring, that all peoples that have arrived at any degree of civilization have been drinking peoples, have invented some kind of intoxicating drink. It is, therefore, most bravely concluded that strong drink is a civilizer. A grog-shop, then, is a centre of civilizing power. Need one argue against such a statement? It reminds one of Lord Brougham's case concerning Tenterton Steeple and Donneby Sands. In former times, there was a harbor at Donneby; the sea filled the channel. Meantime, a church with a steeple was built at Tenterton. A meeting was called to consider what should be done about the channel, when one man said that he noticed that, as soon as they built that steeple at Tenterton, the channel filled up, and moved that they tear down the steeple. All peoples that have become civilized have drunk strong drink: therefore, strong drink is a civilizer. Mark another fact. All peoples that have become civilized have stolen, been licentious and adulterous, and have lied; therefore, stealing, licentiousness, adultery, and lying are civilizers.

Now, let us look at the facts concerning domestic wines and their influence upon drunkenness in the countries where they are raised and made. This will be a fair putting of the case, to put it at its best. Paris, the city of *wine*, where the light wines abound, where more wine is consumed than in any other city in the world, in 1863 consumed seven gallons distilled spirits for each man, woman, and child. That surpasses us. She produces 1,089,000,000 gallons of wine in 1865, yet consumes more brandy and other distilled liquors per head than any other nation on earth. This indicates that wine does not wean men from strong drink. If it does, they had better not be weaned, judging by the poverty, wretchedness, and godlessness that characterize France, especially the wine-growing sections.

There is an impression that France is a temperate nation. Men ride through the country in the better class of cars and see little of it, because the matchless police remove the nuisance ; but let them live there, and live with the people, and they will change their minds. Listen to the witnesses:

Our author, J. Fenimore Cooper, says: "I came to Europe under the impression that there was more drunkenness among us (Americans) than in any other country. *A residence of six months in Paris changed my views entirely.* I have taken unbelievers about Paris, and always convinced them in one walk. I have been more struck by drunkenness in the streets of Paris than in those of London."

Horace Greeley wrote from Paris: "That wine *will* intoxicate, *does* intoxicate, that there are confirmed drunkards in Paris and throughout France, is notorious and undeniable."

M. Le Clerc says: "Laborers leave their work, derange their means, drink irregularly, and transform into drunken debauch the time which should have been spent in profitable labor."

A French magazine says: "Drunkenness is the beginning and end of life in the great French industrial centres. At Lille, twenty-five per cent. of the men and twelve per cent. of the women are confirmed drunkards."

The Count de Montalembert, Member of the Academy of Natural Sciences, said in the National Assembly of France: "Where there is a wine-shop, there are the elements of disease, and the frightful source of all that is at enmity with the interests of the workman."

M. Jules Simon: "Women rival the men in drunkenness. At Lille, at Rouen, there are some so saturated with it that their infants refuse to take the breast of a sober woman."

Hon. James M. Usher, Chief Commissioner of Massachusetts to the World's Exposition in Paris, in 1867, says: "The drinking habit runs through every phase of society. I have seen more people drunk here than I ever saw in Boston for the same length of time. They are the same class of people, too."

Hon. Caleb Foote, of Salem, Mass., writing from Paris, after large investigations, "denies, in toto, the theory that the people of the wine-producing countries are sober."

Dr. E. N. Kirk, of Boston, says: "I never saw such systematic drunkenness as I saw in France during a residence of sixteen months. The French go about it as a business. I never saw so many women drunk."

Surely there is no lack of testimony. Look at other wine-growing countries:

Rev. E. S. Lacy, of San Francisco, six months in Switzerland in a wine-growing section, says: "Here more intoxication was obvious than in any other place it was ever my lot to live in."

Before the Legislative License Committee of Massachusetts, Dr. Warren, of the Boston Biblical School, seven years a resident in Germany, says: "Drunkenness very common; every evening drunken people stagger by my house."

Rev. J. G. Cochran, Missionary to Persia, says of a wine-producing section: "The whole village of male adults will be habitually intoxicated for a month or six weeks."

Rev. Mr. Larabee, another missionary to Persia, confirms the statement. Even priests coolly excuse their own irregularities by the plea of drunkenness.

How in Italy? Cardinal Acton, Chief Judge of Rome, says: "Nearly all the crime in Rome originates in the use of wine."

Thirty-five or forty years ago, England attempted to suppress drunkenness by licensing ale and beer. More distilled liquor per head now than then. The consumption of distilled liquors has increased in the last fifty years one hundred and seventy-five per cent.

Turn to America. How fares it in California? The experiment fails. A State convention of the friends of temperance, in October, 1866, resolved against wine-growing. Conventions of Congregational ministers and lay delegates, same month, reached the same result. They are fully convinced that the hope of temperance based on wine is delusive. This case has been tried till the State exceeds, perhaps, all others in corruption.

Com. Wells: "California, with her cheap wines for temperance, in the year ending June 30, 1867, sold fourteen times, per head, as much alcoholic stuff as Maine did, and more than any other State."

These are the facts concerning the wine-growing countries. The idea of a substitute of wine for alcohol in the interest of temperance is absurd. I have protracted this part of the argument because the enemies of this law are seeking to have wine and beer excepted from the law. But do it, and you kill the law; and this is what they seek. Beware! If you make wine and beer abound, drunkenness will much more abound.

Against this evil plan we can only thunder the facts that the countries that manufacture and drink most wine use most distilled liquors, and have the largest per cent. of beastly, wife-beating, child-beating drunkenness. Husbands may tell their ragged and pleading wives that they can stop. They guess they know who drives. They can stop if they will, but the fact remains. The 60,000 drunkards that annually die were all moderate drinkers before they settled down into old tubs. They all tippled a little before they guzzled. There is no disguising the fact: once drinking, there is no way out but to face about and let it alone, or go through into hell. When a pair of dice are thrown, and 999 out of 1,000 turn double sixes, you are bound to believe the dice loaded. This awful game of perdition turns up death 60,000 times a year. Are you willing to believe that any dose is safe? Will slow scuttling keep a ship afloat better than no scuttling? You who tipple are the ones that need to be alarmed. 'Tis not the worthless sot that desolates the land; it is the respectable drinker. This is where the evil is conceived and born. Beware of the beginnings of evil. Wines can never advance the temperance cause by being substituted for distilled liquors.

The third mode of treatment is that practised in Illinois and many other States. It is the LICENSE SYSTEM. This justly assumes that the traffic is wrong, and must be controlled. I am bold to say that this is the chiefest if not the only virtue in the entire system. I object to the license system, that *it does not control the trade.* It does not limit the sale of liquor. Do you ask for proof? You can have it on this very block, within a stone's cast from this spot. There is not a section of this city where there is any dearth of saloons. There are in Chicago two thousand—one for each one hundred and fifty people. There is not a man living in this city whom the law has restrained from drink. It does not restrain the business.

Again: *It helps to make this systematized murder respectable.* Good citizens do not engage in killing their fellows. Reputable men do not go into this work of making criminals and paupers. This awful work is disgraceful. License legalizes it, and cloaks it with public sanction. They become public servants, doing the public will.

Again: *It is an unjust monopoly.* If it is right for one man in one hundred and fifty to sell liquor, the other one hundred and forty-nine have the same right. If it is wrong for the one hundred and forty-nine, it cannot be right for the one. Legislatures have no power to make rights. Rights are as old as God. And no conclave, no Congress, no Parliament, no Sanhedrim, can give a man a right to murder his fellow for his money, even though he does drop a part of the price of his crime into the public coffers.

Again: *It involves the right to license gambling-houses and houses of ill-fame.*

Again: It becomes itself a school of vice. The law is a public educator. If it proscribes a crime, it puts the fatal seal upon that crime, and the children grow up with the conviction of the evil of that crime. Establish the prize-ring by law, and your sons will be more apt to be bruisers. This is fearfully true of the license law. Therefore, for these reasons, the license law fails, and must for ever fail.

The fourth course *is by prohibition.* I will not discuss this, for it is not now within our reach. But allow me to say, I believe in prohibition. We have the right by the law of self-preservation. Again, the Supreme Courts of some of the States have decided in its favor. The safety of the State is the supreme law. *Moreover, it is not a failure.* It actually empties jails, almshouses, and poor-houses. It stops the sale of three-fourths of the liquor, and stops nearly all the crime. Take the general statistics. Maine, Vermont, and Massachusetts, with 2,250,000 population in 1860, sold, under prohibitory law, $43,-022,754 worth of liquor during the year 1867. New Jersey, Rhode Island, Maryland, and Wisconsin, with 2,225,000 population, sold the same year, under license-law, $137,886,445 worth of liquor. Prohibition is not a failure.

We now approach the last experiment as embodied in the new law. Three questions arise. First, Is it right? Second, Is it wise? Third, Is it possible? Let us answer in detail. It is right, because all that favors prohibition favors this, as the greater includes the less. The first fact is this. Intemperance is *an evil,* therefore this restraint can do no harm. The experiment is safe. It is the case of a man on a burning vessel—it is entirely safe to take to the landing. Whatever comes, to stay is to die. The change here can do no harm; we take no risk. Again, we have the right. This inheres in us; we have the right to protection. A man tries to bring his cattle from Texas to our market; we stop him, because they infect and damage our herds. A man tries to bring the quintessence of ruin into my home to infect my sons. I have a right to stop him; are not my sons as sacred as my oxen? An assassin crawls into my room and raises his dagger above my wife. He dies, if God gives me grace and strength to kill him. A wretch crawls up to my brother and undertakes to poison him. Have I not a right to stop him? A man comes to my hen-coop to steal my chickens. The law says *Joliet.** He comes to my angel-coop to steal my angels. Have I not a right to protect them? Have I not as divine a right to defend my children as I have to defend my chickens? More than this, the Supreme Courts of many of the States declare this right. The people are *sovereign.* They have supreme right to stop crime. Prohibition is an old right: China forbade the use of wine eleven hundred years before Christ, and it is a stranger there yet as a beverage. Carthage banished it from the camp. Plato approved this law. Lycurgus made it shameful to use it; slaves were intoxicated and exhibited to the youth. Romulus sentenced women to death for intoxication as the beginning of adultery. Mohammed

* State prison.

prohibited it twelve hundred and fifty years ago. Governments have always had the right to punish and prevent crime.

This is not all vague generalities. This law is based on the principles of common justice and common law. A leading jurist of this city, Hon. Judge Goodrich, has given me his opinion of this law since its enactment.

He says: "It is justified upon principles fundamental to all social and governmental organizations. In entering into society, every individual surrenders certain of his natural rights, such as the vindication of his wrongs, the protection of life and of property, in consideration that society will insure to him the peaceable enjoyment of his unsurrendered rights, and indemnity for all wrongs done to him.

"One right surrendered is the privilege of doing anything, though personally beneficial, or pursuing any occupation, the natural or probable results of which are, or are likely to be, injurious to other members of society; and society in return is bound to prevent such acts, and provide for remuneration for all damages occasioned by such acts. This right and remedy should be extended to wives, mothers, minors, as well as to men and adults. Unless society afford this protection and these remedies, it cannot be maintained, for it fails to keep its terms of the compact.

"Hence, if a man erect on his premises a dangerous or unhealthful business, or nuisance society can remove it, and the injured party can recover damages resulting directly from the same.

"So we say, If the natural result or probable result of the sale of intoxicating liquors to minors, or persons liable to intoxication, is to inflict any injury upon the person purchasing it, or other persons, society is bound to prevent it, or afford to the parties damnified adequate compensation for the injury sustained.

"If it takes away the means of maintenance from those dependent upon the party to whom sold, or maddens his brain so he inflicts injury upon others, society is bound to give them a remedy of compensation.

"This law is just to the vendor, and is founded on well-established principles of the common law.

"The law holds a man responsible for the consequences of an act which he had reasonable ground to know would be the result of the act, and, doing the act with such knowledge, is held to have intended the consequences; therefore, as a vendor of intoxicating drinks knows its sale to a minor or habitually intoxicated person usually produces acts of violence, pauperism, etc., he should be regarded as having intended to produce such results, and liable for the injurious results."

This is definitively stated, vol. i., "Starkie on Evidence," p. 51: "In case of crime, it is reasonable to infer that a man intended and contemplated that end and result which is the natural and immediate consequence of the means which he used." *Therefore, for the foregoing reasons we conclude that the law is right.*

Next, *Is it wise?* Is it a law that, enforced, will reach the object aimed at? In my judgment, it is wise, because it *treats the business like any other crime.* It does not dignify it by the name of law, nor protect it by the arm of the government. It does not turn the rumseller loose in society as a teacher on the footing of public approval to mould and educate our children. It brands him as an enemy. It does not let him lift a hand or foot till it takes hostages from him for good behavior; and thus it says, "This monster must be watched. He may slay or ruin somebody. Beware!" It looks on him as a mad dog in the highway. It runs after him, crying, "Mad dog, mad dog." This puts a sort of Cain-mark on him to start with. Society says, "I am not able to slay him, but I will cry after him, wherever he goes, Murderer! murderer! so the youth in the land may not be deceived." It is like a certain old English livery-stable, in which a police-officer was stationed. Of some gentle horses he said to the owner, "Hire them, and make a living, and be blessed." Of one black, untamed beast he said, "If you hire him out, you shall pay damages." It discriminates against the black beast. A man can sell groceries, and the law says, "Amen, good citizen;" but if he sells alcohol, it says, "Dangerous! beware of the black beast."

It is wise, *because it strikes the rumseller where he*

lives—in the pocket. It wastes no strength in sentimentalism. It moves to conquer. It means business. It comprehends the character of the enemy. Nothing but striking the profits can be understood, so it aims low; and, if I mistake not, it will slay these things, rumsellers, by the thousand. The law accepts the situation, admits that every sentiment of humanity is dead, that moral obligation has lost its power, that honor has long been forgotten, that common justice is only a myth of the past, that there is no footing in such a soul but in the low sense of loss of the blood-stained gains.

So the law is wise in striking the rumseller where he lives—in his pocket. Touch the profits, and he feels; make it unprofitable, and it will cease. It is not a missionary enterprise, it is all for gain.

It is wise, because it applies the recovered money to the injured. It does not put this money into the public pocket. I have little faith in the policy that will allow a man to destroy a whole neighborhood, send a hundred men to jail and a hundred families to the poor-house, and stop a score of factories, for the small income the murderer pays on his booty. Nor do I see how the Sate can innocently barter the blood and health and character of my brother or son for a few dollars for the treasury. I have more faith even in the poor wretch who, in the confessional, while confessing and paying a few pence for absolution, was stealing the priest's watch and purse. It is here a penny in, and a thousand dollars out.

But this law gives its recovered plunder not to the State, which has but doubtful right to it, but to those who suffer the wrong and need the help. It keeps that mother from pauperism. It feeds and schools those helpless, innocent, wronged, and robbed children. It applies the funds exactly where they are most needed, and, therefore, we conclude *that it is wise.*

It is wise, because it cuts down through all subterfuges, and *makes good its securities.* Wherever it is possible to sell or give away this deadly drug, there it can seize the very soil for damages. It stops not at the cat's-paw, but it reaches all the parties. The landlord who divides the profits in rents must now divide the responsibility and damages as he has always shared the guilt. Nothing can be clearer than that the man who furnishes the den is a *particeps criminis*, and should be so held. Some men rent their buildings for deadfalls, and fancy that they are free from guilt. But I can see no moral difference between your letting a saloon into your building and your tending the bar yourself. In both cases you pocket the profits, and your hiring some widow's son to dose out the poison for you does not lessen your guilt. The victims sinking into a drunkard's hell may fasten their frenzied hands upon you, and, crying, "Thou art the man," drag you into the same condemnation. This law recognizes this great fact, and holds the property liable, *and so is wise.*

Again, it is wise in making no distinctions in liquor. Chemists are not needed to define the various kinds. It is one simple question: Did the man who drank your liquor do any damage? If beer and wine do no harm and do not intoxicate, then there will be no damages. If the man who drinks beer does not break down my fence, you will not have to put it up again. Why do these men resist? It is because they know that wine and beer are dangerous and ruinous, and ought to be held responsible.

Again, it is wise in *touching off this shell with a six months' fuse.* It gives its friends a chance to rally against a foe already in the fort and always ready.

Is it possible? Can it be enforced? This is the leading question. I wish to answer that it *can and must be enforced,* because it receives the *support of the good men of all parties.* It was introduced into the House by one party, and into the Senate by the other. Sometimes party spirit carries men over into opposition to a good thing, because it is of the opposite faction. But in this case it breaks into all the old party lines and makes a party for itself, and comes to the people with a tremendous endorsement from the strength of the State.

The fact that it is a law of the State must be its surety. It is purely a question of *public sentiment.* If the people are convicted for the law, all the powers of lager and whiskey and of darkness cannot resist it. Awaken the people, impress them with the majesty and authority of law, set them for its defence, and its victory is inevitable. I think we need a revival on this question of law.

The way to despotism is through anarchy. Law is our only safety. Let me sail on a sea of fire rather than on the sea of chance and chaos. We are drifting toward the breakers. In the *home* there is a letting down of authority. Children are certain they know more than their parents, and, by the pulseless hand with which the parents guide them, I think the children are right. God has put you in charge. They are not your guardians. They resent correction as an insult. All this must be cured. In the home must be laid the foundations of law and authority. The best thing a people can have as insurance for the future is a solid conviction of *the authority of law*. It is not a question whether my personal rights can be served, but what is the demand of the public good. My sidewalk may hold me, but it must hold also the public. My cellar-way may be sufficiently guarded for me, but it must also be safe for the stranger. The public good is the supreme law And enacted law is the judgment of the majority as to what is the public good. So the individual can have no alternative but to obey the law while it is law, or suffer the penalty. Let this be instilled into every mind, and there will be no difficulty in enforcing the law on temperance or on any other subject. It is purely a question of public opinion. This is always resistless. Government is always the creature of the public will. The government of the Celestial Empire would last in America about one-sixteenth of one second—just long enough to touch ground. It would hold this Yankee nation about as long as a sheet of tissue paper would keep down an eruption of Vesuvius. The public sentiment is absolute. No law can be valid without this support. Let the mayor issue a proclamation forbidding Christian people from assembling to worship next Sabbath morning, because he was opposed to it. What would happen? I can tell you what would happen. Unless such action was demanded by the public good, on account of som. plague or peril, and so had the approval of the people, next Sabbath would see us all in our places, and such a mayor in his place in Jacksonville or at Elgin. The public will is supreme. This is always the final arbiter. This makes the people invincible. "You may destroy the cities to the last hamlet, desolate the country to the last cabin, wipe out the press to the last page, and you have done nothing. There still remains the human mind, pure as the light and unapproachable as the sun." And in its supreme decisions are the decrees of destiny. Thus you may burn the buildings from Jefferson Street to the Lake, and from De Koven Street to Fullerton Avenue, and you have not burned Chicago. All that is not Chicago. Chicago is in the heroic bosoms of the heroic people, in the everlasting purpose, in the almighty energy that camped like savages on the prairie, without stool or tent—planned by the light of the burning fortunes new railroads, new depots, new elevators, new hotels, new churches, a new city, and a new civilization. Fix this sentiment for this law, and then the gates of hell shall not prevail against it. The whole question is one of public opinion. This, I think, is right, or can be righted by the first of July.

Suppose I indicate how I think it can be done. First, on the general question of respect for law for the long future. Teach your children to respect it, teach them to respect your authority, and teach them to respect the law while in school.

Again: Let *your influence be solid against excusing great criminals.* These local aldermen that have sold themselves and the public trust should have fair trial and fair chance like any other thieves, and, if convicted, suffer the extreme penalty of the law. They have nominally served the public for nothing, now make them do it actually. This is not so harsh. If it seems harsh, that seeming is proof of its necessity. This poor day-laborer is sick, and so without income, and his babes are hungry, and in desperation he snatches a man's money, and runs. He is dogged into the penitentiary. These scoundrels steal the city poor, and take away public confidence, and breed contempt for law. I say, in God's name, do not shield them, but send them to their reward. To secure this, let men in trying places know that they have your sympathy and support. Without regard to party, let honest men say to the faithful judges and officials, "God bless you," and "We will support you."

The press have a large share of responsibility

in this matter of public opinion. There is great hope in the general tone of the press on this law. Some editorials have been clear and manly for the law. These forces mean victory in July. The Press is the Third House, but the people are the Fourth House.

Another fact: You come in contact with large numbers of laboring men. You meet them in their shops and at their work. A few words judiciously spoken will prepare them for right action when the time comes. If the law is to be resisted, men must be found to leave their work, and mass and combine against it. Now, you can prevent many from doing this. If the great working-class say that the law shall not be enforced, its execution will be difficult, if not impossible. But if they say, "It must be obeyed," or even keep out of the crowds and at their work, its enforcement will be as certain as destiny. Every man do his duty like a man, and this benign and equitable law will hedge this awful traffic with mortal and fatal disabilities.

Mobs may threaten, but they must finally obey. I would put deliberate emphasis upon this. If men cannot obey the law, the way is open. They can return to the old despotisms, and they can go without passports too; and they can take the fortunes they have made here. But if they stay, they must obey the law. I had rather be a thousand years longer in reclaiming the wilderness, than see it seized by brutality, and beastliness, and crime.

Possibly some of you are saying, "I approve the law, but my family is safe, and I will not take any risks of ill-will by taking sides. Let those who are exposed enforce the law." Brother, you are exposed. This traffic is an infernal machine stored under your bed. Your thoughtless boy may light the fuse when you least expect it. There is no safety with the thing about the premises. Is it just the fair play which we all approve and demand to ask our representatives to take the chances of defeat or censure in enacting a good law, which we approve and the public safety demands, and then we ourselves shirk the responsibility and leave the law unenforced? Is it manly for us to send them out on the forlorn hope, and then, when they have made the breach and hold it, we desert and refuse to march in with the main army? All honor to the men who have breasted the storm and secured such advantage to the cause! Blessings from many a humble widow whose son shall be saved to her, and from many a poor orphan thus furnished with protection and possible schooling, shall come upon their heads. In the humble homes of poverty, where piety and virtue struggle against want and degradation, where God's tall and tender-footed angels keep nightly watch, there their names shall be mentioned. And yonder, when the reckoning comes, think you this vote shall be forgotten? I tell you, nay. The Judge himself shall say, "Inasmuch as you have done it unto the least of these my little ones, you have done it unto me." I had rather have my name on that affirmative vote than be the representative of a compromised and drunken constituency for a thousand years. All honor to the men who enacted the law, and let us show ourselves worthy of such representatives. To-night, brothers, after this long survey of this momentous subject, I call upon you, in the presence of this great criminal—in full view of his malignant character; of the vileness that stamps the poison itself; of the frauds that are practised in its manufacture; of the deadly counterfeits that deepen its malignity; of the insanity that makes its victims fairly fly to ruin; of the 1,000,000 wrecks that stagger, and ooze, and leer, and bloat, and fester, and fall downward; of the 60,000 poor creatures that yearly fill drunkards' graves on their way to the drunkard's doom; of 2,000,000 children that are left worse than orphans, cursed with an inheritance of rags and shame; of the 3,000,000 of women who have millstones tied about their necks and are thus cast into the social sea; of the 200,000 broken-hearted ones that yearly march to the poor-house; of the 200,000 convicts that are annually sent to jail; of the 200,000 orphans annually bequeathed to public charity; of the 450 suicides that are caused by this evil spirit; of the 700 murders that horrify the year; of the 1,350 rapes that are committed by this demon; of the 12,000 lunatics that are made in this fire; of the great company of idiots that are spawned by this monster; of the millions of homes ruined and all the homes threatened by this invader; of the public schools, robbed of 2,000,000 children; of seven-eighths of all the crimes of the land committed by this evil inspiration; and of the enormous sum of $2,607,491,866 annually taken from the public comfort and expended in wretchedness and crime —in the presence of all these fearful facts, I call upon you, in this day of probation, in this house of God, by the absolute need of prompt action, by the utter failure of indecision, by the worse than failure of many substitutes, and by the right of self-preservation; I call upon you, in the name of the countless victims who are bound in this wretched habit, in the name of the wearying, watching mothers whose sons are imperilled, in the name of some young men here to-night who may yet wreck all beauty for time and all hope for eternity, in the name of some fair and hopeful maidens here to-night who may yet mourn and pine in the squalor and misery of the drunkard's hovel, in the name of earth desolated and heaven forfeited by this crime, and in the name of Almighty God, whose eye is upon us, and at whose judgment-bar we must shortly stand—I call upon you to maintain and enforce this law at all costs! Out of these awful responsibilities we cry from our hearts for ever and for ever, " Everlasting war against rum, and eternal death to alcohol!"

DRINKING FOR HEALTH.

"DRINK no longer water, but use a little wine for thy stomach's sake and thine often infirmities."—1 TIM. v. 23.

TIMOTHY was a temperance man. He would not use anything in the shape of liquor, from fear of self-injury and hindering the Gospel he preached. So abstemious was he that it required a positive command from his spiritual father to induce him to touch even wine.

Paul was a temperance man. He was so careful as to his example that he would refrain from eating "*meat*" if it caused a weak brother to stumble. And, no doubt (so anxious was he that Timothy should be "blameless"), he had enjoined upon his son in the Gospel the strictest temperance. But now, as his health was giving way, he exhorted him to use "no longer water [*only*], but a little wine."

And *what was this "wine"?* Was there *alcohol* in it? Probably none at all. Investigation has of late been very thorough as to the wines of the Bible; and the conclusion reached is that they may be divided into two distinct classes—the harmless and the pernicious, or the unfermented and the fermented.

All the principal Biblical critics who have made the study of this subject a specialty, have reached the result expressed by Professor Moses Stuart: "My final conclusion is this, namely, that, whenever the Scriptures speak of wine as a comfort, a blessing, or a libation to God, and rank it with such articles as corn and oil, they mean—they can mean—only such wine as contained no alcohol that could have a mischievous tendency; that, wherever they denounce it, prohibit it, and connect it with drunkenness and revelling, they can mean only alcoholic or intoxicating wine. If I take the position that God's Word and works entirely harmonize, *I must take the position that the Bible before us is such as I have represented it to be.* . . . I cannot refuse to take this position without virtually impeaching the Scriptures of contradiction or inconsistency."

Now, would Paul have advised the use of fermented and intoxicating wine? Did he not know what Philo, Aristotle, Pliny, and other credible authorities, nearly contemporary with himself, tell us, namely, that "intoxicating wines were deleterious to health, and produced headaches, dropsy, madness, dysentery, and stomach complaints; while other wines were salubrious and medicinal, and particularly commended for enfeebled and diseased stomachs"? How absurd to suppose that Paul would recommend Timothy to use poisonous wines, when the unfermented and harmless were every way better! In any view of the case, however, here is cold comfort for wine-bibbers; for even if there were a moiety of alcohol in the drink recommended, yet it was to be used strictly as a medicine, and Timothy was expressly *ordered* to take it by an *inspired apostle.* I agree with another, that "as the recommendation here was not for gratification, but for medicine, and to Timothy personally, a sick man, and only a little at that, it gives no more countenance for the beverage use of wine for any one, and especially for those in health, than does the prescription of castor-oil by the physician for the beverage use of that article."

But what shall be said of the *drinking for health* which is now so common? Few are aware of its prevalence. The use of "pure wine," as it is called, has been put forward as a preventive of intemperance; and "mild stimulants" and "healthful tonics" are dabbled with by thousands to-day who a few years ago knew nothing of their use

Our homes are becoming fountain-heads of drunkenness. Wines and other drinks are on the tables, not only on special occasions, but regularly; and wives, mothers, and sisters, instead of frowning upon their use, encourage it by their example. Indeed, the increase of intemperance among women themselves, both in England and America, is becoming alarming. A recent article in one of our secular papers says:

"It is worth our while to see how this matter stands. There is such a sense of chivalry towards the weaker sex and faith in their purity among

Americans, that a statement that drunkenness existed to any appreciable amount among educated women would be received with disgust and incredulity. Yet there are certain facts which it is high time should be taken at once into the gravest consideration by both the pulpit and the press. To physicians they are, unfortunately, but too familiar. Among these is the too large proportion of female patients in insane asylums who have become so from the use of stimulants. The American fashionable woman, as we all know, drinks often, at her own table, wines of a strength which her European sister would not dare to touch. She 'mixes her liquors,' too; in her teens is a connoisseur of champagne, delicately sips sherry-cobblers and Roman punches; and all this with her in-door life, her limp constitution, her bilious habit, and under climatic influences which, to the strongest man, make alcohol a poison. There are certain quiet 'ladies' restaurants' in all the seaboard cities, so quiet and modest in appearance that gentlemen are not tempted into them, where respectable women resort for the stimulant which is probably inaccessible at home. Deaths from *mania a potu* have occurred this winter, and that not in the debased lower classes, but among cultured, delicately-reared women; some of them young, generous, lovable girls. The baby at the breast is dosed nightly with soothing syrups; the sickly school-girl has her 'drops' night and morning; while for the innumerable ailments of the married woman there is a mantel-shelf full of tonics, elixirs, and bitters, German and native, all warranted 'free from a drop of alcohol mixture.'"

I wish that church-members and so-called temperance people were not among these tipplers. But many such are tampering with strong drink. How common it is for gentlemen in the chophouses and restaurants to call for liquor at lunch, while at home they daily use wine or ale "as a *medicine*"—of course! Not a few pastors must say with one, "The deepest anxiety I feel for several of my flock is, lest they fall under the dominion of the cup, which is a mocker, and which upsets a Christian's brain just as soon as any one's."

Now, what is the cause of this drift towards drinking for health? And who is directly responsible for it? Three parties are chiefly blamable; viz., the regular medical profession; the irregular or "quack" medicine venders; and the people themselves.

1. *Heavy blame attaches to authorized medical practitioners.*—The great Dr. Rush declared that "no man should be able to say that he made him a drunkard by recommending spirits." Would that this could be said *generally* by physicians! The medical profession enrolls great numbers of self-denying, philanthropic, learned, and conscientious men—never so many as now; and I am glad to say many of them are among the stanchest advocates of temperance, both in theory and practice. But still beyond question, the

injudicious and indiscriminate recommendation by physicians of alcohol as medicine and a beverage is a principal source of prevailing intemperance. Forty years ago, Dr. Pye Smith said that "the permissions of *some* medical men, *too careless of physical and moral results*, have given great impulse to spirit-drinking, and have caused an estimate to be attached to spirituous liquors beyond their value as a medicinal drug." Since then the evil has gone on increasing, until we have a sort of medical epidemic in spirit-drinking for sanitary purposes. Mr. Beecher's statement of the case is scarcely extravagant:

"Doctors, like every social body, are subject to tides of fashion; and just now the tide sets very strong in the direction of alcoholic stimulants —particularly of Bourbon whiskey. Everybody has, first or last, one of three complaints. Everything is either neuralgia, or heart-complaint, or dyspepsia, with the doctors; and Bourbon whiskey seems to be the great wholesale stimulant. The minister whose nervous system is deranged by too close application to his professional duties drinks Bourbon whiskey—the doctor told him to. The merchant who has overtaxed his powers of body and mind by confining himself night and day to his business drinks Bourbon whiskey—his physician told him to. The lawyer whose brain is perpetually at work, and intensely at work, drinks Bourbon whiskey—his doctor told him to. *Everybody that feels bad is drinking Bourbon whiskey under medical prescription!* The indiscriminate and almost universal prescription of it, I know, cannot be right. I think that matter has gone full as far as fashion will justify, and that physicians should begin to hold back, and to discriminate, and to make fewer cases in which this all-healing remedy is applicable. Otherwise, under the cover of a medical prescription, we are going to have a deluge of whiskey on the land again; for as soon as it is found out that the physician prescribes whiskey for everything, men will not go to him any more, but will buy it in large quantities and at wholesale rates, and administer it themselves!"

At a late annual meeting of the Pennsylvania Medical Society, Doctors H. Carson and W. W. Townsend, in a written report to the society, said:

"Every physician whom we know personally, and all of whom we have heard, use and recommend the use of alcoholic liquors in some form in their practice. The great majority use them freely, in trifling as well as in grave cases; in the cases of drunkards as well as total-abstinence people; on the child of a day and the parent of threescore and ten. They prescribe them in diseases of the kidneys, lungs, heart, brain, stomach, and every other organ, and yet they know full well that diseases of those organs have been produced thousands of times by those very agents. They recommend them to the weak and the dyspeptic; the aged because they are aged, and the young because they are young; the nursing mother because of the drain on her system (natural though it be and healthful); to those who are given up as hopeless because they are dying, and to the convalescent because they are convalescing, and they cannot forego the opportunity to show them how porter, ale, or whiskey will 'build them up.' The effect of such a course is to impress the community with a high opinion of the valuable medicinal, life-giving properties of alcoholic liquor."

It is well for all to know that by eminent physicians this dosing with stimulants is thoroughly discountenanced and denounced as an outrage. I could readily bring forward a long list of high medical authorities who hold that *pre*scription here ought to be *pro*scription! If your doctor orders you to take stimulants, it is of no disadvantage to you to be aware that other physicians would order you to throw them into the fire! There is *not* such uniformity of opinion here as to justify your blind adherence to medical advice. Hear what physicians themselves say. I give you a few quotations from their written testimonies. Beginning at home, listen to what one of your own townsmen has said: "I am a physician. Medical men, you say, occupy towards the subject of temperance a position that is professional and peculiar. Doubtless this is so. Knowing what they do, there are responsibilities resting upon them solemn as death. I shudder almost to think what mischievous potency there is sometimes in a mere touch of their finger. Many a credulous wretch, tottering on the verge of the abyss, has thereby been pushed headlong. The crude utterance of some rash oracle of medicine has dug many a grave, and kindled many a fire, unquenchable as hell." *

Says Dr. Charles Jewett: "A fruitful source of error, and often, it is to be feared, of fatal mischief, is the almost unquestioning credence given by the masses to the opinions of their family physician, without stopping to consider how far those opinions may be influenced by his habits, associations, and unreasoning prejudices. Personally, I have no doubt but that tens of thousands annually in this country are hurried out of existence by the uncalled-for and mistaken use of wine and brandy. No one but a physician of pretty extensive observation, and one personally free from the influence of alcoholic liquors, can fairly estimate the amount of mischief caused by the almost indiscriminate prescription of such liquors under the general but false notion that they are tonic or possessed of supporting power."

Dr. Carpenter, an eminent physiologist and physician, says: "Nothing in the annals of quackery can be more truly empirical than the mode in which fermented liquors are directed or permitted to be taken by a large proportion of medical practitioners."

A physician in Edinburgh, alluding to the frequent cases of forming an appetite for strong drink by its prescription, says: "No man who

* Dr. Abraham Coles, Newark, N. J.

knows the effects of this liquor, as they are now in thousands of cases existing, can possibly doubt that multitudes had better have died a hundred deaths than been ensnared as they have been by means of it."

You see, then, that there is ground for hesitancy before you accept the advice and follow the prescription of a physician recommending wine, ale, or brandy for yourself or a dependent. Believe me, the remedy in this case is oftentimes worse than the disease; and you may well imitate that young American soldier who, when exhausted and shivering, was presented by his officer with a glass of wine, but said: "No, sir, thank you; I would rather face all the cannon of the enemy than take that liquor."

And, if I here address a physician not thoroughly "booked," let me ask him to consider a few facts bearing upon this subject. Dr. Gairdner, of Glasgow, speaking of the cases of young persons afflicted with typhus fever, and treated altogether without alcohol, states that out of 189 cases only one died, and that one was in a dying state when admitted to the hospital. If those cases had been treated with a small amount of alcohol, as practised in Glasgow in the years 1861 and 1862, he shows that *six* or *seven* would have died. Had they received the greater amount of alcohol given in Glasgow in 1847, *nine* would have died. Had they received the still larger amount of this poisonous liquor given in the London Hospital, *nearly twelve* would have died. Had they been in the hands of Dr. Todd, "who advocated alcohol in typhus in the highest degree," Dr. Gairdner shows that not less than *thirty to thirty-five* of them would have gone to their graves! This is a fair specimen of Dr. Gairdner's carefully and far too cautiously stated results, as demonstrated in his tables of statistics and his reasoning on them. Instead of really *no* deaths among 188 patients treated without alcohol altogether, you have at least *thirty* young persons sent into eternity by its use!

In 1864, the venerable surgeon of Nottingham, England, Dr. Higginbottom, published a *résumé* of his experience, in which he says:

"For about thirty years I have not once prescribed alcohol as a medicine; so that I have now fully tried both ways, with and without alcohol; and I am now fully of opinion that a more dishonest or cruel act cannot be inflicted on a patient than to prescribe or order alcohol as a medicine. So strongly am I convinced, that I should consider myself criminal if I again recommend alcohol, either as food or medicine."

He adds: "During my long practice, I have not known or seen a single disease cured by alcohol; on the contrary, it is the most fertile producer of disease, and may be considered the bane of medicine and the seed of disease. It is destitute of any medicinal principle implanted by the Creator in genuine medicines. "I have found acute disease sooner cured without alcohol, and chronic disease much more manageable. "I have never seen a patient or any person injured by leaving off alcoholic fluids *at once.* I should as soon expect, as a Dr. Scott has said, 'killing a horse by leaving off the whip and spur.' I have not heard from my professional brethren, or from any of my patients, that my non-alcoholic treatment of disease has occasioned a single death. My greatest trouble has been, for many years, in preventing patients from being destroyed by the use of it. I do not say the *abuse, for I consider the use the abuse.* "No person can form any idea, except from experience, of the superiority of the practice of medicine and surgery when alcohol is banished from it."

Dr. L. M. Bennet, M.R.C.S., says:

"I believe there is no curable disease (chronic or acute) but what may be treated and cured better without alcohol than with it. . . . *During the last twenty-five years, I have not once used it as a medicine or recommended it as a beverage;* and, although I have had great experience in the treatment of dyspepsia, fever, exhaustion from the loss of blood, and profuseness of purulent discharges, I have found all those complaints and conditions *much more easily removed without alcohol.* . . . From all the observation and experience I have had for a period of thirty years, I have come to this conclusion—that intoxicating drinks in any quantity, however small, are unnecessary to maintain health; that they are neither necessary nor desirable to support the frame under excitement, nor to recruit it when exhausted ; that, when a necessity exists for the use of a stimulant in the treatment of disease, *a safer, more certain, and effectual substitute can be found ;* that the mortality in disease will always be in proportion to the amount of alcohol used in the treatment, and that the entire disuse of it as a medicine would prove highly beneficial to mankind."

My limits forbid reference to other authorities to the same effect.

2. Passing from the medical profession proper, I speak of the *irregular or quack doctors* as responsible for the tippling habits of the day. They have flooded the country with their decoctions under the names of Cordials, Tonics, Strengthening Bitters, Buchu, Plantation Bitters, Schiedam Schnapps, Liebfrauenmilch, Lachryma Christi, Santa Cruz, Golden Bitters, and the like, which they blazon forth everywhere with a prodigal waste of money. Almanacs and other pamphlets are thrust under the door-sills, and distributed from country-stores, filled with glowing descriptions and certificates of "remarkable cures"; and to read of these "scientifically prepared stimulants," "wholesome cordials," "tonic alteratives," "life-reviving bitters," "pure and genial restoratives," and the catalogue of the ills for which they are a *sure remedy*, one would almost wonder why men ever die with such "elixirs of life" within their reach!

Now, the simple truth is, the entire catalogue of these so-called remedies and restoratives sought to be palmed off upon the innocent public are vile compounds. In many cases they are chiefly bad whiskey, and in all cases it is *alcohol* (without being so-called), which the purchaser swallows; and *this is the reason* WHY it is swallowed. Though often advertised as "temperance bitters" with but "just enough spirits to preserve them," they were inert without liquor, and would lack consumers. People buy them *because they like the brandy that is in them!*

The quantity of these bogus remedies that are sold is almost fabulous; and untold multitudes have found their *bitters* to be *biters!* The epitaph upon their tombstones might be written (as with one poor victim): "I was well; and I would be better; and here I lie!" Or living, they have found an acquired appetite for strong drink fastened upon them, which is often worse than death.

I agree with another, that these preparations, whose names are paraded on every picturesque rock along our great thoroughfares by pandering scoundrels, are rum, *rum*, RUM, with a little something added to disguise it. To advertise these things is to encourage intemperance; and to suffer them to go unexposed is to leave the community the prey of a subtle and most damaging evil. All these promises of rejuvenation, all these pretences of ability to revitalize worn-out men, are miserable shams. All these preparations for men and women that claim the power to do such wonderful things, are scarcely disguised abominations of intemperance, are fit only for deception, and are a shame and disgrace to any respectable store or respectable family. And it is high time that *this outrageous hypocrisy*, under the color of medicine, should be exposed, and trodden into the ditch from which it came, and to which it belongs.

3. But, after all, *the people themselves* are chiefly responsible for this growing custom of drinking for health. They acquiesce in alcoholic prescriptions by the medical profession, and support by their patronage the villanous compounds which would otherwise prove profitless. Mothers are knowingly giving liquors in some shape to their infants (besides taking it themselves), and tens of thousands of otherwise sensible people have come to believe that they must have some strong drink.

A little must be taken for "weakness of the stomach," and a "faintness" and "goneness" of feeling when they get up. It must be sipped with the lunch and drunk after dinner to "help digestion"; and they must have "a night-cup" before they go to bed! It would be a curious spectacle if the cellars, vaults, closets, and garrets of all the houses around us were to disgorge the filled and empty bottles that they contain, marked with some inscriptions of porter, ale, wine, tonics, bitters, and the like!

Now, assuming that I am speaking to some who have not much considered this matter, let me ask two questions:

1. *What are you drinking?* I have answered the question as to the compounds sold for strengthening and remedial purposes.

But how about lager-beer, which has become so much of a beverage? Possibly in its use you think you are taking nothing intoxicating. That is a mistake. There is alcohol in lager. The percentage is small; but yet it is sufficient to induce an appetite for something stronger, and to do directly an injury to health. A glass of this beverage is not as injurious as a glass of whiskey or gin, because it contains a far less quantity of alcohol; but an ounce of alcohol is just as hurtful when diffused through six glasses of lager as when imbibed in two glasses of rum or brandy.

Says a competent authority: "The question 'Does lager-beer intoxicate'? is a thing not to be argued. I might as well attempt to prove that two and two make four. It is gross and palpable to sense. I am amazed at the effrontery—I scarcely know a parallel to the audacity—of those who deny it."

Perhaps you say, "I use a little *wine*." Very likely it is *pure* wine that you think you are using. Are you sure of it? Did not Addison long ago tell us of philosophers "daily employed in *the transmutation of liquors;* and, *by the power of magical drugs and incantations, raising, under the streets of London, the choicest products of the hills and valleys of France, and squeeze claret out of the sloe, and draw champagne out of an apple*"? Who does not know that nine-tenths of the wine consumed is but brandy (or something worse) under another name? In France and other European countries are extensive establishments for the *manufacture* of all the choicest varieties of wines; and you may as well know that, when you have paid a round price for wines *imported direct from the wine-growing districts*, and in *original packages*, you are yet most likely paying for what never smelt a grape! I do not say that there are *no* pure wines; but I say that adulteration is the law, and purity the exception; and that wines are so skilfully "doctored" with well-selected drugs as to escape even chemical tests as to their quality. An able writer goes so far as to affirm that "wine has become a myth, a shadow, a very Eurydice of life. *There is no such thing, we verily believe, as honest grape-juice wine remaining—nothing but a vile compound of poisonous drugs and impurely obtained alcohol;* and all our beautiful Anacreontics are merely fables like the rest; for wine hath died out from the world, and the LABORATORY IS NOW THE VINEYARD."

There is perhaps nearly a hundred times as much "PORT" wine (so called from Oporto) sold and drank as can be made from all the grapes raised in the region of Oporto, including the whole Douro Valley.

Says a writer: "If the Douro River were a thousand miles long instead of only sixty, it could not furnish grapes enough to make all this ocean of 'port' wine. The whole world of fashionable topers, and invalids, and imbeciles are drinking wine made out of the little handful of grapes grown on the banks of a small creek in Portugal! The miracle of feeding five thousand souls from 'five loaves and a few small fishes' is as nothing compared to this!"

I spoke of the *manufacture* of wines abroad; but it should be known that *our own country* is the largest "wine-growing district" in the world! Here are furnished a *million times* more baskets of champagne [with exact imitation of foreign brands!] than are put up of the pure juice in all the champagne districts of Europe! By passing the oil of whiskey through carbon, a Madeira is made at a profit of 500 per cent. which few can tell from the genuine. With neutral spirits, or even with whiskey, vinegar, sulphuric acid, beet-root, alum, lead, logwood, potash, cider, copperas, and the like, are produced wines at trifling cost. Of these and other wines, New York City annually manufactures to the value of $8,000,000: all of which are admirably adapted to Timothy's weak stomach!

"It is a notorious fact," says one of our daily journals, "that even the California champagnes have been driven from the market by 'doctored wines,' or have themselves been 'doctored' to meet the popular demand. Madeira *grows* 30,000 barrels of wine yearly; and America alone *drinks* 50,000 barrels of 'Madeira' wine!

Perhaps you drink the "best *brandy*"; but very unlikely! A chemist lately analyzed a bottle of pure brandy [as was alleged], and found in it alum, iron, sulphuric acid, essential oil of some kind, tannic acid, Guinea pepper, burnt sugar, lead, and copper, with a nitric ether, basis of whiskey. This is the delicious mixture which, by the aid of a pretty label and a little sealing-wax on the cork, passes for Old Hennessy, London Dock, Martel, or Seignette brandy.

Is it *whiskey* that you take?

Some whiskey seized a few days ago in Newton, Mass., was found to be thus compounded: Ten gallons of kerosene, three pounds of potash, one ounce of strychnine, mixed with soft water. Promising stuff to drink for health! Twenty-five per cent. of the alcoholic strength you get in whiskey is often but *strychnine* strength.

Are you a drinker of *porter, ale, beer?* Would you could see what becomes of the thousands of bags of *cocculus indicus* [the rankest poison, without any known antidote] imported into this country to be used up in breweries! Would you could see the Brewers' Guides and various recipes which the liquor manufacturers keep hidden away! They would read something like this:

Ingredients of a Warming Nature.—Pepper, capsicum, cloves, ginger, spice, vinegar, acetic acid, tartaric acid, citric acid, butyric acid, cream of tartar, nitric acid or aquafortis, sulphuric acid, prussic acid, sulphuric ether, nitric ether, acetic ether, spirits of nitre, oil of vitriol, oil of turpentine, oil of cassia, oil of caraway, oil of cloves, extract of japonica, extract of bitter almonds, extract of orris root, extract of angelican root, grains of paradise, multum, poppy seeds, juniper berries, aloes, cochineal, black ants, and Spanish juice.

To give Taste and Astringency.—Bruised raisins, dried blackberries, dried peaches, dried cherries, orange-peel, coriander seed, white oak bark, tannic acid, kino, rhatany, catechu, caraway seed, cardamom seed, fennel seed, wormwood, alum, copperas, sulphate of iron, and sulphate of copper.

For Beers without Malt or Hops.—To prevent sourness, use sugar, honey, molasses, licorice, alum, opium, gentian, quassia, aloes, cocculus indicus, amara, tobacco, and nux, for hops; saltpetre, jalap, salt, maranta, green copperas, marble dust, oyster-shells, egg-shells, sulphate of lime, hartshorn, shavings, nut-galls, potash, soda, etc.

To correct Unnatural Tastes.—Lime-water, carbonate of lime, carbonate of soda, nitrate of potash, caustic potash, pearlash, saleratus, sugar of lead, and litharge.

For Coloring Matters.—Burnt sugar, beet-juice, dried apples, dried peaches, elderberries, molasses, red saunders, logwood, and sulphuric acid.

A pretty list indeed!

These facts convey some idea of *what it is* that you are most likely drinking if in the use of liquors:—a "heterogeneous conglomerate of poisons, drugs, and dye-stuffs"!

I proceed to another question:

2. *Why do you drink?* let me ask. *Have you*

investigated and properly considered the effects of liquor drinking upon health?

Think of introducing into the stomach, and into all the delicate ramifications of that frame-work so fearfully and wonderfully made, the "poisoned poisons" and the "fluid nastiness" which I have described! Nor flatter yourself that *your* liquors are pure, for adulteration, as I have said, is all but universal; and the cry of one is well founded, that "the people ask for pure spirit, but nauseating and maddening and death-dealing stuffs are sold in its stead. They ask for stimulants, and are given strychnine. They seek exhilaration, and are treated to insanity. They crave refreshment and inspiration, and are mocked with inebriety and madness."

But passing this by, *what is alcohol itself?*—for you will bear in mind that this ingredient is in all spirituous liquors [including wine, porter, ale, beer, cider, etc.] This *makes* them spirituous. And this alcohol is a *poison.* It is a poison produced by fermentation, *i.e.* a process of decay, or rottenness. Dr. Munroe, of England, says: "Alcohol is a powerful narcotic poison; and, if a large dose be taken, no antidote is known." And again he says: "A small quantity of pure alcohol, injected into the veins of an animal, has caused immediate death; showing alcohol to be a dangerous and deadly poison."

There is not a medical or chemical authority in the world that does not pronounce alcohol to be a poison, and one of the deadliest known.

But you say, "Are not poisons sometimes useful as medicines [which is granted], and may not *my* health be promoted by its use?" I have already shown that many learned and skilful physicians never use it, even as a medicine, and do *not* consider that under any circumstances it is necessary to health. But let me ask, *In what respect* are you benefited by strong drink in any form?

It does not give strength. If you are stronger for taking it, it is but excitation for the moment. You have *irritation*, not strength, and you consume to-day the capital for to-morrow—you run in debt to nature:

> "Prodigal of life, in one rash night
> You lavish more than might support three days."

You are strengthened just as the whip strengthens the horse. As if you would give your horse the spur that irritates for the corn that feeds!

Certainly there is no *food* in pure *alcohol;* no one pretends it. How much is there in the beverages supposed to build up the body and increase vitality? The following are some of the analyses, by chemists, of drinks in common use:

STRONG ALE.			PORT.		
	oz.	grs.		oz.	grs.
Water	18	0	Water	16	0
Alcohol	2	0	Alcohol	4	0
Sugar	2	136	Sugar	1	2
Acetic acid	0	57	Tartaric acid	0	80

MILD ALE.	oz.	gr.	BRANDY.	oz.	gr.
Water	18¾	0	Water	9½	0
Alcohol	1¼	0	Alcohol	10½	0
Sugar	0	280	Sugar	0	80
Acetic acid	0	38	Tartaric acid	0	120
PALE ALE.					
Water	18	0	GIN		
Alcohol	2	0	Water	16	0
Sugar	0	38	Alcohol	4	0
Acetic acid	0	40	Sugar	0½	0

This must be *very* nourishing!

There is more food in one bushel of barley than there is in 12,000 gallons of the best beer. So says Baron Von Liebig. He adds: "Beer, wine, spirits, etc., furnish no element *capable* of entering into the composition of blood, muscular fibre, or any part which is the seat of the vital principle." And Dr. T. K. Chambers, who is physician to the Prince of Wales, the heir-apparent to the throne of England—and therefore supposed to be the first-class physician, says, "It is clear that we must cease to regard alcohol as, in any sense, an aliment (a food), inasmuch as it goes out (of the body) as it goes in."

Dr. Lees says: "There is more real nourishment in a threepenny brown loaf than there is to be found in a barrel of Allsopp's ale, containing three hundred and sixty-five gallons, and costing $175!"

Liebig says: "We can prove, with mathematical certainty (as plain as two and two make four), that as much flour or meal as can lie on the point of a table-knife is more nutritious than nine quarts of the best Bavarian beer; that a man who is able daily to consume that amount of beer obtains from it, in a whole year, in the most favorable case, exactly the amount of nutritive constituents which is contained in a five-pound loaf of bread or in three pounds of flesh."

"It is a mistaken notion," says Dr. O'Sullivan, "that ale, wine, or spirits communicate strength, and it is disgraceful to see medical men endeavor to propagate the error."

Says Mr. Parton: "When we have taken from a glass of *wine* the ingredients known to be innutritious, there is scarcely anything left but a grain or two of sugar. Pure alcohol, though a product of highly nutritive substances, is a mere poison—an absolute poison—the mortal foe of life in every one of its forms, animal and vegetable. If, therefore, these beverages do us good, it is not by supplying the body with nourishment."

Possibly you are of the opinion that alcohol is a *heat-producing* fluid, and you use it for that. But this is a fallacy. Says Dr. Lees, "Alcohol cannot possibly yield a single unit of heat to the blood. Everybody must see that, as the coals and chips that *fall out* of the grate are not the fuel that actually boils the kettle, so a substance like alcohol, which is constantly *cast out* of the bodily furnace, cannot contribute to the warming of the living house."

Dr. E. Smith says: "The action of the *skin* is lessened. It neither warms nor sustains the body, [though] the *sensation* of warmth is increased. In other terms, alcohol burns the nerves, but casts a wet blanket over the vital fire."

A "drink," then, to keep off the cold, and the "warming of the stomach" which tipplers speak of, are pleasing delusions. Insensibility for the time being to external influence is all that is gained—not a particle of real warmth.

Dr. Rae, who made two or three pedestrian tours of the polar regions, and whose powers of endurance were put to as severe a test as man's ever were, is clear and emphatic upon this point. Brandy, he says, stimulates but for a few minutes, and greatly lessens a man's power to endure cold.

But you say, "I take a little stimulant *to help digestion.*" Then you are behind the day—you are not posted—for the popular fallacy you hold is now thoroughly exploded. Do you not *preserve* things, that is, keep them from dissolution, by alcohol, as when you preserve a piece of meat or an animal or a reptile in it? But the *digestion* of substances taken for food is the *dissolving* of them by means of the pepsin or gastric juice furnished in the stomach for that purpose. And how can a thing at the same time *prevent* and *promote* decomposition or dissolution; or, if you so call it, digestion? This is absurd, and the truth is, that stimulants *hinder* digestion. The stomachs of men dying after two days' steady drunkenness have been opened, and the food was found wholly undigested—*preserved*, as snakes are, in alcohol! Mix gastric juice into crushed meat, and it readily dissolves; put in beer or wine instead, and it dissolves but little; put in alcohol, and you *preserve* it! This tells the story.

If you say a glass of brandy or light wine gives *relief* after an excessive meal, I will tell you why: *not* because digestion is aided, but because the stomach is *narcotized* or *stupefied.* The nerves are deadened for the time, and, therefore, you do not feel pain. The same is true when a sense of hunger and exhaustion from want of food is relieved by a drink of spirits. In both cases, a few drops of laudanum or a small dose of morphine would produce a precisely similar effect; that is, narcotize the gastric nerves, so that oppressive cravings, or pain, is not felt.

In the words of Dr. McCulloch, then, "how mischievous is the drinking of alcoholic drinks, particularly during or after meals! How absurd the popular, and too often *medical,* delusion that they assist or promote digestion! And how atrocious the quackery of prescribing these drinks for such a purpose! So far from truth is all this, that Professors Todd and Bowman, in their great standard work on 'The Physiological Anatomy of Man,' declare that, 'were not these drinks rapidly absorbed from the stomach, it would be utterly impossible that digestion could go on in those who use them.'"

Even Mr. James Parton says: "With regard to this daily drinking of wine and whiskey, by ladies and others, for mere debility, it is a delusion. In such cases wine is, in the most literal sense of the word, a 'mocker.' It *seems* to nourish, but does not; it seems to warm, but does not; it seems to strengthen, but does not. It is an arrant cheat, and perpetuates the evils it is supposed to alleviate."

I know it will be said by some to all this, "But I *look* better, healthier, and am more fleshy for my wine, or beer, or whiskey." Ah! that may be the very thing that should alarm you. Do you know of a disease called 'fatty degeneracy'—solid muscle turning to fat? The blood and the walls of the heart get loaded with fat, and death is imminent. It is asserted by a high authority, that three-quarters of the chronic diseases in England, and a large proportion in America, are in some way combined with fatty degeneracy, and chiefly with those who use ardent spirits.

Settle it in the mind, then, that no spirituous liquors can be conducive to good health. They do not give strength; they do not add warmth to the blood; they do not assist digestion. The best trainers strictly forbid their use to those striving for the highest physical development; and the brute creation are healthy without them. As says Dr. Cummings: "In the *natural* world, the blackbird, thrush, canary, and nightingale drink nothing but water, and smoke nothing but fresh air. A grove or wood in spring echoes with feathered musicians, each a teetotaler, ever singing and never dry."

Preposterous is it to imagine that men will

thrive on what no other living thing can be made to touch!

> "Oh! madness to think use of strongest wines
> And strongest drink our chief support of health;
> When God, with these forbidden, made choice to rear
> His mighty champion strong above compare,
> Whose drink was only from the limpid brook."

I go further, now. *All alcoholic drinks are positively injurious.* Says Mr. Parton (whom I quote simply because he is not, technically so-called, a temperance man, and therefore with some his testimony may have more weight): "All that has yet been ascertained of the effects of alcohol by the dissection of the body favors the extreme position of the extreme teetotalers. A brain alcoholized the microscope proves to be a brain diseased. Blood which has absorbed alcohol is unhealthy blood—the microscope shows it. The liver, the heart, and other organs, which have been accustomed to absorb alcohol, all give testimony under the microscope which produces discomfort in the mind of one who likes a glass of wine, and hopes to be able to continue the enjoyment of it. The dissecting-knife and the microscope so far have nothing to say for us — nothing at all; they are dead against us."

Forty-five physicians of Cincinnati have stated as follows: " Ardent spirit is not only unnecessary, but absolutely injurious in a healthful state of the system. It produces many, and aggravates most, of the diseases to which the human frame is liable. It is equally poisonous with arsenic, operating sometimes more slowly, but with equal certainty."

"Time would fail me," says Dr. Sewell, "were I to attempt an account of half the pathology of drunkenness. Dyspepsia, jaundice, emaciation, corpulence, dropsy, ulcers, rheumatism, gout, tremors, palpitation, hysteria, epilepsy, palsy, lethargy, apoplexy, melancholy, madness, delirium tremens, and premature old age, compose but a small part of the catalogue of diseases produced by ardent spirit. Indeed, there is scarcely a morbid affection to which the human body is liable, that has not, in one way or another, been produced by it."

I know that some habitual drinkers live to old age, but it is because they have remarkable constitutions, and very often those who *seem* to be well are fearfully unsound. Were their bodies transparent, they would see the footprints of the enemy *inside* long before they are discovered outside.

And now, let not any one oppose against these stubborn facts of modern science the flimsy pleas for drinking which were urged in the days of the former ignorance which God winked at.

It hath been said by them of old time, we may use all "the good things of God." But investigation shows that alcohol is *not* a thing of God. The Creator never made it! It is not found in all the fields of nature. Sir Humphry Davy says of alcohol, "It has never been found ready formed in plants." Chaptal says: "Nature never forms spirituous liquors; she rots the grape upon the branch, but it is *art* which converts the juice into wine." And if God *had* made it, it were a "good thing" of his only in the sense that arsenic and other rank poisons are. Adders and lizzards are "good things" of God; but shall we *eat* them?

It hath been said by them of old time: "The Saviour made wine at the marriage at Cana, and used it at the institution of the Lord's Supper." But it never has been proved that the wine which Christ made was intoxicating, and never can be. It was "good wine," because it was pure and sweet, nutritious and harmless. Pliny expressly says that a "good wine was one that was destitute of spirits." It was the pure juice of the grape. And this was the character of that used at the Supper. It is a shame that any intoxicating wine is ever brought to the table of the Lord.

Again it hath been said by them of old time: "It is not the moderate use, but the *abuse* of a thing that is to be deprecated." But, as Dr. Alden says, "to a man in health there is no such thing as a temperate use of spirits. In any quantity they are an enemy to the human constitution." And besides, what *is* "moderate use"? How hard a thing to define! More yet, "moderate" use is almost certain to become immoderate. A slumbering appetite may be awakened; and you may go on from bad to worse. Well said old Augustine: "Drunkenness is a flattering devil, a sweet poison, a pleasant sin, which whosoever hath, hath not himself—which whosoever doth commit, committeth not a single sin, but becomes the centre and slave of all manner of sin."

What unnumbered millions, from simply saying, "A *little* will not hurt one," have come to ruin! The only safe course is total abstinence. More yet, your *temperate* drinking is the chief support of drunkenness. O "respectable" men and women!—and professed followers of Christ!—your brother's blood cries to you from the ground!

> "From east to west
> A groan of accusation pierces heaven.
> The wretched plead against you; multitudes,
> Countless and vehement, the sons of God
> Your brethren."

Granted that you can drink with safety to yourself, yet you *must* meet and answer this question: *Can you do it with safety to your neighbors?* You *know* you cannot! And I tell you there is an awful accountability incurred by those who by the manufacture, license, sale, or use of liquors keep alive the fiend INTEMPERANCE, filling this world and the next with woe, and

> "Fierce as ten furies—terrible as hell!

Let us be rid of such responsibility. I call upon *young men* to be *pledged* to temperance, and to aid in every way in advancing the cause. I call upon *professing Christians* to take high ground against that evil which leads to the fall of more ministers and church-members than all other causes combined. I call upon *physicians* (in the words of an honored member of that profession) "to put forth their utmost power to induce a healthier and happier relation between temperance and hygienic philosophy than now exists. Let them *speak out*, and first put down the quackery *within* their profession, and then they will find that they have more power to put down that which is *without*."

I call upon the *rich* and the *influential* to beware of the decanter on their tables and sideboards. It is a startling fact that nearly 2,000 of the applicants for admission to the Inebriate Asylum at Binghamton have been *rich men's daughters!*

I call upon *woman* to exert in this behalf her holy influence. O wives, mothers, sisters, forget not the misery of your sex from strong drink, and frown down this curse upon the home and the social circle.

And, finally, I call upon *every one* to forswear for ever all that intoxicates, and to help uplift everywhere the white banner of temperance, remembering that word of inspiration: "NOR THIEVES, NOR COVETOUS, NOR DRUNKARDS, NOR REVILERS, NOR EXTORTIONERS, SHALL INHERIT THE KINGDOM OF GOD."

SCIENTIFIC CERTAINTIES

(*NOT OPINIONS*)

ABOUT ALCOHOL.

"It biteth like a serpent, and stingeth like an adder."—Prov. xxiii. 32.

WHAT I know about alcohol by experience would make a very short chapter. It would be only one word. And that word would be *nothing*. A pledged abstainer from my boyhood, I have kept my pledge; through college; at those enormous feeds called public dinners; in the West, where the only use for water is to run steamboats; amid the solvents of all restraints in foreign lands, where many forget their morals, and remember that the land flows with wine and lager—amid it all, I have kept my pledge, and am not sorry. "Where ignorance is bliss, 'tis folly to be wise."

But we have other sources of information than experience, viz., observation and evidence of others. And what we learn by evidence, and thus accept by faith, is, to what we know by experience, as a thousand to one.

I propose to put science on this stand to-night,

and let it tell us something about the effect of alcoholic drinks upon the human body. I do not propose to speak of the unwordable horrors of delirium tremens, nor of the nauseous loathsomeness of drunkards, nor of the hopeless slavery of men who feel that there is a law of habit, reinforced by desire, in their members stronger than their power of will, imposing a servitude under which they groan and burn, but from which they cannot break. These men are not here to be benefited by the recital of their woes. They know them infinitely clearer than we can tell them. And if their sorrow could be put into words, it would be useless; for it is a well-established fact that very few of them can be permanently reformed. All men of experience in temperance reforms testify that an exceedingly small percentage of cases supposed to be reformed can be regarded as permanent. They have an unquenchable fire within them, and, cover it as you may, it breaks out with volcanic energy. There is no hope for man in the thickening meshes of this habit but in one of two things: the first is the converting grace of God, making him a new creature: the second is six feet of gravel.

Neither do I propose to speak of those abominable compounds of poison and filth that are perfectly solvent death insurance agencies. Nobody ever endorsed, much less drank them. None of us ever saw a man who drank any port wine that was not made in Oporto. Oh! no. He was confidentially assured of its genuineness by the highly respectable dealer, who was induced to part with his rare treasure, not for the man's money, but by his needs.

It was said in England, forty years ago, that the only way to get pure port wine was to go to Oporto yourself, raise the grapes, press the wine, put it into the cask yourself, and ride on it all the way home. But the age has grown so much in honesty, especially in reference to alcoholic beverages and the men who deal in them, that one can now have full assurance of the purity of wine, from the simple word of its respectable dealers.

The question we wish to consider is, what alcohol does in the living body—alcohol in any wine really from Oporto, or innocent of any grape; in any whiskey really from Bourbon County, or, having made a voyage to France and back, has "suffered a sea change into something rich and strange," and is called brandy—what this does in the living body.

If I were to call human witnesses upon the stand, and question them, I could get any number of opinions, endorsing any number or order of theories. There are plenty of advocates for the use of arsenic—men, and possibly women, who declare it to be essential to the highest civilization. Some take enough every day to kill several men unaccustomed to its use. But these are only individual opinions, and they are worth next to nothing.

Can we produce an unquestionable authority, measuring by a reliable standard, drawing conclusions no man can gainsay, uttering judgments that will be law, though one hundred men who feel the halter have no good opinion of it, declaring perfect truth, though a thousand men's experience declare the contrary? Yes, indeed. After one hundred men have guessed at the weight of a stone, according to their ignorance or wisdom, weakness or strength, put it on the scale, and silence every one of them. Never ask a man who has the shakes, or who has got out of them into fever, what is the temperature. Look at the thermometer. And when a man says of wine, "I like it, it does me good, could not get along without it," tell him what he thinks is of little consequence. What says the standard? "For there is a way that seemeth right unto a man, but the end thereof are the ways of death."

So we turn to Science, and ask her if she can give us a true answer. She says, Yes. I believe it. Science is accustomed to exactness. It measures to a ten-thousandth of an inch. Astronomical measurements are worthless that allow so much error. It measures to a millionth of a second. It detects a ten-millionth of a grain diffused through a dozen pounds. It can make solid silver float invisibly in a transparent fluid, yet its eye sees every atom of it, and gathers it to a solid again, no particle being lost. As easily can science see every particle of alcohol in a living body. It tells what the far-off stars are made of; much more what is right under its eye. Science is the realm of certainties, not opinions. Theories are not science. It is not a theory that water is composed of oxygen and hydrogen: it is a fact. And men hang their all and shape their conduct from these certainties, in defiance of opinion, their own or that of others. Science says, the world spins like a top, flies like a rifle-ball, and men believe it in defiance of every sense. It says water will explode by fire terrifically, and men believe it. The captain drives his ship at full speed in the blackest night and thickest fog, thousands of lives besides his own hanging on his act, because science told him at sunset that the land would not be reached before morning. And if he rushes on ruin, no man blames science, but that man's interpretation of it.

Now, if science can give us any certainties about the effect of alcohol on the living body, we will depend on them. If it says use it, we will use it, in spite of all temperance advocates, teetotal societies, dictates of fashion, and thunders of pulpit or press. If it says refrain, we will refrain, spite of the power of habit, the calls of a clamoring appetite, the interest of innkeepers, the demands of distillers, the necessities of political machinery, the quibbles of quacks, the delusions of those doctors who are willing to throw physic at us if we throw fees at them. Yes, in spite of the charms of Circe and the devices of the devil, we will refrain.

It makes no difference what our experience is. That experience is not long enough to make up a full account. Something may seem to stand to the credit of alcohol, but the debit side cannot be made up till we are underground. That is too late to be of any use to us. It may serve as a terrible example to others. But none of us wants to put all our sum total of possibilities into the terrible example business. We have better use for our capital. As was said before, there are plenty of men whose experience, in their estimation, tells in favor of the daily use of arsenic, opium, and absinthe. But we know that experience is not ended yet. And when it is, there will be a terrible balance on the wrong side of the ledger. They may be feasters at a royal banquet to-day: they will be swine to-morrow. No, neither your experience nor mine is the standard. Science is. And we now lift up the hand, and vow, God being our helper, to bring opinion, influence, and practice to the true standard.

Now, what certainties has science on this subject? King Alcohol, you have practised at your bar a great while: now stand up at the bar of Science, and be acquitted and welcomed, or convicted and banished, according to the evidence.

Science assures us that alcohol is never changed into any other compound in the living body. Hence it can never be food or fuel. It is never appropriated by any organ for its sustenance. It remains alcohol everywhere and always. It is alcohol when it goes in, while it stays, and when it comes out. The theory that it is in any sense food is distinctly disproved, and has been everywhere abandoned. The theory that it acts as "respiratory food"—proposed by Liebig as a mere theory, but never experimented upon by him, the theory defended by Governor Andrew for hire, long after it had been disproved has been abandoned. The theory of MM. Bouchardat, Sandras, and Duchek has been routed, horse, foot, and dragoons, by Buckeim's little army of facts. The simple truth remains, that alcohol is never appropriated to any use in a living organism. It goes in an enemy, it remains an enemy, it is cast out as an enemy, or, too strong, it conquers the citadel and destroys the life.

When a country is invaded, its commerce and varied industries must stop, that the invader may be cast out. When alcohol invades the kingdom of man, digestion, assimilation, and growth nearly or wholly stop, that the foe may be routed. Swallow a needle, and the system puts it out the nearest way; between the ribs, if it point that way; through the foot, the furthest way, if it point thither; but it puts it out. Swallow alcohol, and the system puts it out by every possible way to void it. The blood carries it to the lungs, and scents the surrounding air for hours with pure alcohol. It goes to the kidneys, and they throw it out. The whole skin exudes it. The whole man smells like a distillery. What cannot be immediately thrown off is deposited in liver and brain, the blood actually refusing to carry it when a place of deposit can be found. Pure alcohol that will burn can be collected from liver and brain. If more alcohol is forced upon a system than can be expelled, it puts the system into a state of inflammability, that only requires to be ignited to be consumed.

Neither can it be urged that it is only the excess, over and beyond what the system can assimilate, that is thus thrown off, as in the case of food. Not a particle is assimilated, because it cannot be found in stomach, blood, breath, urine, perspiration, liver, or brain, in any changed condition: it is alcohol always. If it is only the excess that is thrown off, we ask what an appropriate amount might be; for a single ounce of brandy will set a man exuding alcohol from every excretory organ in half an hour. An ordinary bottle of weak, French wine will keep the lungs at work eight, and the kidneys fourteen, hours to void the excess. Of course it is impossible to collect and measure every atom thus discharged, but the amount actually collected has so nearly equalled the amount drank as to justify the conclusion that no particle was appropriated to permanent use.

If, then, men will insist on paying from five cents a glass to fifteen dollars a bottle for compounds to pour on the ground and into the air, it becomes important to inquire whether he had better make a filter of his body through which to do it.

The fact, that two and a half ounces of alcohol injected into the stomach of a dog will kill him about as quick as a rifle-ball, and a pint of its dilution, called rum, has about the same effect on a man, adds interest to the investigation.

We now invoke science, that seems to have an almost omniscient eye tracing matter through all its protean changes, through solids, liquids, gases, visible and invisible, ponderable and imponderable, to tell us what alcohol does in the living body. It responds, first, negatively. It has no power to digest food. Put a pound of raw beef into alcohol for twelve hours, and it loses four ounces of water, but the beef is simply hardened, and no approximation made toward digestion. So well known is this fact, that fishes and snakes are put into alcohol to preserve them indefinitely from decay. A cask of snakes, toads, etc., was forwarded, a few years ago, from Oregon to the Smithsonian Institute at Washington. On the way, the sailors, who were very fond of grog and not very delicate about its previous associations, drew off the liquor and drank it. A deceased English admiral was once returned home in a cask of spirits. On the way, the sailors were constantly drunk. The utmost vigilance of the officers failed to discover their source of supplies. At length, one of the tipsy sailors let out the secret by saying, "We have tapped the Admiral." Do not shudder at that; for, if the published receipts of liquor manufacturers have any truth, such liquors are clean, compared with that which is set before men and women in the homes of elegance to-day.

Now, who supposes that the fluid which would prevent snakes and men from digestion in the cask would digest food in men?

Neither does alcohol ever assist digestion by causing a greater flow of gastric juice, or by any other means. You have all heard of St. Martin, the man with an extra hole in his stomach, and of Dr. Beaumont, who peered in through this hole upon some of the most secret operations of the inner man. It was then seen that even the small amount of alcohol in a glass of beer retarded digestion. The flow of gastric juice was arrested, and the organ sought to protect itself against the liquid fire by exuding an enlarged supply of mucus as a sheathing. He saw the stomach give immediate evidence of inflammation on the introduction of spirit. It flushed fiery red like the tell-tale face of an angry man. Possibly the stomach was vehemently angry at such treatment. He says, after drinking hard every day for eight or ten days, the stomach would show alarming appearances of disease, and yet the man would only feel a slight headache, and a general dulness and languor. Were the stomach as able to report its condition as the inflamed eye, few men could endure many glasses of spirit. But feeling is no guide.

These observations of his have been signally confirmed by posthumous examinations. We herewith present representations of the stomach in health and in disease.

The opening in the first shows the inside with a delicate peach bloom, like the cheek of beauty and health. The second shows a section of the same inside surface, after moderate drinking.

DIAGRAMS OF THE STOMACH IN VARIOUS CONDITIONS.

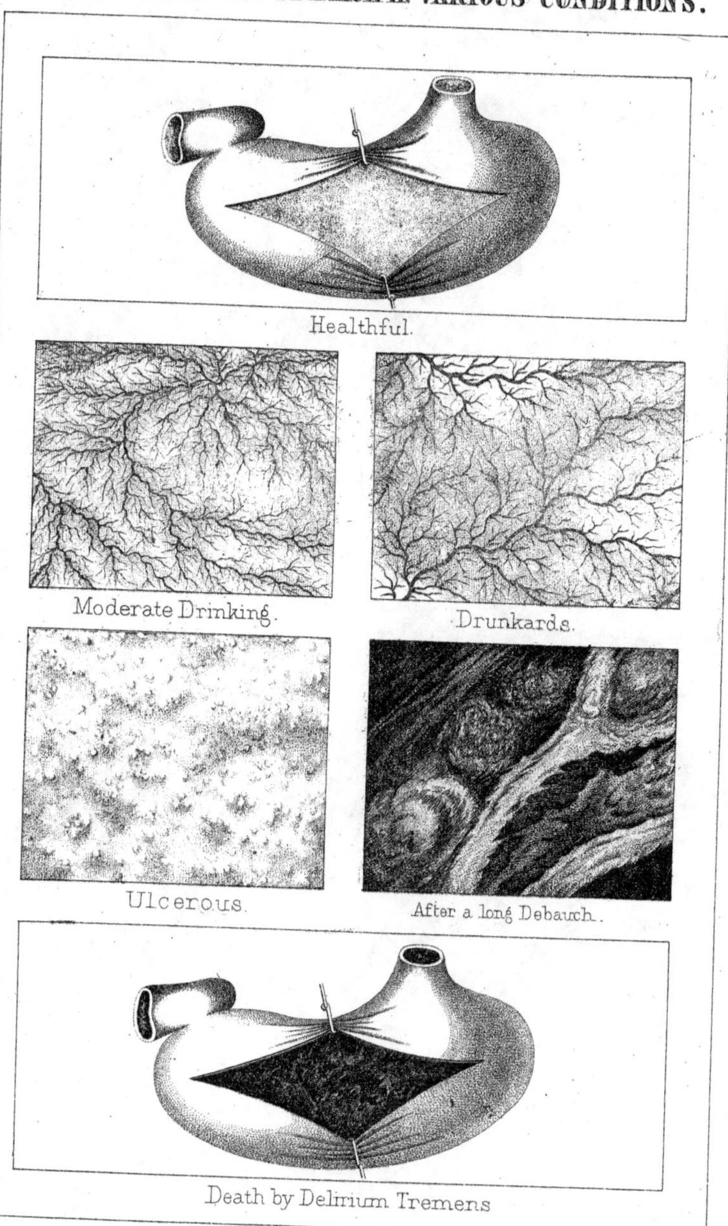

Eng.d on Stone by A. Tolle.

Every vein is inflamed and injected with blood like a blood-shot eye. The third shows the greater inflammation of the drunkard, with deadened blue spots of incipient ulcer. In the fourth we observe the veins have been covered with ulcerous exudation. The fifth shows a surface torn, as it were, by violence, and partially repaired by vital energy. It looks like the volcano-rent surface of the moon, or the cicatrices of half-healed wounds. The sixth has the blackness and putrefaction of death before death comes. "An enemy hath done this." Who could expect efficient work from an organ thus abused? Not only can it not freely yield gastric juice, but the least degree of alcohol mixed with gastric juice diminishes its digestive power. Some dogs have made themselves valuable by laying down their lives in the cause of science One was killed some hours after taking five ounces of meat and one and one-fourth ounces of proof spirit. The meat had not begun to digest. Dr. Figg found that the process of digestion had not commenced twenty-four hours after the reception of food in people who had kept themselves drunk during that time. It is impossible to nourish the body till this enemy is cast out.

Neither is alcoholic drink a source of strength. Trainers of men for feats of strength invariably forbid all kinds of ale, beer, porter, wine, rum, brandy. They cast out the whole legion of devils at once. Dr. Brinton says, "A moderate dose of beer or wine would, in most cases, at once diminish the weight which a healthy man could lift below his teetotal standard." Milo, the Samson of Italy, and his forerunner, the Samson of Judea, were both total abstainers. This is small comfort for weak backs and weak heads that try to strengthen themselves with bitters, cordials, and wines. The only use for them is when one has too much strength and can find no possible use for it. Then alcohol may be safely recommended to reduce it with rapidity truly astonishing.

Neither is alcohol a producer of heat. I might quote volumes of testimony from experience in Canadian and Russian winters, from travellers on Arctic and Antarctic ice, to show that alcohol is death to men exposed to a temperature ranging toward 100° below zero. But that would be experience, and we are not willing to take anything that has a shade of uncertainty about it just yet. We have too huge a pledge pending to take any body's experience or opinion. What is *fact?* Here comes Science, thermometer in hand, and she shows that alcohol actually reduces the temperature of a body receiving it. That is what we wanted to know. And now we *know* it. If we were receiving testimony and not mathematical certainties, we would produce the testimony of Sir Charles Napier, and a host of surgeons in the East Indian army, that alcohol is equally death for men who have to face the heat of a tropical sun. But since we are not willing to introduce anything that any man can gainsay or pretend to contradict, we will return to our certainties.

Let any constant abstainer draw off a little of his blood, and microscopically compare it with the blood of the recent drinker, and he will be confirmed in his abstinence. The one is full of bright, round, electric disks of life. The other has bedraggled fibres, pale in color, shapeless in form, deprived of power to absorb oxygen and eliminate carbon—a devitalized condition of the life-giving fluid that must result in a devitalized condition of the tissues it feeds. The pipes that supply the city with water are no longer filled with bright, sparkling water from the sky-kissing hills, but a turgid stream from the dye-houses, distilleries, slaughteries, and the sewers of the cities above us is offered to our lips.

Another certainty. Lallemand and Perrin proved that a small dose of alcohol would cause globules of fat, clearly distinguishable by the naked eye, to float in the blood. The result is another clear change in the constitution of this vital fluid. This fat is deposited instead of real muscle, producing what is called fatty degeneration. Take your microscope again, and examine a very fine section of a temperate man's muscle. It is firm, elastic, of bright-red color, in parallel fibres, with beautiful crossings. That muscle means business, and is able to do it. Now, take a similar section of a man who indulges in intoxicating drinks, and you see at once a pale, inelastic, flabby, oily aspect. Fat has displaced fibre. This especially takes place in the involuntary muscles, such as the heart and those concerned in breathing. After such degeneration, it is not strange that the heart should stop its work mid-beat and never act again. It requires no excitement, no sudden shock, for that mass of fat, that ought to be muscle, to cease responding to nervous influence, and so cease working. It may be in the street, in quiet conversation, and especially in sleep, this man, a picture of health, suddenly dies, and men say, "What a mysterious dispensation of Providence!" We had better say, "What a dispensation of—the other one!" Or better still, "What an inevitable result of taking intoxicating drinks!"

Let us continue our consideration of certainties. By actual measurement, it is found that alcohol has twice the tendency to the brain that it has to any other organ. You can tell the brain of the drinker the instant you put knife to it. Alcohol and alcoholic induration are found in different parts of the brain in different individuals. Now, a brain is divided into—1. A *cerebrum*, by which man perceives, remembers, judges, wills, and dictates movements; 2. A *sensorium*, which takes note of all impressions on organs of sense; 3. The *cerebellum*, which regulates and equilibriates locomotion. And, 4. The *medulla oblongata*, which directs and excites respiration. Now, man shows incapacity from the lowest degree up to absolute stupefaction, according as one or more parts of the brain are congested and incapacitated

by the deadly agent. Some are clear-headed, when an affected cerebellum refuses power to walk; some have an unconquerable desire to burn houses, steal, or murder, according to the organ affected. Indeed, "mental acuteness, accuracy of perception, and delicacy of senses are so far opposed by the action of alcohol, that the maximum efforts of each are incompatible with the ingestion of any moderate quantity of fermented liquid." Which is Dr. Brinton's elaborate English for, You can do nothing nice when drunk, even in the least degree, and you are terribly liable to commit murder, arson, robbery, libel, etc., which are far from nice.

Again, a proper dose of alcohol brings instant death by its action on the nerves. That is a certainty. You can try it, but never will try it but once. Now, smaller doses have a proportional effect on the nerves. If you only want to tremble with palsy—to feel every nerve a line of fire, take only wine cordial. If you want to "see more devils than vast hell can hold," try something stronger, and oftener. It will come, and may last for ever.

I here close my certainties about alcohol. I allow no man to dispute one of them, They are all sure as a two-foot rule, ponderable as pig-iron, inevitable as the tax collector. We make no allowance for varieties of constitution, peculiarities of temperament, diversity of habit, differences of alcoholic concomitants. These conclusions are sure as fate, viz.: Alcohol never digests food, nor helps digest it; never assists the body to permanently resist cold; brings no increase of strength; vitiates the blood; emasculates the muscles; indurates the brain; harms the nerves; never acts as food, either alimentary or respiratory, but is always and everywhere a poison, in sickness, and in health, and the vital powers try their utmost to throw it off, even to the extent of perishing in the attempt. Now, these are facts, not opinions; certainties, not deductions. No man can gainsay them. Neither are there any counter-facts.

Do you ask me if there is no room for alcohol as a medicine? That is quite beyond my ability to answer. Every imaginable thing has been crammed down human throats under the delusive idea that it is medicine. I have a receipt for "A famous spirit made out of human skulls," warranted to cure every ill that flesh is heir to. But the inventor of it died two hundred years ago. And we have all known of famous spirit that has been distilled into human skulls that proved a panacea for every good that flesh is heir to. Since there are no *certainties* about the possible usefulness of acohol as a medicine, we will examine the most recent *opinions* of doctors. The most trustworthy of them have given up its usefulness, except in two instances.

It seems to be proved, by the history of the Parker family in Massachusetts, that a tendency to pulmonary consumption is checked by keeping a man always intemperate, and often drunk. I presume that would be the case. He would be preserved in spirit. Alcohol is confessedly an "arrester of metamorphosis." But my opinion is, that the man had better get ready and die. I should prefer it for myself and for my friends.

The other instance is that of a man who has had an intermittent fever. The disease is spent. The vital forces will go down to zero at six o'clock, and the man die; but if he escape dying at six o'clock, his vital force would be two above zero at seven o'clock. In that case, alcohol, as a stimulant, may be given at six o'clock, thus borrowing one from the vital force at seven o'clock, and so escape utter bankruptcy of life by heavily discounting the future. Well, perhaps we might, but it is only an opinion, and no certainty after all.

What we especially desire you to observe here is, that, from calling spirit "the water of life," one hundred years has proved it to be the fire of death, and physicians confess it in all but these two instances. If we will be content to wait till such an exigency arises, few of us will know the power that biteth like a serpent and stingeth like an adder.

Having thus admitted a brace of opinions, allow me to come down from things mathematical, sure, and minutely measurable, and introduce a single deduction on the other side, which has, nevertheless, all the force of a demonstration. That drinkers of all grades are a terribly vitiated lot of humanity is seen in the sureness with which contagious diseases smite them down. "Four-fifths of those who were swept away by the dreadful visitation of the cholera, in 1832, were addicted to intoxicating drinks." Drunkards and tipplers were searched out with such unerring certainty as to show that the arrows of death were not indiscriminately flung. In St. Petersburg and Moscow, the whole population ceased to drink spirit, so sure were they that they drank death. Out of 1,200 attacked in Montreal, not a drunkard recovered. Out of a thousand deaths, only two were members of a temperance society. And at that time every temperate person was a member. Of 30,000 victims in Paris, nearly every one was a user of intoxicating liquors. Nine-tenths of those who died in Poland were of the same class. In some towns every drunkard was swept away. Monsieur Huber saw 2,160 persons perish in twenty-five days in a town in Russia. He says: "Persons given to drinking were swept away like flies." In Tiflis, containing 20,000 inhabitants, every drunkard fell. Dr. Sewall stated that, of 204 cases of cholera in the Park Hospital, New York, there were only six temperate persons, and they recovered. Out of 366 who died in Albany, 326 were habitual drinkers, while of those who drank no spirit whatever there were only seven. If you want to be insured against the cholera, you can find plenty of offices that will do it, not societies to pay you something after you have died of it, but to insure you against having it. You will find these offices anywhere they give you a chance to sign the pledge. And if you want to be insured to die of it, there are plenty of offices glad to do it. And they will insure you, if you don't want to die of it, if you go there. You will find the office easily. There is one in any liquor-store. It makes little difference whether it be Bedford Street or Chestnut Street, the insurance is about the same.

Having thus considered the indisputable certainties about alcohol (not including the last two items), it is time to determine our future line of conduct, for consideration is vain without determination. Surely, knowing that alcohol is evil, only evil, and that continually, what shall we do about it? Why, for every one who has seen these certainties, there are but two things possible. First, banish the wine-cup, dash it away at once and for ever. And that is just what you and I now do, my friends. And let *all* the people say amen. The only other way is to say, "I confess the certain injury, but I like the rare exhilaration, and mean to indulge in it." Very well. That is your matter—and God's. Say then frankly, not "I take it for my health, or for my brain"—if your brain had not a felt deficiency, you never would want it; but say, "I take it for the fine exhilaration, for the ecstatic thrill of nerve, for the airy fancies that troop the brain, for the winged lightness that could let me walk on flowers, for the sense of kingliness that takes the place of carking care." Then say, "For this, I'm willing to take what follows: the real pain that succeeds champagne, headache, nausea, induration of brain, trembling of nerve, weakening of muscle, vitiation of tissues, gloomy thoughts for my airy fancies, unutterable loathing of self for my fancied kingliness of a moment, black horrors, delirium, and—hell, if I go too far."

But there are some of you who are not influenced by these certainties. You would not believe the multiplication-table if it were now presented as a new thing, and it went against you interests and tastes. You insist on putting your experience against the fact of the earth's revolution. What can be done for you? Not much. Nevertheless something. Weigh probabilities fairly. Never incline the beam with the weight of your own inclination. And if you really conclude that alcoholic drinks are best for you, do not conclude that they are best for everybody else. While you insist on the usurped rights of rum, take care that you are not trampling on the rights of men. Rum has long asserted that one insults a man to refuse his invitation to drink. Let us remember that the one invited has a right to decline. An officer of the crown of England once sent me a glass of wine, at a public dinner. I acknowledged the gift, and never touched it. While explaining my course to him afterward, I could see that I had risen one hundred per cent. in his estimation. If I had not seen it, he would have sunk two hundred per cent. in mine.

A member of this church called upon some government officials with the expectation of making large contracts for goods. They immediately invited him to drink. He declined. They insisted with oaths that he must drink. Then he *refused.* Thereupon one of the half-drunken fools tried to force him, declaring that he would buy no goods of him if he did not drink. Then said the other, "You buy no goods of me," and walked away. The next morning, the fiery madness having been slept off, the officers made most unexpectedly large contracts, because they had found, to their surprise, a man true as steel, a man that could be trusted.

It is claimed to be a breach of politeness not to partake of the punch on the side-board of your host. It is a contempt of his providence, an insinuation against his good taste. Not so. A host always provides a scraper outside the door. But it is no breach of politeness, when I come clean-footed from the carriage, that I do not stop and rasp for five minutes on that scraper. I do not need it, nor his punch-bowl either. Guests have rights as well as hosts, and, if hosts will drink, let them never tempt the guest whom hospitality binds them to protect.

We have had a subtle influence of death in our midst the past winter. It has spread its dark wing over our city, and men feared as they passed under the cloud. This awful influence has penetrated all sorts of homes. Satin damask curtains can no more keep it out than the broken windows of poverty. It climbs up high marble steps, as well as pours down the passages of underground dens.

There is another subtle influence of death in our midst all the time. It puts more in the grave every year, in our city, than the plague referred to. It penetrates the palace as well as the hovel. It takes daughters and wives as well as husbands and sons. It leaves a darker shade of sorrow, and a worse inheritance for children. It is death, but that is a small part of its horror. It is sad to mourn a dead friend, but tenfold worse to mourn a living friend. And yet it spreads and spreads. New graves are opened for its victims every day. New homes are invaded with its foul breath and blasted every day. And—O amazement beyond words!—we have eight thousand shops in this city devoted to this deadly plague's perpetuation and spread.

MY NAME IS LEGION.

"He said unto him, Come out of the man, thou unclean spirit. And he asked him, What is thy name? And he answered, saying, My name is Legion: for we are many."—ST. MARK v. 8, 9.

IT is announced to us, by divine authority, that "for this purpose the Son of God was manifested that he might destroy the works of the devil." For the accomplishment of this result, not only was his own personal ministry designed, but also the ministry of his Gospel, and the maintenance of his church and people through all the ages of their history upon the earth.

The Saviour's purpose is to break up the whole dominion of Satan over the souls of men, and to annihilate his power, however exercised, and by whatever instruments maintained. He illustrated this purpose, and his power to accomplish it, in many instances of his personal ministry. The incident here before us is but a single instance of this beneficent design and action. This illustrates the subject which I have in hand, and gives an encouraging view of the Saviour's power and the Christian's duty.

The case presented to us here was an unusual demonstration of fierceness and power in the evil spirit, and of melancholy suffering in the poor victim of his rage. It is said of the latter that "he had been often bound with fetters and chains, and the chains had been plucked asunder by him, and the fetters broken in pieces. Neither could any man tame him. And always, night and day, he was in the mountains and in the tombs, crying out, and cutting himself with stones." A legion of devils had taken possession of him; and they exercised their malice and their strength for his destruction.

Jesus met this wretched victim of Satan, and his gracious salutation of authority sounded instantly for his relief—"Come out of the man, thou unclean spirit." "And he that was possessed with the devil, and had the legion, was found sitting, and clothed, and in his right mind."

This was the stand of Jesus. This was his relation to the works of the devil, and to the miseries of men suffering under his power. May we not see in it, the duty of his servants and disciples, and the relations in which they should be arrayed, in reference to similar spirits of evil which are oppressing and enslaving the souls of men? May we not here learn the responsibility and obligation of the Christian Church, in regard to those who are destroying the earth?

Surely they are not to participate in the works of the devil. They are not to make their gains by trafficking on his side in human suffering and blood. They are not to cover up, conceal, excuse, apologize for, the cruelty of his dominion over men corrupted and enslaved by his power. Still less can they be permitted to offer themselves and their children as victims upon his altar.

They are bound by every relation in which they stand to the Lord whom they profess to serve, to set themselves against every evil work, both in abstinence from its temptations, and in hostility to all its attempts. They are willingly arrayed on the side of the Captain of their salvation, as pledged to the utmost extent of their influence, to break down and destroy, all the instruments and means by which this enemy to man prevails for the destruction of mankind.

To trace out this destructive dominion of Satan in all its branches, in a discourse like this, would be impossible. There is, however, one grand agency of his for evil and ruin to man which may well be called LEGION. All the miseries and madness of human life are seen flowing from it and produced by it. There is no shape of suffering or sorrow for man which it does not habitually create. This mighty power of destruction is seen ruling in the land in which we dwell, and dragging down to a dark and hopeless grave, more victims perishing in their guilt, than all other agencies of evil combined.

This is the EVIL SPIRIT OF INTEMPERANCE—the Moloch of our age and nation.

The character and influence of this spirit of evil I would attempt to display in some of the *results of his work*, some of the *abodes of his labor*, and some of the *victims on whom he preys*. The view is so extensive that it will be impossible to do more than to recount some of the conceded facts of its immense exterior. The fearful catalogue of personal details of individual and domestic sorrows it would be beyond our power to enumerate.

I. Consider some of the RESULTS of this evil work.

Behold the establishments in our land for the shelter of absolute pauperism, containing more than 300,000 persons supported at the public expense as an inevitable burden. Remember that at least one-half of this vast number of paupers have been driven there as the direct victims of intemperance. Then realize that you cannot compute the wandering poverty in this nation, at less than a similar amount, or varying from a similar division; and you have as the result, in this land of intelligence and self-government, 300,000 persons reduced to absolute beggary, and in most cases to hopeless beggary, and laid as an immovable charge, and burden, and tax, upon the industrious and temperate remainder of this people by this legion of destruction.

Go look at more than 20,000 lunatics as they appear before you, either sheltered by private kindness, or confined by self-defending cruelty, or wandering in sorrow, and learn that more than one-half of these have lost the reason with which they were endowed by a gracious Creator, under the tyranny of this demoniac oppression.

Go examine more than 30,000 criminals confined

in your public prisons, under various sentences of guilt and violence against their fellow-men, and hear that more than 25,000 of these prisoners of public justice have been directly brought there by this cruel demon of intemperance.

Go hear 95 out of every 100 wretched beings who are convicted and sentenced under charges of capital crime, acknowledge for themselves, in the despair of their condition, that they have been stained with blood because they had first been stupefied with rum.

Go calculate, if you can, the amount of taxes and pecuniary burdens which have been brought upon the community who are peaceably and soberly laboring for their own and for the public welfare, by all this array of violence, of poverty and crime. Not less than fifty millions of dollars are annually expended in the direct payment for the poison which has produced this work of ruin. More than thrice that sum is annually paid to guard the community from the effects produced by this direct expenditure for the gratification of crime; to remedy the evils which it has produced, and to shelter the wretched beings who have been ruined by it.

Remember that all this immense sum has been paid, and all these enormous burdens have been borne, by the toil, the labor, and the self-denial of the sober and industrious remainder of our population.

In this limited calculation, which every serious investigating mind will acknowledge comes far within the truth, every laboring, temperate father of a family is compelled, by direct and indirect taxation upon his toil and self-denial, to support at least one other family rendered vagrant, idle, impotent, and hopeless, by this fearful traffic in RUM.

Thus does this demon of intemperance grind down honesty to pay for crime; make labor in the upright become the slave of guilty idleness in the corrupt; and compel the prudent and faithful servant of God and friend of man, to bear a tax for the support of the victims of his rage and power; a tax which eats into the heart and consumes the very vitals of honorable and industrious effort, for those whom God hath committed to its rightful charge.

Yet again, go look at the results of this power of destruction upon the immediate victims of this cruelty. There are more than five hundred thousand—it may be more than one million—of drunkards in these United States. Of these at least thirty thousand in every year go down to the darkness, gloom, and eternal despair of a drunkard's grave. An average of more than three in every hour pass from time into eternity, with all this load of hopeless guilt, to meet a God whom they have despised and a judgment which they have defied. Within the single hour of one meeting for the public worship of God, the open grave has received three immortal victims of this demon of intemperance. Since this century began, more than two millions of drunkards in this land of boasted liberty and refinement have been driven by this enemy of man down this dark abyss.

All of these were once the objects of human tenderness and love. They were bedewed by a mother's tears of joy, and bathed with a mother's kisses of affection. They were a father's hope, and the anticipated props of a father's age and weakness. Life to them opened as sweetly, promised as fairly, and was looked upon as eagerly as for any others of their race. Their youthful blood was as fresh, their infant blush as innocent, and their appetites as docile, as others around them.

They have been driven away before this demon of intemperance, since these eyes of ours have seen the light, from the very soil which we inhabit —if there be truth in God—to a hopeless and dark eternity. Could you see this vast multitude of wretched beings, separated from the residue of the community, congregated together in some great common field of blood and sorrow, what a spectacle of horror would they present! But could you see them individualized and separate, dispersed among their friends and kindred, each united in his vileness by ties tender and indissoluble to other beings—often to beings of the purest virtue, of the liveliest sensibility, and of the loftiest hopes—what gauge could measure the extent, what arithmetic could sum up the amount, of the misery comprehended within your field of vision?

Could you number the concealed tears which have flowed from so many sleepless eyes, as God, in his watchfulness, numbers them; could you hear those stifled sighs which escape from such sorrow-wounded hearts, as God hears them, could you bring into your view the despairing anguish of their own eternity, as the wages of their sin are measured out to them, you might then, but not till then, estimate something of this one portion, of the fearful amount of evil which this demon of intemperance has accomplished for mankind.

But you must return from the grave where you have left these victims of a hopeless sorrow, and sit down with broken-hearted widows, whose life of sadness, almost worn out by the violence, and exhausted by the waste of the living drunkards, has been rendered finally incurably wretched, by the despair which has settled upon their ignominious graves. You must look upon the orphans whose poor hearts have been so early taught to fear the cruelty of those whom they were made to love, and who must now struggle with a load of want and anguish which has been bound upon them by the very hands formed for their support. You must look upon parental hopes all blighted, upon family honor stained and gone, in the furrowed aspect of fathers whose hearts have been broken in their age by the very ones who were given to them to hold up their declining steps and to cheer their feeble, sinking years; and of mothers whose tenderness, never dying, cannot repress the secret cry, "What, my son! What, the son of my womb! What, the son of my vows! Would to God I had died for thee, my son, my son!"

You must multiply these Bochims, these valleys of weeping, sometimes by this whole number of buried drunkards. You must go further: you must go look at the youthful female victims of unholy lust—daughters who were once as innocent and as free from guile as the purest of their sex, and who have been sacrificed in that horrible immolation which buries them in oblivion, and darkness, and unchanging sorrow, ere yet the youthful period has been exchanged for the full years of maturity.

You must multiply these wretched victims, as we have thus considered them, to an extent of which I dare not speak. My soul sickens at the thought. My weary heart turns off with shuddering from the view. You must go forward and stand with all these at the judgment-seat of the living God, where the whole tale of secret wickedness shall be told, and the whole recompense of its varied iniquity shall be brought out to public gaze and to open light.

You must look into the horrors of the second death, where the enemy and his victims are bound together in everlasting despair, and God is known in his consuming holiness as taking vengeance on the ungodly, and in destroying those who have destroyed the earth. All these fearful results must be considered before you can fully estimate the results which have been accomplished by this demon of intemperance, whose name is Legion, even within the limited space of earth included in your own country, and the short period of your single generation.

You must then consider the world in its extent and its history, and the conclusion will be forced upon you, as with the thunder of overwhelming truth, that all other agencies and instruments of Satan combined, WAR, PESTILENCE, FAMINE, and DISEASE, have not more effectively cut off the life of man, and crowded the dark chambers of eternal woe, than this single demon of intemperance, the spirit which may well adopt this comprehensive title, "MY NAME IS LEGION."

II. We will proceed to consider some of the ABODES of his labor, the residences which this evil spirit has chosen upon the earth, in which to establish the operations of his power, and the machinery by which he labors to destroy mankind. In this view, you may begin at the bottom of the scale, but you cannot stop there. If you ask him, "Legion, where dwellest thou?" he will answer you, "Come and see."

He will lead you to those low and filthy haunts, in your vilest quarters, where beggary and vice are entwined together; where the most depraved and brutish of their species mete out the destructive drug to haggard want and tattered wickedness, for the poor price which has been snatched by theft, or for the last remnant of the recompense of stinted labor, plucked from the mouths of children famishing for bread and starving in the cold;

while this infernal demon sits in the bosom of the guilty seller, and scornfully laughs over a traffic in which both the appetite of the buyer and the gain of the seller are equally dedicated to him and directed by his will—and says, "See where I dwell!"

He will take you to his higher courts, in your gilded bar-rooms, and your lofty and fashionable hotels, where men are willing to pay extravagantly for the pedigree of his craft, and give of their substance in proportion to an imaginary excellence and rareness of his provision; where he has so calculated his dealings with his agents and his victims, that he makes the often enormous rent of his glittering habitation arise from the clear profit of the crime which he has thus taught.

An infidel philosopher once said: "Vice, deprived of its grossness, loses half of its guilt." So this spirit has taught in these higher halls of his display. Here he contrives to combine every possible element which may make this trade of soul-killing which he teaches, in the highest degree attractive and effectual. There you see the demon again at home, amidst the glitter of reflecting plate and the glare of many-colored glass; and rearing hundreds of souls deluded and destroyed, for his own abode; compelling many strong men to bow down beneath his power and to wear his livery and his yoke for ever.

Between the objects seen in these two visits with this spirit of evil, in the mere elements of adornment, the apparent difference is great.

Is there any real difference in the guilt, the crime, the ruin, which mark them and attend upon them? Do all these vast contrasts in the furniture and vessels which are severally employed, establish any unlikeness in the work to which they are devoted? Perhaps! But not in the line proposed. If there be any grade in the degree of guilt, beyond all question, its highest is there where the larger quantity of the poison is dispensed, and where the nobler selections of the human family, doomed and drugged, are betrayed and destroyed.

There would be but little difference of judgment among good men upon this point. The immediate personal retailing of this poison for man's destruction, is acknowledged to be guilt. One individual man reaches it to another, and is instantly connected with the effect which it produces. There is no intermediate agent to divide the responsibility. There is no concealment of the deed effected. He has a single victim before him, and he plunges his pointed weapon into the open breast of the victim whom he destroys. And whether it be a jewelled sword, a silver-mounted stiletto, or a rusty butcher's knife, there is no moral difference to be discovered there.

The trade is altogether everywhere a trade of blood. Its effects are written in blood. Its gains corrode in blood. And there is a voice in this blood which reaches to the skies. And there is *there* an Ear that listens to every wailing which that voice lifts up. And there is a day coming when all these accusations and groans shall be brought out as they are recorded; and God shall judge, not by gains alleged, nor by excuses made, nor by palliations imagined, but in infinite holiness and with unerring justice, the guilt of those who have filled the earth with sorrow, with crime, and woe.

But will Legion stop with these contrasted homes when making the tour of his dwellings? Are these retailing-shops his only abodes among men? Nay, he dwells far more respectably and gainfully than there. If there were not other agents, the trade of these servants would soon conclude. If there were elsewhere no living flowing fountains, these shallow ponds would soon dry up. And there can be no difference in the moral responsibility and obligation of stages beyond these, except the absolute and undeniable principle, that as you increase the quantity, and of consequence the projected results of the evil distributed, you advance the responsibility and the guilt of its distribution.

Will you tell me that the man who shoots a single man with a pistol, that he may strip him for gain, is a murderer; but that the man who discharges a cannon loaded with grape-shot into the midst of a multitude assembled, that he may reap the spoils of many by a single act, is not so?

Will you tell me that the man is justly punished who is found clothed with the garments and the watch of the lonely traveller whom he has enticed to a secret death; but that another, whose gains from the multitude of deaths inflicted by him have been so great that he is obliged to build new houses to contain the spoils which he has gathered from his slain thousands, is innocent?

Legion laughs at the folly of your reasoning. He sees that you could in no way more completely edify and sustain the kingdom of ruin for man, which he is laboring to exalt. No; he will take you where the man, elevated in human computation, has treasured this flood of death in unlimited quantities, has ripened it for years, and parts with nothing but the largest measures at the highest prices; where the smothered conscience, or the sensibility to remark, has lifted the poison out of sight to the very attic of his immense warehouse, or buried it deep in cellared vaults beneath; and the man himself, ostrichlike, has hidden his own eyes beneath the veil, and imagines himself unseen and safe; and will say, "Here have I a home, guarded and unassailable by feeble man."

He will take you where the merchant welcomes with joy the safe arrival of his ship-loads of these instruments of death; or where the manufacturer has invested his millions of wealth, and has famished the bread of thousands in the products of his still. And though he enables the agents of his employ to ride in charioted splendor, or to dwell in palaces which Moorish pride might envy, he will claim the work as all his own. The demon has domesticated himself completely in these extensive haunts of gain. Like the spirit of the storm, he nestles among these original fountains of the flow of death, and declares, with a pride which cannot be rebuked, that his home is there.

Far rather would he that you should nail the doors, and oust the inhabitants of the flaunting taverns along your streets, than shut up one of these great repositories of his instruments of warfare upon the souls of men. The more respectable he can make the trade, the more he can screen his agents from reproach and arrest, the more really and effectually he accomplishes his ends, of destruction to many, and of apparent triumph over the goodness and power of God.

But does this spirit of intemperance even here limit his abodes with men? Legion will lead you further than this. He has respected, guarded, and attractive nurseries for his victims, as well as highly honored agents in his employ. He will go with you to the luxurious tables; to the social entertainments of your highest ranks of society; to the peaceful private abode of many a family circle, dwelling in the wealth and cultivation of earth; where the sweetened poisons of every description, wines of every age and name, are richly gathered and freely and habitually used; where the father puts the bottle to the mouth of the son, and the mother sees, without aversion or reproof, her blooming daughter enticed to taste the poisoned cup; where family habits and the inheritance of age and station have dignified and consecrated the moderate use, as it is called, of these instruments of death.

Here this destructive spirit loves to dwell. These are like the distant, quiet, sylvan shades of the land he rules—a peaceful, flowery, attractive abode, where he gathers the treasures which he robs without suspicion; where he plucks the lambs for his sacrifices, far distant from the altar on which he means finally to consume them. Could he be driven from these deceitful haunts, his work would stop and his power would end. These armies of moderate drinkers are his reserved corps, to be thrust forward in their turn, as the reeling platoons in the distant van of his unfailing hosts fall and perish in death.

Who can see the wine-cup circulated, and youth enticed to contract a taste perfectly unnatural to the human constitution, but fixed and certain in its process when it has taken possession of its victim—a taste which presses on to his ruin with a certainty which a divine power alone can arrest—who can see this without a secret shuddering at the sight, from the perfect consciousness of feeling and conviction of certainty that LEGION is establishing his dwelling and his ruling there?

It is pitiable to hear him deride the victims of his deception for their weakness, and laugh in scornful triumph, over the victory which he has obtained, when they have been persuaded, themselves to defend the very tyranny by which he is holding them in an oppressive subjection, and leading them onward to a final despair. Nor can all the anacreontic songs of human giddiness and degradation, nor all the perverted influence of past generations, too inconsiderate upon this solemn subject, nor all the flimsy attempts to drag the reason of man, and even the Word of the living God to their defence to sanctify these destructive temptations, blind us to their results.

Whereunto will these things grow? These are LEGION'S choice abodes. You will never drive him from the dark holes and hovels which we have just considered until you force him to leave these earlier honored walks. Banish the wine-bottles from your tables, as the chosen refreshment for your friends, and resolve to meet your children and your fellow-men in judgment, without the opportunity for a single perishing drunkard to say, that your example and your invitations first started him on the road to eternal death.

III. From these two wide and comprehensive views we will proceed to recount some of the VICTIMS of the demon's power. And here you must take a far earlier view of this course of certain ruin than the agents or patrons of the evil will readily concede.

You cannot, must not, confine yourselves to a view of the carcasses of these slain, when in the final beggary of hopeless drunkenness they are cast out from men, loathsome, despised, and perishing. A field of battle, when the fight has passed, and blood, and brains, and mutilated limbs are scattered in confusion round, is an awful, shocking sight. None can walk there and see the hundreds of healthful, youthful forms, pallid in death, torn by dogs, the food of vultures, without a fainting of his heart within him, in remembrance of the men who lie before him. But how many more hearts bleed than those which have beat their last pulse on this field of woe! What anguish is elsewhere felt, far distant from this fearful scene! What lifelong anguish will be felt by multitudes who will never actually behold it—by hearts which were bound to these sons, and husbands, and fathers, by the sweetest ties of earthly life!

But if war has slain its thousands, intemperance has slain its tens of thousands. And where is the father who would not prefer to see his son shot down before his face, than to behold him poisoned to a degrading death by these foul harpies whom LEGION has employed?

And who are the men whose fate has thus been sealed in hopeless ruin?

They are young. They were seized and bound while young. Hardly one in hundreds has passed the maturity of his earthly days. Did they begin as purposed, willing drunkards? Nothing was further from their thoughts or their desires. They have waded out most gradually, almost imperceptibly, into the deep. They then looked down upon the inebriate sot with sorrow and contempt, as others now look down upon them. They started with the drop which their fathers gave them, or with the offered glass of friendship, at noon or night, when they lacked the courage to refuse. The demon seized them when they were sheltered, as they thought, far from his abodes, and led them on, his purpose fixed, though yet unknown to them, for their final ruin.

Where did this work of ruin begin? Do not tell me at the tavern or in haunts like that. What gave to pure and innocent youth that taste for taverns? Where did they get the appetite which sought its objects and its pleasures there? You will be compelled to look back far beyond this final limit, and to feel and to acknowledge the responsibility often coming far nearer home. The moderate drinker is but an indentured apprentice to the drunkard. A gracious divine Providence may cripple his ability in his youth, and he may not thoroughly learn his trade. But the habitual glass, however apparently refined, signs his indenture. And no one who starts in the imitation of the craft, or who leads another, to take a single step in its clearly marked line, has power to define the limits of the course.

These victims of ruin are often, I might perhaps justly say are habitually, selected from the most promising, generous, social, and affectionate of our young men. Genius, education, family, profession, friends, furnish no abiding obstacle or sure defence. When the degrading appetite has been formed and whetted, it bursts through all these bonds. The noblest and most cherished sons of our best connections are here cast out to perish with the vilest and the basest of mankind.

No one who has mingled long and intelligently with men, especially with young men preparing for active life, can be ignorant of this fact. Our colleges are living records of the frequency of this destruction. Our congregated business establishments in large cities present an enormous catalogue of victims.

The venerable Dr. Nott said: "A friend of mine once gave me the number and the names of a social club of temperate drinkers, which existed in the city of my residence, and of which, when young, he was himself a member. And I have since remarked how, bereft of fortune, of reputation, of health, and sometimes even of reason, they have descended, one after another, prematurely to the grave, until at length, though not an old man, that friend alone remains, of all their number, to tell how he himself was rescued from a fate so terrible, by the timely and prophetic counsel of a pious mother. And I have remarked also, how those pupils of my own, who, in despite of warning, admonition, and entreaty, have persisted in the use of intoxicating liquors while at college, have, on entering the world, sunk into obscurity, and finally disappeared, from among their rival actors, once their companions, rising into life. And, when searching out the cause, I have, full of anxiety, enquired after one, and another, and another, the same answer has been returned—"He has become a sot"; or, "Gone a sot into the grave."

Such testimony as this could be corroborated

by a thousand similar recitals. Such death-beds, where genius has been sacrificed, professional character thrown away, and early virtue trodden down, by this demon of evil, have been heard in groans of anguish, and in curses of the most fearful character, upon the early tempters to the ruin, and upon the early indulgence in the temptation, as the source of all the misery produced. Such scenes as these might be summoned in vast numbers to testify that this agent of destruction spares no station, and has bound his victims with cords which are rarely broken, when the habit of drinking has once been formed, or the confirmed desire for the poison has been acquired.

God grant that we may never live to see our sons and daughters, so precious in our sight, cast out to perish under the destroying power of this Legion demon! But if we would avoid this terrible sorrow, let us avoid all connection with the habit or the trade. Let us remember that he plucks the lambs from the flock at home, and selects the victims for his holocausts when they and theirs least expect his approach. I can but say earnestly to those who hear me: "If you will save the souls of your children from the destruction, or yourselves from all participation in the ruin, banish the 'accursed thing' from your habitations; lock up the tempting bottles from their sight; and neither have, nor use, nor offer upon your tables, this unnecessary inducement to vice, this direct provision for impoverishment of the health, poison to the bodies, and destruction of the souls, of yourselves, and your children, and your friends."

We have thus taken a survey of some of the *results*, some of the *abodes*, and some of the *victims* of this Legion spirit of evil. Allow me now to ask, what is the duty of the servants of Jesus Christ, our Lord, in reference to this awful system of destruction for man? When this gracious Saviour met the legion that had taken possession of the poor victim of his tormenting power, his instant attitude was opposition; his immediate language was rebuke; his command, clothed with resistless power, was, " Come out of the man, thou unclean spirit."

Jesus did not participate with him, unite with him, apologize for him, compromise with him. He would " have no fellowship with the unfruitful works of darkness." What, then, should be the stand of his ministers and servants now? We can give no other answer, with a clear conscience, than just the stand which the Lord himself assumed: have no connection with the demon of intemperance in any shape, but to oppose, to resist, to rebuke him.

Would that gracious Lord, were he now upon the earth with us, unite in making or drinking that fiery liquor which his own Word had declared to be "a mocker," against which he had solemnly warned the children of men when it displayed "its color in the cup"; to the effect and operation of which he had assigned " vomiting," " filthiness," "redness of eyes," "woes," "babblings," and "wounds without cause"?

How awful is such a thought! Would he partake with men of this world in draughts like these? Could he walk among the perishing thousands of our people who have been degraded and slain by strong drink, and give the sanction of his example to the pleasurable use of this instrument of death? Would he furnish the shelter of his name and his authority to this fearful trafficking in human blood and the souls of men? Let us not be deceived. The followers of Jesus must take another stand than this.

Their own character and influence on earth demand an entire separation from the traffic in intoxicating liquors, and a total abstinence from their use. The Christian minister or the Christian professor in uniting with either cuts off immediately, and justly, his influence for good among men, and takes upon himself a responsibility which he will find it hard indeed to bear.

There is so much knowledge upon this subject, and so much suffering has been endured in connection with it, that no man can now plead the excuses, or the ignorance of former days. The effects of the drinking of intoxicating liquors are known to be only evil, and immediately evil. No man is ignorant of this. The man who aids the circulation of these poisons well knows that the streams which he sends forth can only operate in their measure and degree to destroy mankind. A venerable Chancellor of the State of New York said years ago; "The time will come when men will as soon be found engaged in poisoning their neighbors' wells as in making or vending intoxicating liquors to be used as a beverage in health."

I would appeal to all who read what I have written: Separate yourselves from this whole system of sin and human misery. Banish the temptation from your families. Wash your hands from all the gains of the traffic. Give your unchanging countenance and aid to the efforts which are made to arrest the power of this ruin, and to rescue the victims of its dominion. Then the remembrance of the stand which you have taken will awaken no sorrows, no misgivings, in the retrospections of your coming hours. The thought that you leave behind you an example and a witness, a family trained to temperance, and encouraged and pledged by the whole weight of your own influence in the line of a total abstinence from strong drink, will plant no thorn in the pillow of sickness and add no pang to the trials of your departure.

There is no stopping-place in this path of intemperance but this—TOTAL ABSTINENCE. The movement in the indulgence once commenced is ever onward and downward. The thirst created is quenchless. The appetite produced is insatiable. You may not be permitted to complete the whole process; but never forget that it is an unceasing, accelerating progress. Your own safety is in withholding yourself entirely from its power

Your usefulness is in setting yourself unflinchingly against it.

If this LEGION DEMON must rage and will rage, let him never be permitted to charge you with the degrading, responsible fact of your willing countenance, or your cowardly silence or indifference.

THE

CHRISTIAN SERVING HIS GENERATION.

"David, after he had served his own generation by the will of God, fell on sleep."—ACTS xii.. 36.

THE great stream of human history, as it flows down through the ages, is fed by the tributaries of individual lives, which differ in character in each particular case. Some rise almost at the very margin of the river into which they run, and, after a short course, lose themselves in its waters. Others flow on with even and gentle current, through banks of rich fertility and luxuriant beauty, and at length emerge into the common stream, in a vale of peace and loveliness, like the sweet "Avoca" of which the poet sings; while others still, rising far up on the mountain heights, come tearing down through the valleys, breaking themselves continually into foam as they leap from rock to rock, and at last, all panting and out of breath, as if in haste to run their course, rush into the general current. And some there are which in their one career pass through many of these different phases. Away up in some mountain moorland they begin their course in lonely grandeur; then, coming down into the plain beneath, they are broken by many a fall, seething like a caldron as they roll over rough and rocky beds, and between rugged and precipitous banks;

thence they come out into some broad and level table-land, where they rest themselves awhile in calm and quiet flow; but out of this again they rush, and anew they tumble, and toss, and are broken, until at length, just before they join the great primeval river, they resume their placid current, and at the meeting of the waters there is no sound of strife, but, instead, a quiet hush of melody which sings of peace.

Of this last kind was the life-course of that illustrious man of whom mention is made in my text—the inspired poet-king of Israel, David. Its opening hours were spent in the pleasant solitude of shepherd life; and who among us has not often had before his eye a vision of that fair-haired boy, of ruddy countenance, waking with his reed the echoes on the slopes of Bethlehem, or singing as he passed on before his flock and led them to the quiet water's edge, "The Lord is my shepherd, I shall not want"? Then the scene is changed, and we find him at the court, seeking to "minister to the mind diseased" of Saul, and calming, for the time, his troubled soul with the soft strains of skilful music. Again the curtain rises, and this time we behold him in the midst of Elah's valley, with a bannered host on either side, and before him the giant Philistine, taunting him with his youth, and boasting that he would give his flesh to the fowls of the air: there he stands, the youthful hero, clad in the unseen panoply of God, and, with a pebble from his shepherd's sling, he fells his haughty adversary to the dust. Next time the scene is in the cave of dark Adullam, whither he has fled through fear of Saul; fierce, cruel, and unprincipled men surround him, and they have made him their captain; yet, in the midst of all their revelry and riot, behold him sitting by the dim light of their watch-fire, inditing one of those divine odes which the church even yet delights to sing. And now a new act of this great life-drama begins, and the scene opens in a royal palace; there are corridors and passages glancing with cedar wood, and there, in the foreground, are companies of warriors, telling each of the martial prowess of their lord—when lo! the door of an inner chamber opens, and we behold the king himself, with the book of the law unrolled before him, and, as he rises reverently to lay it past, we hear him say in the rapt fervor of devotion: "Oh, how love I thy law! it is my study all the day." But a darker change comes over the palace; a man of God is seen before the king; he tells a simple story, drawn from that shepherd life in which the royal heart is yet so deeply interested—a story which unfolds a wrong of the deepest and most wanton kind; and when, with righteous indignation moved, the king pronounces a most terrible sentence, the stern prophet answers: "Thou art the man." In a moment the fountains of that great heart are broken up—the monarch falls upon his knees, and with a cry of penitence, which has come sobbing down through the centuries to us, he says, "Have mercy upon me, O God; have mercy upon me." But now again the scene is changed. He has fled before an unnatural and rebellious son, and stands at Mahanaim's gate; his faithful friends insist on fighting in his cause, but they will not have him exposed to the dangers of the field; and as rank after rank passes on before him to the deadly strife, he says, "Deal gently, for my sake, with the young man"; but ere that day departs, we see him in the chamber over the gate, pacing the floor with agony, and crying in grief of the wildest kind, "O my son Absalom, my son, my son Absalom! would God I had died for thee, O Absalom, my son, my son!" And now, "last scene of all," we behold him lying on his death-bed, and having placed the crown upon the head of Solomon, and given him a solemn charge, he takes once more the harp he loved so well, and tunes it to this touching strain: "Although my house be not so with God, yet he hath made with me an everlasting covenant, ordered in all things, and sure; this is all my salvation and all my desire;" and so he fell asleep, and was gathered unto his fathers.

Such are the main features of that life which is so briefly summarized in the words of my text: "David served his own generation." It is not, however, my intention to dwell further upon the incidents of the Psalmist's history, but rather to fix your minds for a little on the principle which underlies this description of his career, and on its particular application to the great cause which I mean to-night to advocate. It will be evident at a glance that there is here established a connection between a man and his generation, such that the nature of the duties which he is called on to perform is determined by the character of the age to which he belongs, and the circumstances in which his lot is cast. It may indeed be said that the age in which a man lives has fully as much influence upon him as he can have upon it, and in a sense that is true; but it is also true that the character of a man's times fixes, to a very large extent, the form of that service which he is required to render unto his God, so that thus the service of God, and the service of our generation, rightly understood, must be for us identical. The moral law, indeed, in its great essential principles of love to God and love to our neighbor, continues unalterable, but the modes which our obedience to that law assumes must be settled by the circumstances in which we are placed. The priest, the Levite, and the Samaritan, had they been brought together into conclave, might all have agreed as to the abstract meaning of the command, "Thou shalt love thy neighbor as thyself"; but for the Samaritan, the fact that the poor traveller lay before him half-dead, interpreted the law to mean, "Help that suffering one as you would wish to be helped if you were in his place," whereas to them it seemed to say, "Pass by on the other side." He read the law through the circumstances in which he was placed; they read it abstractly, and without any reference to the case before them. He served God by serving the unfortunate man; they were neither serving him nor serving God. Duty thus comes to be the application of the unchanging principles of the Gospel to the ever-varying circumstances of society; hence, it can never be stereotyped, but must be altered in its outward form, ever as the changing character of the time requires. Thus, it is always the Christian's duty to "hold fast that which is good," and "earnestly to contend for the faith once delivered to the saints"; but in the case of an Athanasius, that duty meant to defend the doctrine of the Trinity; while in the days of Luther, it signified to hold up the doctrine of justification by faith. Both of these men held the same great gospel truths, but the circumstances of their times called upon each especially to hold fast that with which the name of each has become identified. Now, the same thing holds in regard to efforts for the moral and spiritual well-being of mankind. It is always the Christian's duty "to do good unto all men," and to seek "to have compassion on the ignorant, and them that are out of the way"; but the particular form which his performance of that duty assumes must, of course, depend on the circumstances of those whose good is especially sought. The path I take in going after him who is out of the way must, in the very nature of things, be regulated by that which the poor wanderer himself has chosen, otherwise I may as well not trouble myself about him. I must go *after* him, if I would overtake him; but if I take another direction altogether, there is no likelihood that I shall ever benefit him. Hence, if I really mean to carry out the principles of the Gospel at all, it is incumbent upon me, not only to understand what they are, but also to consider what are the special evils of my generation, and by what special application of these principles I am to meet them. Even as, in perfect consistency with the general principles of medical science, the remedy is changed to meet the disease; so our efforts of practical benevolence, if they would be of any avail, must take their shape and direction from the evils that are rampant in the land. The traditional things of the past, therefore, will not avail for the exigencies of the present; the kind of instrumentality which was called into existence by the evils of a hundred years ago, will be utterly useless in meeting those of to-day; and things which might then be safely enough left undone, may now be, yea, are, imperatively demanded of us. Here, then, is the problem which we have each to solve, if we would really serve the present age; we must ask, "What interpretation is given to God's law by the requirements of our time?" What does the "Go-thou-and-do-likewise" of our Lord to the lawyer mean now for me? Where shall I find for myself in these days the counterpart of that poor half-dead traveller? and what for me corresponds to the oil and the wine and the money which his benefactor gave? Where shall I find him? I discover him in that little ragged Arab prowling about the streets of the midnight city, his hand against every man's, and every man's hand against him—a waif of humanity floating all uncared-for down the dark river of iniquity; and I open for him a ragged school. I discover him in that down-trodden sister standing at the corner of the streets, with the mark of infamy on her brow, and the scorpion-sting of misery at her heart, an outcast from society, an object of loathing even to herself, compelled to sin for bread: I open for her a home of safety, and go forth at night to bid her come and welcome to its comfort. I discover him in the tenant of that filthy room, the air of which, poisoned by noxious impurity, is eating out the strength of his manhood, and sinking him at once into physical and spiritual degradation; and I seek to raise for him a more comfortable and better ventilated abode. I discover him in that poor besotted drunkard in his cheerless home—if home it can be called—whence peace, and happiness, and love have long ago departed. I discover him in that drunkard's wife, whose pale, careworn face declares how the canker-worm of sorrow is eating at the heart, and bringing her down with sadness to the grave. I discover him in that drunkard's child for whose poor diseased and sickly body the grave is already opening wide; and I become a total abstainer, and gird myself to do battle with the causes which have produced such dire results.

In this service of our generation, however, where there are so many evils to contend against, it is expedient that there should be division of labor. Accordingly, as temperance reformers, the special department which we have chosen is that of dealing with drunkenness and its causes;

but, while this is the case, we must not be understood as disparaging or in any way underrating the importance of those other spheres in which our excellent friends are working. Whatever be the particular object for which they are striving—whether it be sanitary reform, or the building of a better class of houses for the working-classes, or ragged-schools, or midnight meetings for the reclamation of the fallen, or the promotion of a better system of holidays and recreation, or the bringing about of more thorough understanding between employers and employed, or the improvement of our commercial morality, we regard them as fellow-workers with us, and ourselves as fellow-laborers with them. We are working to each other's hands; their success will strengthen us, and our success will strengthen them. We have selected intemperance simply because it so constantly confronts us, and because we find it allied to all the other evils of our time; but, far from being jealous of their movements, we wish them all success, and bid them cordially God-speed. With this explanation, then, I proceed to show how we seek, as temperance reformers, to serve our generation and our God.

I. We seek to do so, in the first place, by reclaiming the drunkard. It will not be disputed by any Christian that we should endeavor to save the drunkard; nor will it be denied that there is an urgent call upon us to use all the means in our power for this purpose, from the immense number of those who are addicted to intemperance. The only question is as to how to do it. Now, there are here a few plain principles which have always been very satisfactory to my mind, and seem to settle the case. Abstinence is for the drunkard a physical necessity, if, at least, he would conquer his habit. For his habit is an appetite as well, having this peculiarity, that the least quantity of ardent spirits taken by him will act as a spark on gunpowder, and set the whole man on fire with the desire for more. Hence, if I wish to deliver him, I must endeavor to get him never to touch strong drink. But before I can prevail on him to be an abstainer, I must make his position, as such, an honorable one. He will never assume it if his doing so be cast up to him as a disgrace. He will rather die in his intemperance than become an abstainer to be pointed at by the drunkard and the moderate drinker alike, and to hear it said regarding him: "That man had to give up tasting strong drink to save himself from drunkenness." As Lieutenant Blackmore discovered that the poor fallen woman, much as she loathed her degradation, loathed still more the prison system that prevailed in the penitentiaries, and preferred to die in her sin rather than to be saved in such a way, so have we found it to be with the drunkard. If we mean to save him, therefore, we must stand on the same platform with him. Just as the Son of God, when he wished to save men, stooped himself to be a man, yet without the sin of man, so—I speak it in all reverence—we, if we mean to deliver the drunkard, must stoop to put ourselves on a level with him, while yet we are not partakers in his sin. We must make abstinence respectable by ourselves joining with him in his abstinence. We must do *with* him what we ask him to do for himself. The old temperance societies of thirty years ago failed because the drinks they permitted fed the appetite they wished to destroy. But, in like manner, the moderate drinker of our day will also fail to cure the drunkard by asking him to abstain, if he do not so far identify himself with him as to abstain along with him. Somewhere about thirteen years ago, the Sailors' Home, one of the noblest institutions in Liverpool, was discovered to be on fire. It was past midnight; all the inmates had retired to rest, and were startled out of their slumber by the terrible alarm. The flames spread rapidly throughout the building, and from every door and window volumes of smoke streamed forth, so that, when the fire-brigade appeared upon the scene, it was at once apparent that nothing could be done to save it, and the whole energies of the force were directed to the rescuing of those who were as yet within it. A dense crowd of onlookers had already gathered round, and many stout-hearted men came forth and volunteered their services in the perilous enterprise. A company of marines landed from a man-of-war at anchor in the Sloyne, and gave themselves right earnestly to the same noble work, until at length ninety-seven souls had been snatched by them from the jaws of death, and it seemed as if the whole were saved. And now men breathed freely as they looked upon the gorgeous spectacle of that massive building wreathed in fire; but hark! a piercing shriek is heard high over the shouts of the multitude; and yonder, on one of the upper ledges of the building, five men are seen calling for help. As soon as possible, the longest ladder on the spot is placed against the wall, right underneath where they are standing; but, alas! it reaches only to a point some twenty feet below the parapet whereon they are. An agony of disappointment wrings the heart of every onlooker as hope for their deliverance is sinking fast into despair. "Stand back," cries a resolute and courageous man, as, with another ladder on his shoulder, he places his foot upon the lowest round, and prepares with it to ascend to their relief. On him now all eyes are fixed. They watch him until he has reached the top of the long ladder, and there he joins to it the one which he has borne with him. But, ah! how bitter the disappointment again! it also is too short. What now is to be done? There is no time to lose; so, taking the ladder up, he raises it until it rests upon his shoulders, and there, at the height of well-nigh fifty feet from the ground, standing on the one ladder, and *adding his own length to the other* which he carried, he calls to them to come down over him. The multitude beneath hold their breath in astonishment, afraid to utter a sound, lest they should mar the self-possession of the men; but when, one after another, they have descended in safety, the air is rent with a most deafening cheer which makes the welkin ring. Thus, brethren, thus must we save the drunkard from the devouring fire—the ladder even of abstinence will be too short unless we *add ourselves to it*, and make over ourselves a pathway for him into safety.

II. But, in the second place, we seek, as temperance reformers, to serve our own generation by endeavoring to do away with the drinking customs of society. No one can deny that the drunkard's appetite is at once created and strengthened by practices that are still, to a large extent, common and fashionable in the land. It is not quite by accident, therefore, that there are so many annually ruined by intemperance among us: it occurs as the natural and inevitable consequence of customs to which the great majority do willingly conform. When we examine into those dreadful catastrophes which are perpetually occurring in the midst of us, and which we write down to the account of strong drink, we find that they are connected with an undercurrent in society, and that they are but the outgrowth and development of a system of things which is upheld and encouraged by all classes alike. At the critical turning-places of life, we meet these drinking customs as invariably as in our large towns we see a gin-shop at the. corners of the streets; and though a young man enter upon the world untainted with the drunkard's appetite, he is gradually habituated to the use of strong drink by the very frequency with which it forces itself upon him. It dogs him from his cradle to his grave; it haunts him at home and abroad; it presides in the workshop and in the market-place; business cannot be transacted without it; pleasure cannot be enjoyed without it; wherever he goes, the bottle is the central object of attraction, and so he becomes enamored of it before he dare confess it to himself; he is on the outermost edge of the whirlpool before he is aware, and once there—

> "Vain! vain is his struggle, the circle now wins him,
> Round and round in its dance the mad element spins him."

Do I speak what is not true, my brethren, in all this? I ask every one of you to look back, for a few moments, to the beginning of his own career. Think of those who lived with you, long ago, in the same street of your native town; of those who played with you in the games of your childhood; of those who sat with you on the same form at school; of those who wrought with you in the same workshop, studied with you in the same class, or entered with you on the same profession. Trace out their after-history as far as you are able; how many of them have fallen before this dreadful drink—and how did they fall? Not from any inherent liking for it at first—not from any want of intellectual ability—not from any original deficiency in moral training—but because they were caught in the meshes of these abominable customs, and ensnared before they knew they were in danger. Who has not known even ministers of the Gospel, who, in the outset of their labors, gave high promise of usefulness and success, but were ruined by nothing else than conforming to the drinking customs of their congregations, and at length thrown off, as worthless and dissipated wretches, by the very individuals who had helped to make them so? To attempt, therefore, to put a stop to drunkenness without dealing with these customs is very much like trying to cure the disease by simply treating the symptoms, while nothing is done to reach the seat of the evil. When a man is all covered with blotches and blains, his physician does not simply try to close up these by external applications, for as soon as one disappears another forms; but he finds that the whole system is deranged, and sets himself principally and especially to put that right, well knowing that the healing of the ulcers must follow as a thing of course. Now, the drunkenness of our times is just analogous to such ulcerations on the human body; it betokens that the entire system of society is diseased; and, if we mean to do any good to our generation, it is to that we must strenuously apply ourselves. And how are we to do it? Personal abstinence may accomplish much; and we will not undervalue it, for we know that wherever one such abstainer appears at a dinner-table or in company, the drinking proceeds slowly; the wheels of the bottle drag heavily; there is a non-conductor at the feast, and the glory of it forthwith departs. It is something thus to put the moderate drinker on the defensive, and force him to apologize for his position, but still, mere individual abstinence will not here suffice; we must bind ourselves to have neither part nor lot in the matter; we must give no countenance whatever to these pernicious practices, and publicly declare that we will neither give nor take strong drink as an ordinary beverage. This is the position abstainers have taken up, and, as it seems to me, it is the only one which can enable us to say that we, at least, are no longer responsible for the intemperance of the country. In this way alone shall we be able to elevate the moral tone of the community, and cure that diseased state of the social system out of which intemperance has sprung. And surely, in a land whose fields have run red with the blood of those who laid themselves on the altar for the cause of liberty, there can be no valid objection raised against the bond of this our covenant, for slavery was not more detrimental to the interests of the nation than intemperance is to its moral and spiritual well-being. But why need we argue this point? Have not the effects already produced by the temperance movement clearly proved that, in this department of our labors, we have taken the proper course? Let any one contrast the public sentiment, in the matter of these customs, in these days, with the views which were held and acted on thirty, or forty, or fifty years ago, and he will at once discover how much progress we have made. It may be said, indeed, that all this is due to a higher tone of religion existing in the midst of us, and I admit it; but then, I contend that this higher spirituality has taken shape and form in the action of our temperance societies, and that through them, mainly, its influence has been exerted. Now, in all this there is certainly much to encourage us; but "there remaineth yet very much land to be possessed." God, by this partial success, is only showing us that we are working in the right direction, and by the right instrumentality; therefore let us work on. Time was when the work had to be done in the face of the bitterest opposition, the most biting sarcasm, and the most withering scorn; but now that we have silenced all these batteries, shall we think of giving over, and resting on our guns? Nay, verily, let us not slacken our exertions until these practices shall be numbered among the things that are obsolete and effete, and the bottle and the glass shall be labelled, and laid by on the shelves of our museums, as the relics of a bygone age. We may not, perhaps, live to see this time, but "it's coming yet for all that," and ours shall be the satisfaction of having done our part to hasten its approach; if we may not, like Solomon, build the temple of temperance, 'tis ours, like David, to fight the battles by which are to be obtained the materials for its construction.

III. But, thirdly, we seek, as temperance reformers, to serve our generation by dealing with the traffic in strong drink. The traffic and the customs are closely interlinked. They act and react upon each other—the customs feed the traffic, and the traffic perpetuates and increases the customs; hence it would be useless to attempt to do away with the one without dealing with the other. And it is in this department of our labors that we have the greatest difficulty to contend with, for here we have the law of the land coming in and giving its sanction and protection to the dealers in strong drink. The readers of John Bunyan's "Pilgrim's Progress" will remember the scene in the house of Interpreter, where Christian is shown a fire which continues to burn brightly in spite of the efforts of an individual to extinguish it by constantly pouring water into it; and, when he can give no account of this apparent anomaly, he is taken to the other side of the wall, where he beholds another man perpetually supplying it with oil. That scene has a sacred significance in the experience of the Christian; but, ah me! it has its counterpart, too, in the devil's edition of his pilgrim's progress. Behold it here! policemen, magistrates, judges in their several departments, and temperance reformers, by their special efforts are all seeking to throw water on the devouring fire of intemperance which is burning constantly in the land, but all seems to be in vain. Why? Because, when we look on the other side, we discover licensing bureaus pouring in oil to perpetuate the flame. Was there ever a more palpable instance of building up with the one hand what we are seeking to pull down by the other—of undoing by one act what is sought to be accomplished by another? One can have some admiration for Penelope, as we see her sytematically unweaving by night the web which she has woven in the day, for it was her constancy to her absent lord that prompted it; but when men's temporal and eternal interests are at stake, and when we see individuals in authority making thus a plaything of the souls of men, it is impossible for us to restrain our indignation, or to forbear asking the question: "Shall the throne of iniquity have fellowship with us, which frameth mischief by a law?" How long, then, is this state of things to continue? So long, and only so long, as the people of the land permit it. Let us rouse them, therefore, from their indifference; let us endeavor, by every means in our power, to awaken them to a right idea of their duty in the matter, and stir them up to demand a general law which shall make it illegal to traffic in the souls of men by dealing in strong drink. This, and nothing short of this, is the aim we have set before us. This is the "Sabbath and port of our labors," and till this be accomplished we are determined not to slacken our efforts, nor "to bate a jot of heart and hope, but still bear up, and steer right onward." Each point we gain shall become a battery, from which we shall assault another outwork; and thus, by ever-narrowing parallels, we shall press in and in, until we breach the very citadel of drinkdom, and plant upon it the standard of our victory. We seek no easy and superficial success; we have learned to labor, but we have also learned to wait; we are content to make haste slowly, if only we may thereby keep what we have gained; we do not want a victory which shall be worse than a defeat. And when those who will not work with us act the part of Sanballat, and mockingly say, "What do these feeble Jews—will they make an end in a day?" we make reply with Nehemiah: "We are doing a great work, and we cannot come down; why should the work cease while we leave it and come down to you?"

But in prosecuting this arduous work, we are met with many objectors. "You cannot make men moral by legislation," says one. "We can at least insist that they shall not be made immoral by it," we reply; and so, as far as that goes, we are on an equality. "But the law will be broken," say others, "and you will have shebeens and low drinking-places without end." "Not at all," we say, "provided the law rest upon and rise out of the convictions of the people, and do not go before them. Let the people be thoroughly in earnest in the matter, and then we shall see the law thoroughly enforced. But even if it should be disobeyed, what then? Is God to repeal the Seventh Commandment because there are so many houses of bad fame among us? Or are our legislators to relax the vigor of our criminal law because there are so many dens of thieves in the land? Away with all these subterfuges! If you were but in earnest, you would brush them from your path as easily as you do the gossamer of the morning. "But," exclaims another, "it is an interference with trade, and it is cruel to the publican." Now, while we hate the traffic, it by no means follows that we hate the men, and I honestly believe we shall be doing them a deed of loving-kindness by compelling them to seek another occupation. I have lately gone over in my mind the histories of all the spirit-dealers who were in a provincial town in Scotland of about 20,000 inhabitants, some ten years ago, and, so far as I can remember them, there are only three or four of the whole number who have not themselves, or their wives, or their sons, or their daughters, fallen under the curse of strong drink. And in Liverpool, as I was informed by a medical man there, the average duration of life for a man after he begins to keep a gin-shop is not much over seven years. Now, is it cruel to take men out of a trade like that? But even supposing there were no such risks in it to the men themselves, are the interests of the community, I ask, to be sacrificed to the aggrandizement of one class in it? In this matter I am not ashamed to avow myself a protectionist, and I ask the law to give me its assistance. I can prevent a man from storing up gunpowder in the same street with me, and no one calls that an undue interference with trade; but I confess that I would rather live next door to a powder magazine than to a gin-shop; for, in the one case, every precaution would be taken to avoid all danger, while, in the other, every means would be employed to make it greater. I demand, therefore, as a Christian minister, that my flock be protected from the contamination of such places. I claim, as a Christian parent, that my children shall not be everlastingly ruined by the flaring temptations of those gilded gateways into hell.

But now I must conclude, and it shall be with a word—

1. To those who are working with us in this cause. To you, my brethren, I would say, labor religiously in the work. It is God's cause, therefore engage in it as such, and ask his blessing on it. One of the most pleasing features of the Scottish Temperance League, with which I was long connected, was that it took this decidedly religious stand upon the question of intemperance, and sought, in all its movements, thoroughly to acknowledge God. To this I trace all that prosperity which has made it the foremost temperance organization in the world. Let us imitate this, and to this end let there be unity and peace in the midst of us; for as the electric wires will not work in a thunder-storm, so no prayer-message ascends to the ear of God from a disunited and contentious company.

2. And now a word to those who are not working with us. Permit me to ask you why you have not joined us? "Because," you reply, "you put total abstinence in the place of the Gospel." But we do not. I will appeal to yourselves if those ministers who are most prominently identified with this movement are not also as well known for their earnest, faithful preaching of the Gospel. It is the very earnestness of their Christian convictions that has made them abstainers, and, so long as intemperance continues to rage among us, it will always be found that a revived piety develops itself in this direction. Need I appeal to the consequences of recent revivals in proof of this? Why, then, should we be so misunderstood? I

would that men would only look on abstinence as they do on other things. Take, for example, the efforts for maintaining a house of refuge for the fallen. Why don't you go to the promoters of that scheme, and say, "We cannot help you, for you are putting your homes in the place of the Gospel"? "No," you answer, "they put them into these homes, in order to bring them under the influence of the Gospel." And what else are we doing with the drunkard? I believe there is not an abstaining minister who has not in his church members who formerly were drunkards, but were first led by him to abstinence, and then from abstinence to Christ. Behold yonder vessel laboring amid the breakers, and going to pieces upon the rocks; wave after wave is dashing over her, and the crew have taken to the rigging, and are in momentary peril of a watery grave. What means that spirit-stirring cheer rising from the shore? It is the crowd encouraging the gallant men to launch the life-boat, and put out to their relief. But why does no one run to them, and expostulate with them thus: "They will not be perfectly safe in that boat; they cannot be cut of danger until they are on shore, and you are putting the boat in the place of the shore"? Oh! how like drivelling idiocy does your argument sound in such a case as that; but that case, my brethren, is ours. Yonder, stranded on the rock of intemperance, is a gallant vessel, and fathers, mothers, brothers, sisters, neighbors, are on board, with destruction yawning underneath them. Here, in

Christ, is the true and only shore of safety; but how shall we get them brought to him? how, but by this our life-boat of abstinence? Our cry to you this night, therefore, is, "Man the life-boat! Man the life-boat!" and if you be men, not to say Christians, you will give a hearty response thereto. But, oh, if you do not, then come with me to Calvary, and see how your indifference appears in the light of that sacrifice which Jesus made upon the cross for you; yea, come with me to the judgment throne, and see how it will look when the Lord, the Judge, shall say, "Inasmuch as ye did it not for one of the least of these, my brethren, ye did it not for me."

Aunt Dinah's Pledge. 12mo, 318 pages. By Miss MARY DWINELL CHELLIS, author of "Temperance Doctor," "Out of the Fire," etc., ... **$1 25**

Aunt Dinah was an eminent Christian woman. Her pledge included swearing and smoking, as well as drinking. It saved her boys, who lived useful lives, and died happy; and by quiet, yet loving and persistent work, names of many others were added who seemed almost beyond hope of salvation.

The Temperance Doctor. 12mo, 370 pages. By Miss MARY DWINELL CHELLIS, ... **$1 25**

This is a true story, replete with interest, and adapted to Sunday-school and family reading In it we have graphically depicted the sad ravages that are caused by the use of intoxicating beverages; also, the blessings of Temperance, and what may be accomplished by one earnest soul for that reform. It ought to find readers in every household.

Out of the Fire. 12mo, 420 pages. By Miss MARY DWINELL CHELLIS, author of "Deacon Sim's Prayers," etc., ... **$1 25**

It is one of the most effective and impressive Temperance books ever published. The evils of the drinking customs of society, and the blessings of sobriety and total abstinence, are strikingly developed in the history of various families in the community.

History of a Threepenny Bit. 18mo, 216 pages, ... **$0 75**

This is a thrilling story, beautifully illustrated with five choice wood engravings. The story of little Peggy, the drunkard's daughter, is told in such a simple yet interesting manner that no one can read it without realizing more than ever before the nature and extent of intemperance, and sympathizing more than ever with the patient, suffering victim. It should be in every Sunday-school library.

Adopted. 18mo, 236 pages. By Mrs. E. J. RICHMOND, author of "The McAllisters," . . . **$0 60**

This book is written in an easy, pleasant yle, seems to be true to nature, true to itself, and withal is full of the Gospel and Temperance.

The Red Bridge. 18mo, 321 pages. By THRACE TALMAN, . . **$0 90**

We have met with few Temperance stories containing so many evidences of decided ability and high literary excellence as this.

The Old Brown Pitcher. 12mo, 222 pages. By the Author of "Susie's Six Birthdays," "The Flower of the Family," etc., **$1 00**

Beautifully illustrated. This admirable volume for boys and girls, containing original stories by some of the most gifted writers for the young, will be eagerly welcomed by the children. It is adapted alike for the family circle and the Sabbath-school library.

Our Parish. 18mo, 252 pages. By Mrs. EMILY PEARSON, . . **$0 75**

The manifold evils resulting from the "still" to the owner's family, as well as to the families of his customers, are truthfully presented. The characters introduced, such as are found in almost every good-sized village, are well portrayed. We can unhesitatingly commend it, and bespeak for it a wide circulation.

The Hard Master. 18mo, 278 pages By Mrs. J. E. MCCONAUGHY, author of "One Hundred Gold Dollars," and other popular Sunday-School books, ... **$0 85**

This interesting narrative of the temptations, trials, hardships, and fortunes of poor orphan boy illustrates in a most striking manner the value of "right principles," especially of honesty truthfulness, and TEMPERANCE.

Echo Bank. 18mo, 269 pages. By ERVIE, ... **$0 85**

This is a well-written and deeply interesting narrative, in which is clearly shown the suffering and sorrow that too often follow and the dangers that attend boys and young men at school and at college, who suppose they can easily take a glass or two occasionally, without fear of ever being aught more than a moderate drinker.

Rachel Noble's Experience. 18mo, 325 pages. By BRUCE EDWARDS. **$0 90**

This is a story of thrilling interest, ably and eloquently told, and is an excellent book for Sunday-school libraries. It is just the book for the home circle, and cannot be read without benefiting the reader and advancing the cause of Temperance.

Gertie's Sacrifice; or Glimpses at Two Lives. 18mo, 189 pages. By Mrs. F. D. GAGE, ... **$0 50**

A story of great interest and power, giving a "glimpse at two lives," and showing how Gertie sacrificed herself as a victim of fashion, custom, and law.

Time will Tell. 12mo, 307 pages. By Mrs. WILSON, ... **$1 00**

A Temperance tale of thrilling interest and unexceptionable moral and religious tone. It is full of incidents and characters of everyday life, while its lessons are plainly and forcibly set before the reader. The pernicious results of the drinking usages in the family and social circle are plainly set forth.

Philip Eckert's Struggles and Triumphs. 18mo, 216 pages. By the author of "Margaret Clair," **$0 60**

This interesting narrative of a noble, manly boy, in an intemperate home, fighting with the wrong and battling for the right, should be read by every child in the land.

Jug-Or-Not. 12mo, 346 pages. By Mrs. J. McNAIR WRIGHT, author of "John and the Demijohn," "Almost a Nun," "Priest and Nun," etc., ... **$1 25**

It is one of her best books, and treats of the physical and hereditary effects of drinking in a clear, plain, and familiar style, adapted to popular reading, and which should be read by all classes in the community, and find a place in every Sunday-school library.

The Broken Rock. 18mo, 139 pages. By KRUNA, author of "Lift a Little," etc., ... **$0 50**

It beautifully illustrates the silent and holy influence of a meek and lowly spirit upon the heartless rumseller until the rocky heart was broken.

Andrew Douglass. 18mo, 232 pages, **$0 75**

A new Temperance story for Sunday-schools, written in a lively, energetic, and popular style, adapted to the Sabbath-school and the family circle.

Vow at the Bars. 18mo, 108 pages. **$0 40**

It contains four short tales, illustrating four important principles connected with the Temperance movement, and is well adapted for the family circle and Sabbath-school libraries.

Job Tufton's Rest. 12mo, 332 pages, ... **$1 25**

A story of life's struggles, written by the gifted author, CLARA LUCAS BALFOUR, depicting most skilfully and truthfully many a life-struggle with the demon of intemperance occurring all along life's pathway. It is a finely written story, and full of interest from the beginning to the end.

Frank Oldfield; or, Lost and Found. 12mo, 408 pages, ... **$1 50**

This excellent story received the prize of £100 in England, out of eighty-three manuscripts submitted; and by an arrangement with the publishers we publish it in this country with all the original illustrations. It is admirably adapted to Sunday-school libraries.

Tom Blinn's Temperance Society, and other Stories. 12mo, 316 pages, ... **$1 25**

This is the title of a new book written by T. S. ARTHUR, the well-known author of "Ten Nights in a Bar-room," and whose fame as an author should bespeak for it a wide circulation. It is written in Mr. ARTHUR'S best style, composed of a series of tales adapted to every family and library in the land.

The Harker Family. 12mo, 336 pages. By EMILY THOMPSON, **$1 25**

A simple, spirited, and interesting narrative, written in a style especially attractive, depicting the evils that arise from intemperance, and the blessings that followed the earnest efforts of those who sought to win others to the paths of total abstinence. Illustrated with three engravings. The book will please all.

Come Home, Mother. 18mo, 143 pages. By NELSIE BROOK. Illustrated with six choice engravings, ... **$0 50**

A most effective and interesting book, describing the downward course of the mother, and giving an account of the sad scenes, but effectual endeavors, of the little one in bringing her mother back to friends, and leading her to God. It should be read by everybody.

Tim's Troubles. 12mo, 350 pages. By Miss M. A. PAULL, . . **$1 50**

This is the second Prize Book of the United Kingdom Band of Hope Union, and which has been reprinted in this country with all the original illustrations. It is the companion of "Frank Oldfield," written in a high tone, and will be found a valuable addition to our Temperance literature.

The Drinking Fountain Stories. 12mo, 192 pages, ... **$1 00**

This book of illustrated stories for children contains articles from the pens of some of the best writers for children in America, and is beautifully illustrated with forty choice wood engravings. It is interspersed with short stories and anecdotes, and should be in every Sunday-school library and in the hands of every child in the land.

Hopedale Tavern, and What it Wrought. 12mo, 252 pages. By J. WILLIAM VAN NAMEE, . **$1 00**

It shows the sad results which followed the introduction of a Tavern and Bar in a beautiful and quiet country town, whose inhabitants had hitherto lived in peace and enjoyment. The contrast is too plainly presented to fail to produce an impression on the reader, making all more desirous to abolish the sale of all intoxicants

Roy's Search; or, Lost in the Cars. 12mo, 364 pages. By HELEN C. PEARSON, ... **$1 25**

This new Temperance book is one of the most interesting ever published—written in a fresh, sparkling style, especially adapted to please the boys, and contains so much that will benefit as well as amuse and interest that we wish all the boys in the land might read it.

How Could He Escape? 12mo, 324 pages. By MRS. J. NCNAIR WRIGHT, author of "Jug-Or-Not." Illustrated with ten engravings, designed by the author, ... **$1 25**

This is a true tale, and one of the writer's best productions. It shows the terrible effects of even one glass of intoxicating liquor upon the system of one unable to resist its influences, and the necessity of grace in the heart to resist temptation and overcome the appetite for strong drink.

The Best Fellow in the World. 12mo, 352 pages. By Mrs. J. McNAIR WRIGHT, author of "Jug-Or-Not," "How Could He Escape?" "Priest and Nun," etc., **$1 25**

"The Best Fellow," whose course is here portrayed, is one of a very large class who are led astray and ruined simply because they are such "good fellows." To all such the volume speaks in thrilling tones of warning, shows the inevitable consequences of indulging in strong drink, and the necessity of divine grace in the heart to interpose and save from ruin.

Frank Spencer's Rule of Life. 18mo, 180 pages. By JOHN W. KIRTON, author of "Buy Your Own Cherries," "Four Pillars of Temperance," etc., etc., . **$0 50**

This is written in the author's best style, making an interesting and attractive story for children.

The Pitcher of Cool Water. 18mo, 180 pages. By T. S. ARTHUR, author of "Tom Blinn's Temperance Society," "Ten Nights in a Bar-room," etc., ... **$0 50**

This little book consists of a series of Temperance stories, handsomely illustrated, written in Mr. ARTHUR's best style, and is altogether one of the best books which can be placed in the hands of children. Every Sunday-school library should possess it.

Little Girl in Black. 12mo, 212 pages. By MARGARET E. WILMER, ... **$0 90**

Her strong faith in God, who she believes will reclaim an erring father, is a lesson to the reader, old as well as young.

Temperance Anecdotes. 12mo, 288 pages, ... **$1 00**

This new book of Temperance Anecdotes, edited by GEORGE W. BUNGAY, contains nearly four hundred Anecdotes, Witticisms, Jokes, Conundrums, etc., original and selected, and will meet a want long felt and often expressed by a very large number of the numerous friends of the cause in the land. The book is handsomely illustrated with twelve choice wood engravings.

The Temperance Speaker. By J. N. STEARNS, ... **$0 75**

The book contains 288 pages of Declamations and Dialogues suitable for Sunday and Day-Schools, Bands of Hope, and Temperance Organizations. It consists of choice selections of prose and poetry, both new and old, from the Temperance orators and writers of the country, many of which have been written expressly for this work.

The McAllisters. 18mo, 211 pages. By Mrs. E. J. RICHMOND, . **$0 50**

It shows the ruin brought on a family by the father's intemperate habits, and the strong faith and trust of the wife in that Friend above who alone gives strength to bear our earthly trials.

The Seymours. 12mo, 231 pages. By Miss L. BATES, . . . **$1 00**

A simple story, showing how a refined and cultivated family are brought low through the drinking habits of the father, their joy and sorrow as he reforms only to fall again, and his final happy release in a distant city.

Eva's Engagement Ring. 12mo, 189 pages. By MARGARET E. WILMER, author of "The Little Girl in Black," **$0 90**

In this interesting volume is traced the career of the moderate drinker, who takes a glass in the name of friendship or courtesy.

Packington Parish, and The Diver's Daughter. 12mo, 327 pages. By Miss M. A. PAULL, . . . **$1 25**

In this volume we see the ravages which the liquor traffic caused when introduced in a hitherto quiet village, and how a minister's eyes were at length opened to its evils, though he had always declared wine to be a "good creature of God," meant to be used in moderation.

Old Times. 12mo. By Miss M. D. CHELLIS, author of "The Temperance Doctor," "Out of the Fire," "Aunt Dinah's Pledge," "At Lion's Mouth," etc., . **$1 25**

It discusses the whole subject of moderate drinking in the history of a New England village. The incidents, various and amusing, are all facts, and the characters nearly all drawn from real life. The five deacons which figure so conspicuously actually lived and acted as represented.

The Fire Fighters. 12mo, 294 pages. By Mrs. J. E. MCCONAUGHY, author of "The Hard Master," **$1 25**

An admirable story, showing how a number of young lads banded themselves into a society to fight against Alcohol, and the good they did in the community.

The Jewelled Serpent. 12mo, 271 pages. By Mrs. E. J. RICHMOND, author of "Adopted," "The McAllisters," etc., ... **$1 00**

The story is written earnestly. The characters are well delineated, and taken from the wealthy and fashionable portion of a large city. The evils which flow from fashionable drinking are well portrayed, and also the danger arising from the use of intoxicants when used as medicine, forming an appetite which fastens itself with a deadly hold upon its victim.

The Hole in the Bag, and Other Stories. By Mrs. J. P. BALLARD, author of "The Broken Rock," "Lift a Little," etc. 12mo, **$1 00**

A collection of well-written stories by this most popular author on the subject of temperance, inculcating many valuable lessons in the minds of its readers.

The Youth's Temperance Banner.

The National Temperance Society and Publication House publish a beautifully illustrated Monthly Paper, especially adapted to children and youth, Sunday-school and Juvenile Temperance Organizations Each number contains several choice engravings, a piece of music, and a great variety of articles from the pens of the best writers for children in America. It should be placed in the hands of every child in the land.

TERMS—IN ADVANCE.

Single copies, one year, . .	**$0 25**	Thirty copies to one address,	**$3 75**
Eight copies, to one address,	**1 00**	Forty " " "	**5 00**
Ten " " "	**1 25**	Fifty " " "	**6 25**
Fifteen " " "	**1 88**	One Hundred " "	**12 00**
Twenty " " "	**2 50**		

Children's Tracts.

A series of forty-five illustrated children's tracts have been published, adapted for circulation in Sunday-schools. Per thousand, **$3.**

Packet of Pictorial Tracts for Children, ... **$0 25**

A valuable packet of 72 of the above Tracts for the Children, suitable for distribution in Sunday-Schools, Bands of Hope, and other Juvenile Temperance organizations.

Miscellaneous Publications.

Forty Years' Fight with the Drink Demon. 12mo, 400 pages. By CHARLES JEWETT, M.D., . **$1 50**

This volume comprises the history of Dr. Jewett's public and private labors from 1826 to the present time, with sketches of the most popular and distinguished advocates of the cause in its earlier stages. It also records the results of forty years' observation, study, and reflections upon the use of intoxicating drinks and drugs, and suggestions as to the best methods of advancing the cause, etc. The book is handsomely bound, and contains illustrated portraits of early champions of the cause.

Drops of Water. 12mo, 133 pages. By Miss ELLA WHEELER, **$0 75**

A new book of fifty-six Temperance Poems by this young and talented authoress, suitable for reading in Temperance Societies, Lodge Rooms, Divisions, etc. The simplicity of manner, beauty of expression, earnestness of thought, and nobleness of sentiment running through all of them make this book a real gem, worthy a place by the side of any of the poetry in the country.

Bound Volume of Tracts. 500 pages, ... **$1 00**

This volume contains all the four, eight, and twelve page tracts published by the National Temperance Society, including all the prize tracts issued the last two years. The book comprises Arguments, Statistics, Sketches, and Essays, which make it an invaluable collection for every friend of the Temperance Reform.

Scripture Testimony Against Intoxicating Wine. By Rev. WM. RITCHIE, of Scotland, . . **$0 60**

An unanswerable refutation of the theory that the Scriptures favor the idea of the use of intoxicating wine as a beverage. It takes the different kinds of wines mentioned in the Scriptures, investigates their specific nature, and shows wherein they differ.

Alcohol: Its Place and Power, by JAMES MILLER; and **The Use and Abuse of Tobacco,** by JOHN LIZARS, ... **$1 00**

Zoological Temperance Convention. By Rev. EDWARD HITCHCOCK, D.D., of Amherst College, **$0 75**

This fable gives an interesting and entertaining account of a Convention of Animals held in Central Africa, and reports the speeches made on the occasion.

Delavan's Consideration of the Temperance Argument and History, **$1 50**

This condensed and comprehensive work contains Essays and Selections from different authors, collected and edited by EDWARD C. DELAVAN, Esq., and is one of the most valuable text-books on the subject of Temperance ever issued.

Bible Rule of Temperance; or, Total Abstinence from all Intoxicating Drinks. By Rev. GEORGE DUFFIELD, D.D., ... **$0 60**

This is the ablest and most reliable work which has been issued on the subject. The immorality of the use, sale, and manufacture of intoxicating liquors as a beverage is considered in the light of the Scriptures, and the will and law of God clearly presented.

Alcohol: Its Nature and Effects. By CHARLES A. STOREY, M.D., **$0 90**

This is a thoroughly scientific work, yet written in a fresh, vigorous, and popular style, in language that the masses can understand. It consists of ten lectures carefully prepared, and is an entirely new work by one amply competent to present the subject.

Four Pillars of Temperance. By JOHN W. KIRTON, . . . **$0 75**

The Four Pillars are, Reason, Science, Scripture, and Experience. The book is argumentative, historical, and statistical, and the facts, appeals, and arguments are presented in a most convincing and masterly manner.

Communion Wine; or, Bible Temperance. By Rev. WILLIAM M. THAYER. Paper, 20 cents; cloth, **$0 50**

An unanswerable argument against the use of intoxicating wine at Communion, and presenting the Bible argument in favor of total abstinence.

Laws of Fermentation and Wines of the Ancients. 12mo, 129 pages. By Rev. WM. PATTON, D.D. Paper, 30 cts.; cloth, . . **$0 60**

It presents the whole matter of Bible Temperance and the wines of ancient times in a new, clear, and satisfactory manner, developing the laws of fermentation, and giving a large number of references and statistics never before collected, showing conclusively the existence of unfermented wine in the olden time.

The National Temperance Society's Books.

Text-Book of Temperance. By Dr. F. R. LEES, ... **$1 50**

We can also furnish the above book, which is divided into the following parts: 1. Temperance as a Virtue. 2. The Chemical History of Alcohol. 3. The Dietetics of Temperance. 4. The Pathology of Intemperance. 5. The Medical Question. 6. Temperance in Relation to the Bible. 7. Historical. 8. The National Question and the Remedy. 9. The Philosophy of Temperance.

Bugle Notes for the Temperance Army. Price, paper covers, **30** cents; boards, ... **$0 35**

A new collection of Songs, Quartets, and Glees, adapted to the use of all Temperance gatherings, Glee Clubs, etc., together with the Odes of the Sons of Temperance and Good Templars.

Temperance Chimes. Price, in paper covers, **30** cents, single copies; **$25** per hundred. Price, in board covers, **35** cents; per hundred, ... **$30 00**

A Temperance Hymn and Tune-Book of 128 pages, comprising a great variety of Glees, Songs, and Hymns designed for the use of Temperance Meetings and Organizations, Bands of Hope, Glee Clubs, and the Home Circle. Many of the Hymns have been written expressly for this book by some of the best writers in the country.

Pamphlets.

John Swig. A Poem. By EDWARD CARSWELL. 12mo, 24 pages. Illustrated with eight characteristic engravings, printed on tinted paper, ... **$0 15**

The Rum Fiend, and Other Poems. By WILLIAM H. BURLEIGH. 12mo. 46 pages. Illustrated with three wood engravings, designed by EDWARD CARSWELL. . . . **$0 20**

Suppression of the Liquor Traffic. A Prize Essay, by Rev. H. D. KITCHELL, President of Middlebury College. 12mo, 48 pp., **$0 10**

Bound and How; or, Alcohol as a Narcotic. By CHARLES JEWETT, M.D. 12mo, 24 pp., . . . **$0 10**

Scriptural Claims of Total Abstinence. By Rev. NEWMAN HALL. 12mo, 62 pp., ... **$0 15**

Buy Your Own Cherries. By JOHN W. KIRTON. 12mo, 32 pp., **$0 20**

National Temperance Almanac and Teetotaler's Year Book for 1873, **$0 10**

Illustrated Temperance Alphabet, **$0 25**

Twenty-four Page Pamphlets. (With Covers.)

Five Cents each; 60 Cents per Doz.

Is Alcohol Food? By Dr. F. R. LEES.
Physiological Action of Alcohol. By Prof. HENRY MUNROE.
Adulteration of Liquors. By Rev. J. B. DUNN.
Will the Coming Man Drink Wine? By JAMES PARTON, Esq.
History and Mystery of a Glass of Ale. By J. W. KIRTON.
Bible Teetotalism. By Rev. PETER STRYKER.
Medicinal Drinking. By Rev. JOHN KIRK.
Drinking Usages of Society. By Bishop ALONZO POTTER.
Fruits of the Liquor Traffic. By SUMNER STEBBINS, M.D.
Is Alcohol a Necessary of Life? By Prof. HENRY MUNROE.
A High Fence of 15 Bars. By the author of "Lunarius."

Packet of Assorted Tracts, No. 1. Comprising Nos. 1 to 53 put up in strong paper covers, making 250 pages, ... **$0 25**
Packet of Assorted Tracts, No. 2. Comprising 53 to 100, making 250 pages, ... **$0 25**

www.ingramcontent.com/pod-product-compliance
Lightning Source LLC
LaVergne TN
LVHW020110110826
845151LV00001B/118

* 9 7 8 1 4 2 5 5 4 3 4 8 8 *